Then to live out all possibilities.

In MEMORIAM

A TRIBUTE TO CHARLOTTE MASON

PARENTS' NATIONAL EDUCATIONAL UNION
26 VICTORIA STREET
LONDON, S.W.1.
1928

ORIGINAL PRICE: TWO SHILLINGS AND SIXPENCE

In Memoriam: A Tribute to Charlotte Mason

First printed and made in Great Britain by Wadsworth and Co.
The Rydal Press, Keighley

Reprinted and updated in the United States of America
Afterthoughts Books
Bakersfield, CA
afterthoughtsbooks.com

ISBN: 0692902872

TABLE OF CONTENTS

Acknowledgements

The World to Come (The Disciple)

Acknowledgements

A few years ago, I discovered *In Memoriam* for the first time. I attempted to read it online, and I fell head over heels in love. Here was Charlotte Mason in the flesh, it seemed! Like I do with all my favorite books, I went searching for a copy—I wanted to touch it and mark it up and add marginalia. Imagine how disappointed I was when I couldn't find an original copy, and the only things available in print were poor-quality, print-on-demand photocopies.

A project like this can't be accomplished by passion alone. It takes people. And not just any people: the right kind of people to do the work.

As time went by, the work grew into the form you see now: the cross-referenced footnotes, the Index of Persons, the translations of phrases, and we put all of the major publications and organizations associated with Charlotte Mason in SMALL CAPS so that her body of work is easily recognizable—we didn't just reprint this book; we improved it (even down to fixing errors we found in the original).

First and foremost, I must thank Hayley Beck, my editor-in-chief, without whom this project would have died in the planning stages. Hayley has the unique ability to drive a project all the way to completion—she dots her i's and crosses her t's, she's great with details, she's a formatting genius, and she loves Charlotte Mason just as much as I do. You can find her at FromYourDeskToMine.com.

Second, I must express my gratitude to the indispensable Alissa Clark (alissadclark.com). Alissa belonged to the same CM reading group as Hayley and me for a couple of years until she moved away. Alissa is a kindred spirit; I've never forgotten her (and never stopped missing her). One of the most notable things about Alissa is her way with beauty. She is an amazing artist both on and off a computer. I knew that if we were going to do this project, we needed Alissa to do the cover. And isn't it amazing?

Third, we are forever in the debt of our wonderful team of proof readers! They literally took months off the timeline of this project. A big thank you to Celeste Cruz, Dawn Duran, Michele Elliott, Katie Freels, Dawn Garrett, Camille Malucci, Virginia Lee Rogers, Kristen Vencel, and Morag Webb—as well as many of their husbands (along with my son, Everett), who served as reading partners for the process. We couldn't have done it without you!

Fourth, I would be remiss if I forgot to thank Wes Callihan for his Greek translation help, and Annie Roy for her French translation help—thank you both for saving us from clunky mistakes. You are much preferred to Google Translate!

Fifth, an extra big thank you to Dawn Duran and Karen Glass who offered much and exuberant encouragement along the way.

And lastly, to my husband, Josiah, whose marketing savvy turned the back cover summary into something worth reading: thank you for lending me your remarkable talents. I have always admired your way with words.

I appreciated each and every one of you!

Brandy Vencel
Publisher
Afterthoughts Books
May 26, 2017

The World to Come (The Disciple)

A child will play all day at what he'll do,—
        When I am big!
        Great hunter will I be!
        That field I'll dig!
His parents look on smiling while he plays,
And with bewildering changes shapes his days.

And we, poor foolish, when we dream and say
        Thus shall it be,—
        Our Father worketh yet,
        And shall not we?
Not eager, we, for crowns or crystal seas,
Or harps or singing or eternal ease;

We would be doing as our Father doth!—
        We have no fears;
        With all our puny might
        Would roll His spheres!
Sure, not for this severely will He chide,
Our Father, who for love of us hath died!

Ye shall go before your brethren and help them,
until the Lord hath given your brethren rest,

O the dear world, sweet life, congenial joys!
        How give them up?
        Though all be sin-defiled,
        Where find we else
The promise we believe our longings hold,—
What work for us in any other fold?

All bright may glow the joys of other spheres,
        But this, our home!
        And would we barter it
        For any gain,
Poorer, less constant, had our substance grown;
Jesus, in separate joy, were less our own.

Continuance, sure, belongs to higher life;
    All fickleness,
    All change, with Death must pass,
    And leave us true:
Less a new life than utmost scope in this,
With help laid on us here, ah, hope of bliss!

Jealous are we, with jealousy unreasoning,
    Over their joys;
    For their gain, sadly bear
    Unbidden loss;
With Him;—in Him;—there all the promise ends:
Ourselves, not Christ, do banish our sweet friends.

Sure, the dim kingdom where we seat our Dead
    Is of the world:
    The heaven of Christ is ruled
    By other laws:
Not cumbrous change in circumstance and place,
But the enraptured vision of His face!

Death opes not heaven's gate; for long ago,
    Soon as the King
    Shone in upon the soul
    Did heaven begin:
A blessed state, a lifting up forever;
Not some far seats when soul and body sever:

Two fuller consummations be there yet
    To this full bliss:—
    Our holy dead have reached
    The second life,—
Where pure eyes see the King in beauty fresh,
And service bears no dragging clog of flesh.

Then to live out all possibilities
     Of love and help,
     Of counsel and support,
     That now but mock
These slow unloving wills: to be unseen
Among our own beloved, a ghostly screen,

And love them with love purely purged from self,
     That, as an air
     Tender, should wrap their lives,
     Nor ever fret
With any waywardness; to lay their cares,
And with pure spirit-promotings, help their
prayers,—

What life were this! Nor only for our own
     Would we have help
     Laid on us, but for all
     Whose pain now moves,
Whose thoughts inspire,—all life that any way,
If only in fond dream, on ours doth play.

And not unowned, or self-imposed, our tasks;
     Ever bidden
     By the dear Word of God,
     Willing His will,
In the low rest of meekness, were our ease:
So, working, should we yet from labours cease.

       *   *   *   *   *   *   *

Poor, ignorant and foolish, what know we
     If this may be,
     Or other, better life?
     We trust in Thee!
Our Father, wilt not smile on us and say,
"Tis but my silly children at their play?"

                       Charlotte M. Mason

PART I

From the Whitsuntide Conference Report, 1922

PART I

Table of Contents

In Memoriam—Charlotte M. Mason

PART I

I: Some P.N.E.U. Principles*
by C. M. Mason

IT gives me and gives us all extraordinary pleasure to meet so many P.N.E.U. members, especially when one reflects on the fatigues of travel through the weary hours of a long, hot and dusty day; for members are here from Ireland, Scotland, Wales, from the most distant as well as the nearer counties of England, and, of course, London has sent a large contingent, notwithstanding the 'Season.'

A few delegates from other educational Societies have honoured us by coming, but the general aspect of this 'great gathering' is undoubtedly P.N.E.U.; we are used to the same aspect in the children, who soon develop what used to be called in my early-Victorian youth 'an intelligent countenance'; and it is that same countenance we see here. Some of those present have upheld our teaching these 30 years and more. Lady Campbell brings a daughter who is a mother and a member, Mrs. Howard Glover does not bring a son who is a father, but we all know Mr. Cedric Glover who carries on our training in Musical Appreciation so brilliantly in the PARENTS' REVIEW, and whom I first met as a 'musical baby' of three!

To our Honorary Secretary[1] and her stalwart supporters we owe it that as a society we have lived in good fellowship for more than a generation.

The P.N.E.U. have taken pains to master a distinctive philosophy of education which some of us believe will do great things for many thousands of children and their homes.

This spiritual edifice, shall I call it, is a sort of coral atol raised by innumerable workers. There is our Honorary Secretary who cares more for our philosophy than even for its results, and who, with her committee, has afforded never failing sympathy and support to every new development. To instance one; when our late deeply lamented friend and

---

* From the Whitsuntide Conference Report, 1922.
[1] Mrs. Henrietta Franklin.

colleague, Mrs. F. Steinthal, succeeded during the last decade in getting a village school in the Yorkshire Collieries to demonstrate that, notwithstanding a very scanty vocabulary and little in the way of cultured surroundings—the children of colliers are just as fit to profit instantly by a liberal education as are those of the leisured class,—the committee led by their Honorary Secretary threw themselves heartily into the new departure and appointed an organising secretary to visit and help these schools. We all know Miss Parish,[2] and some may regret that she gives to the College what was meant, not for the State, but for the whole work of the UNION. Let me reassure them; her work here is just as inestimable, and will perhaps prove as far-reaching as that she did from 'the Office.' Then followed Miss Wix,[3] very able and enthusiastic, now one of Her Majesty's Inspectors of Schools, and lastly, we all know and rejoice in Miss Pennethorne[4] whose brilliant powers and enthusiasm have already effected great things. Then, we have the band of distinguished women, members of the Executive, who have held up Mrs. Franklin's[5] hands for a generation, half a dozen of whom we have with us today: the race of chairmen, treasurers, etc., of the Executive, men of distinction; the last and not the least honourable of whom the Headmaster of Westminster is with us now at the cost of much inconvenience. There are the families with home schoolrooms, so largely and delightfully represented today; the heads and teachers of a great many schools primary and secondary, also well represented; that large and touchingly interesting contingent of families, some of whom are to be found in every one of our dominions and colonies: the 400-500 old students labouring for the cause; our fellow labourers in College, School and Office, who are doing great and original work; perhaps I may make special mention of Miss E. Kitching,[6] my oldest (in service) and not least honourable colleague; in fact, I feel like a drone in a hive of workers, especially when I look at our present Chairman,

---

[2] See pages 60 and 201.
[3] See page 146.
[4] See page 218.
[5] See pages 33 and 113.
[6] See pages 67 and 120.

who comes amongst us like a comet with a tail of some 70 schools, great and small, in the single county of Gloucestershire! Let us all praise famous men, and one more I am sure you will allow me to name who is prevented by illness from being with us—Mr. Willingham Rawnsley,[7] an ever welcome visitor in the schools of Yorkshire, Gloucestershire and elsewhere, who has served us, as have many other friends, by means of many addresses and articles in the Press including the PARENTS' REVIEW.

What after all are those principles which we all labour to advance? Let me first show a tangible result or two, inviting you to look at many such specimens in St. George's room, mostly Christmas examination papers; you notice the bulk of each set, but these are only specimens of what each child could do. The children read many books, probably one question is set on each book; a question which the cleverest crammer could not forecast. Whether they have read 50 or 250 pages, the answers are equally full, clear, accurate and to the point; and what is more, all are touched with emotion. Now, if life were long enough, the children could answer 10 or 20 questions on each book or section of a book, and each child would send in a volume of 200-300 pages of vitalised knowledge all and evermore his own.

As regards the lessons you have listened to with sympathetic pleasure, may I let you into the secret. The children always pay absolute attention, nothing need ever be repeated, no former work is revised; they are always progressing, never retracing their steps, never going round and round like a horse in a mill.

This infinite power of attention in every child (and grownup), our discovery, is one P.N.E.U. principle which puts education on a new footing, and promises the latter-day Renaissance we all long to see. People are becoming in love with knowledge, children and grownups, for of course parents and teachers share the delights of their children. No secondary motive, marks, prizes, place or the like, is required; children work with joy for the pure love of knowledge.

But what then is knowledge? That is a question which as yet nobody has been able to answer. Our approach to a

---

[7] See page 36.

solution is to adapt Matthew Arnold's rather inadequate definition of religion.* *Knowledge is information touched with emotion*: feeling must be stirred, imagination must picture, reason must consider, nay, conscience must pronounce on the information we offer before it becomes mind-stuff. Therefore the current textbooks of the schoolroom must needs be scrapped and replaced by *literature*, that is, by books into the writing of which the writer has put his *heart*, as well as a highly trained mind. That is another P.N.E.U. principle; we try to use none but living books.

Then, a healthy mind is as hungry as a healthy body, and wants a large quantity of fit pabulum; also, the mind, too, hates 'everlasting tapioca,' and must have a very various diet, selected not at random, but according to its natural requirements. Matthew Arnold gives us, again, if not a definition, a rough classification of knowledge: Knowledge of God, of man, of the universe, or, as we might put it, Divinity, the Humanities and Science; these three are the natural requirements of every child of man; so his syllabus must needs be wide, well-proportioned, well-balanced. Here is another P.N.E.U. principle which we act upon with courage and decision because we know of that inexhaustible fund of attention, that hunger and thirst after knowledge and that discriminating taste which can feed only upon literature and art, which are inherent in every child.

For the knowledge of God, the chief knowledge, we use the Bible, Prayer Book, and certain devout and up-to-date commentaries. We avoid what school boys used to call 'pi-jaw.' We do not exhort much, nor appeal to feeling, nor shew pictures, nor introduce models or handicrafts; but the sincere piety of P.U.S. children is remarkable, and is perhaps partly due to the fact that they are never bored but always interested.

From the age of 12 or so, they read a *Life of Christ* in verse; they seem to recognise that the poetic point of view helps them to realise the Divine life, in itself the epic of the ages. A girl of 13½ in her Easter examination tackled the question: *"The people sat in darkness"* ... *"I am the Light of the world." Shew as far as you can the meaning of these*

---

* Religion is morality, touched with emotion.

statements. She was not asked to write in verse, and was she not taught by a beautiful instinct to recognise that the phrases she had to deal with were essential poetry and that she could best express herself in verse?

> The people sat in darkness—all was dim,
> No light had yet come unto them from Him,
> No hope as yet of Heaven after life,
> A peaceful haven far from war and strife.
> Some warriors to Valhalla's halls might go
> And fight all day, and die. At evening, lo!
> They'd wake again, and drink in the great Hall.
> Some men would sleep forever at their fall;
> Or with their fickle Gods forever be:
> So all was dark and dim. Poor heathens, see!
> The Light ahead, the clouds that roll away,
> The golden, glorious, dawning of the Day:
> And in the birds, the flowers, the sunshine, see
> The might of Him who calls "come unto Me."

The Humanities cover a wide field: poetry, the drama, history, literature, biography, languages, essays, in fact where is the line to be drawn?

You have heard in the lessons some instances of the children's quick apprehension, complete comprehension and accurate reproduction of passages, not chosen because they were interesting, but because they followed in each case last week's lesson on the same subject. Many parents and teachers here felt, no doubt, that their children would have 'narrated' in an even more miraculous way; they were right; there seems to be no limit to what these "incredible children"* can do.

But I should like to call your attention to one point which you will see fully illustrated later: this method of narration lends itself amazingly to the teaching of foreign languages, and promises to make of us tongue-tied folk a nation of linguists with copious vocabularies.

The children will read later (*once only*) a scene or two from *Le Bourgeois Gentilhomme* and will narrate it in fluent

---

* Mr. Rawnsley on certain P.N.E.U. elementary schools.

French, grammatically used. The students will listen to a rather long lecture on Molière, from Mlle. Pierson, and when it is finished will narrate it practically without fault or omission. Of course they have never heard this lecture before (though it was delivered to another division of the Senior Class at the Students' Conference a month ago).

Miss Gardner, our Lecturer in Classics, will hear a class construe a passage from Cicero, and they will narrate the passage, acquiring a Latin vocabulary and knowledge of construction in the act. Miss Parish is obtaining results even more remarkable in Italian, and until this year German has been studied to as good purpose.

In Science, too, we have perhaps our peculiar methods; we do a great deal of field work, in geology, geography, botany, natural history, but we also use many living books. French scientists have perceived the poetry of science, and France owns a splendid library of scientific work of the nature of poetry though by no means written in verse; some of these have been translated and we gladly use them, but, also, we have a few volumes of our own, written by our great men of science which fall under the heading of 'the Humanities,' because they are literature of the best; these our children use and they are helped to see what they look at and learn to wonder and admire. Also they narrate what they have read, and as a child in a Council School remarked, "We narrate, and then, we know."

We have, too, quite a code of 'principles' affecting character and conduct, aesthetic development and so on, but the few I have dwelt on, regulating our dealings with mind, are enough for the moment.

Let me add that what Wordsworth calls "The grand elemental principle of pleasure," is not with us confined to joyous occasions; joy reigns in all our schoolrooms, every lesson satisfies the mind-hunger proper to children; they are quite happy and content, and Satan finds *less* mischief there for idle *minds* to think.

II: P.N.E.U., A Service to the State
by C. M. Mason

Yesterday we spoke of some of our guiding principles and how they should influence us individually. But these are days when we feel that we are all due to the country, if only for the sake of our men who have fallen. Many schemes are being tried for the bettering of the nation; we hardly begin to see results yet, and some of us are painfully anxious to do something for which the State will be the better if only in gratitude for all we have received.

What is wanted is a democratic education to include not only the fit, the aristocracy of mind, high and low, rich and poor, but everybody. And now we of the P.N.E.U. are in a position to state that while an academic education will of necessity reach only the fit and few, the humanities in English meet a general appeal. We ceased to count after the first 10,000 children in elementary schools who shewed themselves capable of doing happy and excellent humanistic work, but we know now that history, drama, tale, poems of the best, appeal to everyone.

Mind, capable of dealing with knowledge in its three kinds, knowledge of God, knowledge of man, knowledge of the natural world, science; mind in this sense appears to be a universal possession, and everyone should have the joy and the manifold interests that such knowledge affords. Only a few on the other hand, some dozen, say, in a big school, will excel in academic knowledge, whether mathematical, linguistic or scientific. By all means let these have their opportunity. We shall always want mathematicians and grammarians, but the rest put in their claims too. The stability proper to persons who have read wisely if not very widely should belong to us all. At the present time it does belong to the professional and upper classes, to public school men, for example, who, whatever may be their shortcomings, make themselves felt wherever they are, and do a good deal of the world's work. Home influences, the playing fields of Eton, anything but their school work gets credit for this admirable stability. But suppose that after all their humanistic studies have a tendency to make things seem worth doing even when they are done with little credit or profit; suppose that a sense of duty impels 'the educated classes,' and that, however insistent personal claims may be, they are subordinated to the claims of service; why, here is the very spirit we want to see in all classes of our countrymen; and the direct and very possible way to such a temper of mind is through a liberal education.

We have all heard rumours of educational reconstruction, which possibly affect us as does the rumble of London traffic—we do not analyse the roar, nor consider what it all means. Let me invite you to give your earnest attention to the question of education *en bloc*,[8] because the P.N.E.U. is now being called upon to play a distinguished part in the upbringing of the coming generation: I am not speaking to members now of their own children but of the education of the country, in which we are required to give a lead. We may say with the prince in *Rasselas,* "How the world is to be, not 'peopled,' but educated, is not my concern and needs not to be yours." That has been our attitude in the past, even ours as a SOCIETY; but great things have happened to us: it has been found that our P.N.E.U. way of educating our children is capable of being used with incredible effect on children of all sorts and conditions. Things that have not been done before since the world was are now done through the movement which we are 'in.' Our Honorary Secretary could tell a marvellous tale of children of the slums of a big northern town; so could members of our executive committees; our Organising Secretary could unfold tales which should hold us for days on end. We need not be afraid that such tales would leave us cold; no, education is a vital thing whose pulse we feel, and we can no more listen coldly to a tale of real education than we can to the story of Florence Nightingale or Shackleton, or any other of our benefactors, for we are all one body.

How is it then that only a philanthropist or a philosopher here and there has given much thought to the matter? For the same reason that though the machinery of a great cotton mill is wonderful past all whooping, the wonder stales on us in half an hour and we are chiefly aware of intolerable noise and dust. Our education in all classes of society has become mechanical with only little interludes of interest; the results are remarkable but not interesting; examinations are worked for and candidates pass with distinction; a servant applies (or would apply in the good old days) for a place in as good a letter as any one need write; people, all the people, are

---

[8] Altogether.

educated up to a certain point, but are not as they would say themselves "the better of it!" Education has failed to bring to any class of society, as a class, new interests, keen mental enjoyment, aesthetic pleasure, elevation of character, principles of conduct. A few here and there try to make up for the defects of their education in these respects, but not always with much success. I once dined at the house of a young man who had built a reputation on Keats. We looked up favourite poems to be ready for a feast of enlightened talk. But our host was a mere collector; he had each edition and every commentary and was blank to any remark about the poems themselves. Apparently he has not read Keats at all, but only collected. The education we give makes such an attitude of mind possible.

Let us think of our SOCIETY as one of the "Services," that is, to the State; an idea we are all feeling after. "Save the country" appeals to all. What can we do? Absolutely the first service to the State is to present it with good citizens, and all sorts of schools, nearly all families, are in intention at any rate labouring towards that end.

What are the qualities that go to make a good citizen and how far does a P.N.E.U. child exhibit them? We may for convenience think of the children here, for P.N.E.U. children besides their family traits, exhibit a certain hall mark by which they may be known, a mark composed of many markings: One of the audience suggested 'Integrity' as one of these; you all know how straight your children are about their examinations; how free they are from shifty ways, they know or they don't know, and are quite simple about it. These children do not "ca 'canny"[9] or crib or transgress in any of the venial genial ways common among school children. Is not this attitude which we sum up roughly as integrity what we want in our citizens of all classes?

Again, the absence of self-consciousness, self-conceit, vanity, display, has been noticed in these, who are simply average P.N.E.U. children. These are qualities that should make a citizen put his duties before his rights; and, once more, should not such citizens be an asset to any nation?

This audience has been struck by the children's unconscious obedience, and again, what could a State desire

---

[9] Go slow on purpose or have the habit of going slowly.

more than citizens who obey its laws without knowing it, as
indeed most of us do.

There is a singleness of purpose and motive about them
which augurs well for their future as citizens, and promises
another kind of purity about which we are all a little anxious,
which is best ensured by a well nourished and active mind,
for Satan finds some mischief still for idle *minds* to do.

Another asset offered by our P.N.E.U. children is the
practice of instant absolute attention, what is called
concentration. Think what it would be to the head of a house
or a factory, a ship or a department, to be sure of fixed
intelligent attention being given to every instruction! We all
serve in one way or another, but the capacity to serve is
dependent on the habit of concentration.

We claim that all these and many more of the properties
of a good citizen depend on due nourishment with fitting
knowledge. Let me repeat knowledge (to offer a stumbling
definition) *is information touched with Emotion.* For this
reason it is that only literature and art offer children the
pabulum they require. Who can feel emotion over a
compendium, however praiseworthy? But literature, whether
in the form of history, poetry, drama, scientific treatise,
nourishes the soul; and with all the world in one scale and a
single soul in the other, the scale holding the world kicks the
beam.

A good citizen must know about the laws of his country,
the means of administration, how the constitution has
developed; these things he must learn from a pretty wide
reading of history—English, European, French, Ancient,—the
stirring tales of services rendered to their several countries by
great citizens throughout the ages. No boy reads "How
Horatius kept the bridge in the brave days of old," without
secret resolves and dreamy eyes.

Perhaps the first business of a citizen is to be self-
supporting; we all recognise that boys and girls too should be
brought up to earn their living, it may be by administering
their own estates or by more direct service, and here we are
content to let his self-supporting duty end! But indeed this is
only the beginning; think of the people who bore us by their
inanimity, vex us by their flippancy, and the trivial nature of
their pursuits, who use us as pegs on which to hang an idle

hour,—and we shall see there are other ways of supporting himself which a citizen must practice besides that of providing his own bread and butter.

The mind is inexorable throughout life in its demand for *daily* bread; we do not recognise this fully, and therefore so many old and middle-aged persons become inane, tiresome and incapable of sharing the intellectual interests of their children. The citizen in whose bringing up P.N.E.U. has had a part has had many of his innumerable emotions stirred by his "lovely books," "glorious books," and the emotion of the moment has translated the facts of history, travel, science, the themes of poetry or tragedy, into vital knowledge. That is the *raison d'etre*[10] of narrating; the reader recovers as it were what he has read and looks at it, and in this looking his emotion becomes fired. The Greeks recognised two emotions by the stirring of which tragedy should educate the people; but we try not only to purge but to invigorate the soul, by pity, tenderness, awe, reverence, delight in beauty, noble emulation in heroic action—the hundred impulses that play on the mind (or soul) and by this play, transform the information we receive in *literary form* into the knowledge by which we live.

In seeing that children know good books and plenty of them, we secure delightful fields of thought and reservoirs of interest for their afterlife; the child of the Hall and the hamlet grow up with common possessions, and their good fellowship is secured. The high moral standard, the concentrated attention, of school days are brought to bear on labour for a livelihood, and master and man are alike blessed.

We have tried to show how pictures and music, birds and flowers and trees, geography, local history and geology, the atmosphere of great men (and what village is there which has not bred *one* great man?) public readings like that we have listened to on "George Borrow," the drama, useful and beautiful handicrafts and physical exercises, dances and songs, may become, some home delights, others the joys of the village community. A village Hall or public room and the Carnegie Library are all that citizens brought up in our schools require to make them in every sense, mental, moral and physical, self-supporting.

---

[10] Reason for being, the most important reason.

We have seen how our teachers appear to take a back place while teaching and let children's minds have free play; so, if I may make the suggestion, it is better to indicate to these educated villagers or townsfolk what is open to them in the way of intellectual life than to use leading strings, get up plays for them, lay ourselves out to amuse them in many kind ways; the hamlet may invite the Hall to take part, to sing at a concert, present a character in a play, or the like, but the village community should organise its own pleasures on the sort of healthy lines, perhaps, that we have tried to indicate here for indoor and outdoor life.

You will not say, this is working for posterity, and "What has posterity done for me?" As a matter of fact we all live for posterity and have no other business in the world. But we shall not have to wait for 'posterity' to grow up; what the children know the parents learn also and delight in; so the field is already white to the harvest. An apt nucleus for such work is the village P.U. SCHOOL; already in two or three cases has a PARENTS' ASSOCIATION been set up in connection with a school (owing to Mrs. Franklin's initiative). But Welfare Clubs, Village Institutes and the like are already widely spread and perhaps we may be allowed to introduce a more intellectual element into their working, eschewing lectures, providing concerts and such aids to amusements, and encouraging the people to be their own purveyors—perhaps on P.N.E.U. lines.

A full life makes for content and happiness and these stand for the stability of which the nation is in sore need. All very well, say you, in Utopia! but what of our unhappy country where industry is continually interrupted by strikes, called often enough for whimsical reasons? Education as we interpret it is the only remedy.

We have but to read of the bitter wrongs issuing in the Chartist Riots in Disraeli's *Sybil* for example, to be assured that the people must hold in their own hands an instrument of redress; but education should ensure that this terrific implement shall not be handled impulsively and hastily. What the League of Nations should do to hinder or regulate wars, that I believe we of this one insignificant society may do to hinder strikes. Educate the nation and if strikes come, they will be first well considered by balanced minds; no strike will be called without long and *general* deliberation; we shall have secured that pause in relation to social upheavals that the League of Nations aims at in the prospect of war.

But educate, educate, educate, is the watchword of the day. In what do we of the P.N.E.U. differ from others? Chiefly in two ways. Equal opportunity for all, is the offer of the State; this is no new thing; in countries where there is no hereditary aristocracy, like China and Turkey, it has been the rule for many ages. The Roman Church which is before all things democratic (and socialistic), has always offered unlimited opportunities for the *fit*, according to

> The good old rule, the simple plan,—
> Let him take who has the power
> And let him keep who can,—

a rule as applicable to stores of the mind as of the pocket. The demagogue, the Socialist, the Bolshevist are the outcome of an education snatched as it were by mind-force. We spread education, not for the fit only, but for all; all partake, even to the backward child; and we claim to send out contented citizens, capable of a right judgment in all things, religiously, morally, socially, physically, fit to take their due part in a happy ordered state. Again, the manner of our education differs; schools in general send forth scholars who have learnt 'how to learn'; (they rarely show that they *have* learned this art!) We send out scholars who *have* learned and *do know* and find knowledge so delightful that it becomes a pursuit and source of happiness for a lifetime.

Two thousand years ago it was said to a dozen undistinguished men, "Go ye out unto all the world and preach the gospel to every creature"; and they did. We too have, by the Grace of God, a fragment of this gospel to preach; we who are here and who represent thousands of P.N.E.U. members are vastly better provided as far as numbers go to spread this new Renaissance. Let us be up and doing; the enthusiasm perceptible in this room alone is enough to convert a world; how much more, to make our own people able to prefer (and to act) Shakespeare's plays rather than the trivialities of the Music Hall. Let us do battle with the schools for "a liberal education" for the boys we send to them. We cannot make or find a substitute for the Public Schools—a great national achievement; but we can urge the willing minds of Masters and Heads to afford at least the six or eight hours a week devoted to English and History, to the studies and conditions we have found marvellously effective. For our P.U.S. girls, I do not know that life offers compensation for the loss of the work in the Fifth and Sixth Forms; let them work out their scheme of liberal education to the full, if only that they may be prepared to take up the crusade which I am tempted to urge on listeners so responsive and encouraging. We know the way, we have the means, we see opportunities everywhere—elementary and secondary, private and public schools are open to attack!

Let us part with the pledge—

> I will not cease from mortal strife
>   Nor shall my sword sleep in my hand
> Till I have built Jerusalem
>   In England's green and pleasant land.

and may God be with us in our labours!

(The writer must apologise if these notes contain more of what she meant to say than of what she really said. The friendly attitude of the audience tempted her into informal talk.)

PART II

From the Memorial Numbers
of the Parents' Review

PART II

Table of Contents

PART II

Table of Contents (continued)

PART II

(1) Official Tributes

I

Board of Education
Whitehall, S.W.I.
12th February, 1923

Dear Madam,
      I do not think it is right that I should allow the death of Miss Charlotte Mason to pass without recording officially the deep regret of the Board of Education at the termination of her long and fruitful labours in the field of education, and their high appreciation of the great public services which she has rendered.

We know that Miss Mason started her work very early in life, and she carried it on with unremitting diligence and enthusiasm for over half a century. The fundamental principle of her teaching—a belief in the child's natural powers of appreciation—was unfamiliar in England when she was young. It is far otherwise today, and that perhaps is in itself the best evidence of what we owe to her and the most lasting memorial of her labours. Her influence, diffused through her books and the UNION which she founded, was a source of strength to many hundreds of teachers, and though she did not come into direct relations with the public system of education as administered by the Board and the Local Education Authorities, there can be no question of the profound and permanent benefit accruing to that system from her life and example, and from her efforts to establish and diffuse the principles which she followed. She was a high-minded, disinterested and sincere worker for the advancement of education, who combined a generous vision and a good practical judgment, and on behalf of the President and my colleagues I join with the PARENTS' NATIONAL EDUCATIONAL UNION in deploring her loss and paying tribute to her memory.

Yours very truly,
(Signed) *L. A. Selby-Bigge*
Permanent Secretary

The Honorary Mrs. Franklin
Parents' National Educational Union
26, Victoria Street, S.W.I.

II

Miss Mason was *grande dame,*[11] *grande âme.*[12] Her thoughts and her tastes had lineage. To be with her, to come under the spell of her courteous and considerate self-possession, was to know what it must have been like to meet Madame de Genlis or some other of those great ladies of the *ancien regime*[13] who won fine culture through teaching children and through sharing with them the love of things which are beautiful and true. Miss Mason had a genius for education. She had an inbred good sense and an unfatigued sensibility. Her mind was tempered by great literature. She loved the humanities. She had a very distinguished gift of leadership in cooperation. There was a tenderness, a humility in her self-confidence which recalled Vauvenargues' saying that 'great thoughts come from the heart.' And the greatness of the thoughts she lived with made her greater-hearted as her experience deepened and as the circle of her pupils grew nationwide.

It was fortunate for England to have the guidance which Charlotte Mason gave with patriotic and unselfish tenacity and with gracious *largesse* of heart and mind. What she did, no one else attempted on the same scale. Others who like her were national figures worked through another medium. Lady Stanley of Alderley and Frances Mary Buss were steeped in the same tradition but became preoccupied with the problems of the public secondary day school for girls. Charlotte Mason represented the culture of the homeschool at its best. The writers of her generation had shown themselves a little blind to the beauties of the best home teaching and forgetful of what had been achieved in good private schools, especially for girls. There were not a few private schools in which an attempt was made to reproduce the stimulus and restraining influence of a cultivated home. Charlotte Mason was a witness to their excellence. More than this, she disengaged from her knowledge of their work a reasoned statement of the educational theory of their practice. This, I think, was her great contribution to the

---

[11] Admired old woman.
[12] Great soul.
[13] Old regime or we'd say "old guard".

thought of her time. But she gave something more precious than this. She gave herself.

As our grateful memories of her fall into perspective, we see what rank she takes in the succession of illustrious educators. Like Thring of Uppingham she realised that education is the transmission of life, of the life of the mind, kindled by the fiery particles which lie unquenched in noble literature. Like Thring she longed to give new opportunities to the rank and file, though she was not oblivious of the claims of the elite or unmindful of the value of their gifts. Hers was an unselfish, unexclusive humanism, tolerant of variety, never jealous of superiorities and eager to share in wide commonalty the precious consolations of culture. Born in an age of historical discovery, when the records of the past were being revealed with some assuagement of outworn controversies, history (not least in its appeal to the imagination) was the centre of her intellectual interest. But her standards of judgment were ethical. Plutarch and Sir Walter Scott stood high in her educational canon. Greatness in goodness was her ideal, and her ideal of goodness had in it, like Plato's, a place for beauty of pattern, colour and tune.

Through Ruskin and Thomas Arnold of Rugby, she was in direct succession from Wordsworth. In the luminous summary of principles which she prefixed to her series on HOME EDUCATION, there is much that might be illustrated by passages from *The Prelude*.

> Children are born persons. They are not born either good or bad, but with possibilities for good or evil. The principles of authority on the one hand and of obedience on the other, are natural, necessary, and fundamental; but these principles are limited by the respect due to the personality of children. By the saying Education is an Atmosphere, it is not meant that a child should be isolated in what may be called a child's environment, especially adapted and prepared: but that we should take into account the educational value of his natural home-atmosphere, both as regards persons and things, and should let him live freely among his proper conditions. It stultifies a child to bring down his world to what has been disparagingly called the child's level. In the saying that

Education is a Life, the need for intellectual and moral, as well as physical, sustenance is implied. The mind feeds on ideas and therefore children should have a generous curriculum.

Like Comenius, she believed in a course of reading which is massive and many sided. Like Comenius she had to guard against the dangers of superficiality.

The liberal movement which broke upon education through Rousseau found expression in Miss Mason's work as in that of her predecessors. But it had lost its neurotic excitement. Charlotte Mason was a woman of temperate judgment as well as of eager charity. She was steadied by a deep religious conviction, by the reverence for human personality which has in it the quiet awe of faith in Divine guidance.

The Lake School of Poetry and her own Lake School of Education are not unconnected. She was in the tradition of Wordsworth and the Arnolds. And the gratitude felt for her teaching and example will be extended to those who worked with her and by their loyal activities helped in the diffusion of her ideas.

M. E. Sadler, C.B.
The University
Leeds, February, 1923

III

St. Radegunds
Cambridge
February 16th, 1923

What a wonderful thing personal influence is, or may be! From an invalid couch in a remote part of England, Charlotte Mason reanimated and reformed a large part of education in Great Britain. It needed no long visit to her at AMBLESIDE to understand how this influence made itself felt. In her conversation, even on trivial matters, but still more on the greater issues of life and policy, one became vividly aware in her of a lucid view of affairs, and an intellectual grasp of principles, animated by the inward warmth of sympathy and hope. Surrounded by a group of faithful disciples, she directed the course of many a ship on the education ocean which personally she never saw; and like many supreme organisers of great industries, while apparently at leisure herself, was exactly aware of what was doing in all the provinces of education where her principles were in action. Yet she was no bureaucrat; her practice was as various and elastic as her principles were constant; there was the method and even the letter, but above all the spirit. I hope and think that the chief secret of Miss Mason's ascendancy was the fine ethical quality of her teaching. From AMBLESIDE there issued many an earnest missionary imbued not only with a sense of order, a lover of learning and an insight into rudimentary and growing minds, but above all sanctified by a lofty ethical spirit, a spirit not merely added to her system of education, not merely supplied in parcels of so many hours a week, but penetrating the whole and carrying it into a higher sphere where it was enlarged, warmed, and enlightened. We lament Miss Mason's death, because of our personal loss, and our sense of what might have still been done had a longer life been given to her; but, on the other hand, we may rejoice to know that she lived at a time of change, just when her hand upon the helm was most needed, and that her frail life was spared long enough to make her mark upon England's education and to build up her own people for many generations to come.

Clifford Allbutt
Regius Professor of Physics, Cambridge

IV

Through having common interests in education, literature and religion, I was made acquainted with Miss Mason, and more than once had the pleasure of visiting her at AMBLESIDE. To do so was to be made quickly aware of a mind and spirit that triumphed over difficulties which in many other people daunt their ambition and activity in work. Miss Mason reigned from her couch. And her dominating influence was as much an inspiration as a governing force. She planned and schemed her courses of education, yet never once made more of the scheme than of the spirit of her lessons.

I had good ground for knowing also that to her, more than literature, more even than poetry was Religion itself. This was proved in that work to which she gave much time and effort—the verse paraphrase and comment of much of the Gospel record, and to which she gave the title, THE SAVIOUR OF THE WORLD. Others will write upon and commemorate her system of education. To me let it fall to mention the work dearer to her heart, perhaps, than all the rest.

W. H. Draper
Master of the Temple

V

The Girl Guides,
25, Buckingham Palace Road
London, S.W.I.
February 21st, 1928

It is a very great pleasure to me to write something about Miss Mason and her wonderful work.

Never shall I forget the memorable day in May 1922, when I was at last able to pay my first visit to the HOUSE OF EDUCATION. Its name and fame is so well known in the Girl Guide world, and as a humble worker in the educational field I had long wanted to meet the Founder of the P.N.E.U.

The County Commissioner for Westmorland and I were met on arrival by the kindest welcome from Miss Mason, and her ready interest and willing discussion made me feel at once that, though actually somewhat outside her province, the Guides had her true sympathy and warm approval.

I remember so well one remark she made. After having luncheon amongst the students she took me to sit on the verandah and then leaning gently towards me from her wheeled chair, she said, "You know I am a little afraid of you!" No! not SHE personally of ME personally!—but she meant that the special appeal and romance of the Guides were sometimes apt to tug away enthusiasts from some of their urgent and more matter-of-fact work and studies.

It was an extreme pleasure to me to have had that time in the company of one to whom parents and children will always owe so much. In my mind's eye as I write I can see her sitting with folded hands on the verandah at SCALE HOW watching her students at play, as keenly interested in the game as in everything that makes for the happiness and wellbeing of youth.

VI

We have received the following from General Sir Robert Baden-Powell:—

A FIELD MARSHAL'S GOVERNESS

How did the Boys Scouts start?

Oh well! I believe it was largely due to—whom shall we say?—a Field Marshal's governess.

It was this way; the Brigadier General, as he was at that time, was riding to his home after a field day when from the branches of a tree overhead his little son called to him, "Father, you are shot; I am in ambush and you have passed under me without seeing me. Remember you should always look upwards as well as around you."

So the general looked upward and saw not only his small son above him but also, near the top of the tree, the new governess lately imported from Miss Charlotte Mason's training College at AMBLESIDE.

Her explanation of the situation was that a vital point in up-to-date education was the inculcation of observation and deduction and that the practical steps to this were given in the little handbook for soldiers of "Aids to Scouting." The present incident was merely one among the various field stunts from that book which might be put into practice by her pupils and herself.

For example, they might as another exercise creep about unseen but seeing all the time, and noting down everything that the general did; they might lead him off on some wild chase while they purloined some tangible proof of their having invaded his sanctum. Taken as a warning of what he might expect I daresay the governess's explanation opened the general's eye pretty widely, if only in regard to his own future security against ambuscades and false alarms.

But it certainly opened mine to the fact that there could be an educative value underlying the principles of scout training; and since it had been thought worthy of utilisation by such an authority as Miss Mason I realised that there might be something in it.

This encouraged me in the direction of adapting the training for the use of boys and girls.

From this acorn grew the tree which is now spreading its branches across the world.

The Boy Scout of yesterday (reduced alas by some ten thousand who gave their young lives in the war) is already becoming the citizen of today (and none too soon) largely thanks to the Field Marshal's governess.

VII: A Pioneer of Sane Education
CHARLOTTE MASON*
(From the *Times*, January 17th)

Many hundreds of parents and teachers in all parts of the world will join in mourning Miss Charlotte Mason, who died in her sleep at the HOUSE OF EDUCATION, AMBLESIDE, at noon yesterday. She founded the PARENTS' NATIONAL EDUCATIONAL UNION so long ago as 1887, and strove steadily for more than half a century to create a system of education that should form a balanced union of religious belief and literary and scientific thoroughness.

Her personal influence was probably more widespread than that of any educationist of her time. The loyalty which she inspired was more than could be accounted for by the mere weight and force of her educational philosophy. The HOUSE OF EDUCATION founded by her rapidly acquired a tradition and a spirit radiating throughout the great system which she evolved of "home schools," with many hundreds of children and governesses widely separated in space but one in endeavour, working through the same syllabuses with the same books, and passing by means of test papers, sent to AMBLESIDE for correction, through the same series of grades. Until almost the last it was the pride of Miss Mason's many disciples that she knew all the children in the PARENTS' UNION SCHOOL, looked through their work, and followed their progress. The HOUSE OF EDUCATION has been, incidentally,

---

* By kind permission of the Editor of the *Times*.

the only institution that has offered special professional training to the private governess.

Charlotte Maria Shaw Mason was born on January 1st, 1842, the daughter of Joshua Mason, a Liverpool merchant. After a home education she was drawn to teaching work, and after some experience in various schools and in a training college, at Chichester she began her work as an educational reformer, and eventually founded the UNION associated with her name. The principles which she preached and which she lived to see widely adopted, both in the schools that confessedly carried out her ideas and in schools that tacitly adopted them, were the hunger for knowledge, the use of school life as a deliberate preparation for the larger interests of life, and the cultivation of a natural and earnest interest in nature and art. She continually preached the oneness of education and the universal necessity of knowledge: "Without knowledge Reason carries a man into the wilderness and Rebellion joins company." That is a quotation from a remarkable series of letters on THE BASIS OF NATIONAL STRENGTH contributed to the *Times* in 1921. Knowledge well balanced was her panacea for the dangers of revolution; and such knowledge must be universal. It was the due balance on different sides of education which in her view made for national sanity.

The PARENTS' UNION SCHOOL was founded in 1891 to press forward these principles, and by 1918 Miss Mason's ideas had permeated some 40 elementary schools,* a number of preparatory schools adopted the syllabuses in greater or less degree and became known as P.N.E.U. SCHOOLS, a guarantee to parents that the home point of view would at least not be disregarded. Great praise of the method came from various parts of the country—Bradford, Gloucestershire—and Miss Mason was satisfied to the last that her scheme of education was making considerable progress in elementary as well as secondary schools and in private teaching. Miss Mason's publications include:

- HOME EDUCATION
- PARENTS AND CHILDREN
- SCHOOL EDUCATION

---

* Now over 200.

- OURSELVES
- SOME STUDIES IN THE FORMATION OF CHARACTER
- THE AMBLESIDE GEOGRAPHY BOOKS
- THE SAVIOUR OF THE WORLD (a life of Christ, an issue running into six volumes)
- THE BASIS OF NATIONAL STRENGTH
- A LIBERAL EDUCATION FOR ALL.

Miss Mason's work was not dethroned by the various modern developments in the direction of freedom of education. Together with other educational reformers of today she saw children not as little unwilling receptacles for information, but growing creatures struggling towards the light, eager to learn, eager to work, and too often starved of the means of doing so.

VIII: A Personal Tribute
(from the *Times* Educational Supplement, January 20th)

A correspondent writes: Charlotte Mason was that rare combination:— an original thinker and philosopher and at the same time a wonderful organiser and business woman. She was wise and witty, keenly interested in the things of the world, birds, and flowers, books and people, but with an inner vision for the beyond, and the graciousness of manner and selfless consideration for others which marked the *grande dame* of a passing age. She treated the smallest child with courtesy. She was gracious to the youngest member of her household just as she was to the great of the land who were among her disciples. Her students and all who came under her influence caught the fire of her enthusiasm for her educational principles together with her singlemindedness and humility.

She never allowed her methods of teaching and philosophy of education to be called by her name, but by that of the society she founded to spread them. Thus her work will continue and be ably carried on by those she has trained and appointed for the task. She was at work up to four days before her death, and personally superintended the many arrangements for accommodating the ever-increasing number of students wishing to enter her college. Her end was the passing of a great spirit. With all her powers of mind and heart fresh and keen, memory and apprehension unimpaired, she fell asleep after many days spent for the good of humanity. Her teaching has spread to almost every part of the globe; the pupils of her correspondence school are to be found in home schoolrooms, in private and council schools, and many generations of happy children filled with the joy of living and of learning will rise up and call her blessed.

IX: From Other Papers

There is ample reason for supposing that a great educational effort for the improvement of our methods of teaching our native language and literature will meet with its reward. We are in truth an artistic people, though we are shy of acknowledging it... And that great educator, Miss Charlotte Mason, whose death we are now deploring, has shown us how readily English children respond to the appeal of the masterpieces of English literature.

H. A. L. Fisher

X

Miss Mason and her gospel had a curiously conspicuous way of arousing enthusiasm. The present writer recollects, at a distance of 36 years, the sight of the first issue of the PARENTS' EDUCATIONAL REVIEW and the interest awakened among those parents whom Frances Mary Buss summoned together in 1887 or thereabouts to start the first London branch of the P.N.E.U. Frequently since then one has come across in some remote country vicarage a struggling and not very well-equipped governess who would—on the showing of some sympathy—open out as a glowing adherent of Miss Mason's methods, testifying that, through her influence, teaching had been literally turned from darkness into light; while to meet a student from the HOUSE OF EDUCATION, AMBLESIDE, was most assuredly to meet an enthusiast for education and, as a rule, a lover of children. It is characteristic of the fine spirit of the woman that P.N.E.U. methods and ideals have never advertised her own name; yet to many her death will come with a sense of personal loss.

XI

Of Miss Mason it is difficult for us to speak when there are so many much better qualified to do so. Out of the love in her heart she gave up a long life to the betterment and well-being of her fellowmen, and of late years her influence, her writings and her teaching have spread far and wide throughout the world; very high rank will she take amongst the educationists of this or any other age. But standing out above all this—that which so greatly endeared her to her students, to her staff and to her friends—was her humble, loving, Christian faith and character, the secret which won for her the love of all with whom she came in contact.

PART II
(2) The Union and Its Founder
Haud Immemor[14]

It was in the autumn of 1886 that I first came into personal touch with Miss Charlotte Mason, through reading her book HOME EDUCATION. I was then a young mother, with four children, the eldest of whom was 7, and Miss Mason's exposition of her ideas of what Home Education might be, and should be, was an inspiration to me. A most delightful and interesting correspondence ensued, in which Miss Mason outlined her plans and projects for organising the PARENTS' NATIONAL EDUCATIONAL UNION, and into these Lord Aberdeen and I entered with zest. This accounts for the honour done us by Miss Mason, when she invited us to become joint Presidents of the new ASSOCIATION when framed in 1887. We accepted that invitation with considerable diffidence, being conscious of our own lack of training, and our absorption in public affairs, but at the same time highly prizing the mark of confidence thus shown, and the privilege of being connected with a scheme so full of opportunity and potentiality. Miss Mason assured us that a Chairman of Committee and an Hon. Organising Secretary and other Officers would be appointed to take charge of the practical work of the UNION, and that therefore our regular attendance at Committees would not be required. Her persistence overcame our scruples, and we deeply value the association of our names with hers all through the period of her great life work; and her patience with such truant Presidents as we have been, whilst resident in other countries during many years.

We have had personal experience of the benefits of Miss Mason's beneficent transformation of home education, not only in connection with our own children, but more especially as it has affected our grand children, and our grand nephews and nieces. In particular has this been true in the case of two of our grandchildren, who were faithful pupils of the PARENTS' UNION SCHOOL under teachers trained at AMBLESIDE, during seven years residence in India, and who certainly do the

---

[14] Not forgotten.

utmost credit to the system, to the joy of their proud grandparents.

There will be others, who lived in close fellowship with Miss Mason, who will tell of the miracle of the far spreading influence of that frail life, and how she, invalid as she was, directed and watched over every item of the work and the many developments of the P.N.E.U., of the PARENTS' UNION SCHOOL, the PARENTS' REVIEW, and of the HOUSE OF EDUCATION at AMBLESIDE.

But we yield to none in our thankfulness and appreciation of the magical effects which her genius, devotion and foresight-coupled with her reverence for, and marvellous understanding of child life, have wrought for thousands and thousands of children, to whom the treasures of life have thus been revealed. They will send their tributes of affection and gratitude from all over the world, and be in very truth a "choir invisible" testifying to the

> Immortal dead who live again
> In minds made better by their presence, live
> In pulses stirred to generosity,
> In deeds of daring rectitude, in scorn
> For miserable aims that end with self,
> In thoughts sublime that pierce the night like stars,
> And with their mild persistence urge man's search
> To vaster issues.
>
> *Ishbel Aberdeen and Temair*[15]
> February 12th, 1923

I take the privilege of identifying myself, wholeheartedly, with this tribute.

Aberdeen and Temair
Joint President, P.N.E.U.

C. M. M. - The Friend

When one writes at the end of a close friendship which has lasted 30 years, there is much that one feels to be too sacred to put into words. At the most it is of things of the surface that one dares to speak, of the love and kindness and

---

[15] See also page 183.

sympathy which Miss Mason gave me during all these years one cannot speak. I hope that one day some of the wonderful letters which are among my most precious possessions may be published.

It is perhaps as her 'chela,'[16] as she sometimes called me, that I may be allowed to add my note to the chorus of praise and gratitude that we are raising to her. When as a young mother of 26 I first read a number of the PARENTS' REVIEW and became a member, I at once felt that the P.N.E.U. was the one 'cause' which appealed to me. Though still a young woman I had married so early that I already had quite big children, and I felt sorry that I had known of this rather late.

I was determined to learn all I could and to help others to avoid those first mistakes which so often mean tears and sorrow. Circumstances made it possible for me to make a pilgrimage to AMBLESIDE and Miss Mason at once admitted me to her friendship and taught me so much. It was she who told me to read aloud daily to my children; and how possible a daily half hour is even in a busy life I proved for over 20 years. She introduced me to the delights of open windows and fresh air and of the country *even* when it rains. She shared with me, as through her work and writing with thousands of others, her own love of the beautiful in literature, poetry, art and nature and many owe her some of their greatest happiness because of this.

The first Natural History Club was started in London and those rambles of parents with their children have given a new joy in life to hundreds of homes. Incidentally, Mrs. Perrin's wonderful book of wild flower illustrations is due to these rambles.

We started the first PARENTS' UNION SCHOOL Class in 1894, taught by two of her teachers, and thus through the idea of the combination of families, Secondary and, later, Elementary Schools asked to be enrolled. She inspired and helped all the efforts and always in that wonderful impersonal way.

Her visits to our home every year up to 1914 were the annual festival for all the household; former maids have written saying how her gracious personality filled them with loving memories. The many distinguished people who used

---

[16] Disciple or follower of a guru.

the opportunity of her being in London to sit at her feet and learn, from Board of Education officials to teachers of every kind, have shown the result of such talks in the whole trend of modern educational movements from the Report on the Teaching of English, down to small reforms in private schools. It was her humility of mind together with the power of her educational philosophy which won for her the triumphs that we so rejoice she lived to see. It was when she was visiting in the home of the present poet laureate that she encouraged Mrs. Bridges to produce her copy book and thus give to the world the method of teaching beautiful writing, which she was adopting in her P.U.S. homeschool room for her own children. Of this Miss Mason wrote in the PARENTS' REVIEW in 1899:

> Five years ago, we heard of a lady who was elaborating by means of the study of old Italian and other manuscripts, a 'system of beautiful handwriting' which could be taught to children. We have waited patiently, though not without some urgency, for the production of this new kind of 'copybook.' We have felt that the need for such an effort was very great, for the distinctly commonplace writing taught from existing copybooks, however painstaking and legible, cannot but have a rather vulgarising effect both on the writer and the reader of such manuscript. At last the lady, Mrs. Robert Bridges, has succeeded in her tedious and difficult undertaking, and this book for teachers will enable them to teach their pupils a style of writing which is pleasant to acquire because it is beautiful to behold. It is surprising how quickly young children, even those already confirmed in 'ugly' writing, take to this 'new handwriting.' We shall welcome Mrs. Bridges' efforts in proportion as we feel, with her, that the average hands, which are the outcome of the old copybook writing, degraded by haste, seem to owe their common ugliness to the mean type from which they sprang.

It was on one of her visits to London that she met the 'musical baby' in 1895, and persuaded Mrs. Howard Glover to give to the UNION her ideas on musical appreciation and to set the terminal programme of music to be heard and understood. Miss Mason had the wonderful gift of revealing to parents, student, teacher and child their own innate powers and of helping them to use these to the full. She trusted and believed in us and so we dared not fail her.

But it was 'for the children' that she lived and worked and thus through her, generations of children have learnt the joy of a liberal education, the joy of learning and of serving. To the end our dear teacher was herself learning and serving. She read daily for several hours and was always taking in new ideas which stimulated her thought and helped her to help us.

Her wit and her wisdom, her beauty of spirit and graciousness are with us always, her philosophy and teaching will live and bear fruit. We thank God for His gift to the world of one of His most beautiful spirits—Charlotte M. Mason.

H.F.[17]

Public Elementary Schools

The death of Charlotte Mason, who finished a long life of great intellectual activity by just closing her eyes to wake in another world, has left a void in many a household in which for more than a generation she had been the polestar to which hundreds of eager children and grateful parents looked each day of their lives for direction in their studies, and never looked in vain.

She was a great teacher, and had the genius to think out new methods, and the fruitful ingenuity to set the methods going, and the unfaltering industry to keep them going and growing in spite of the fact that she had to lead an invalid's life for many years, so that by her magic influence she has made a large section of society able to choose the right path in the all-important matter of education, directed to the formation of character and the widening of intelligence as befits those who aim at being useful citizens and God-fearing men and women.

It was in the autumn of 1915 that Miss Mason, to talk with whom as she lay on her couch on the verandah at SCALE

---

[17] The Honorary Mrs. Henrietta Franklin. See also page 113.

HOW was always a real treat, asked me to listen as she unfolded a scheme which she had very much at heart for bringing a new atmosphere into the lives of the children in our elementary schools, and she begged me to go and see for myself the really wonderful work which her method had in quite a short time effected in some of the schools in Bradford, Yorkshire.

She told me that the principle was to teach "by the humanities," that is to say by supplying the children from quite the earliest teachable age with plenty of really good English literature: and she was ready to stake her reputation on the fact that they would understand and assimilate what they read to themselves, and would love to feel that they were getting of themselves daily new knowledge.

I found that Miss Mason had been under no deception. All that she had expected had come to pass and the experiment was already a perfect success.

Now these children were not picked specimens—they were mostly miners' children from the Yorkshire coalfield, but their bright, happy faces showed that Miss Mason's idea that a child was naturally anxious to know, and would be intensely interested in feeling that he was getting fresh knowledge by his own endeavours, through quite a new way of looking at the teaching problem, was a real incontrovertible fact. The treating the child as a pitcher into whom so many facts were to be poured was to be discontinued entirely, and the laborious task of the teacher in lecturing to a class who never tried to give their attention was to be exchanged, to the great comfort both of teacher and pupil, for a system by which the child was the labourer, and pleased to be so, whilst the teacher guided, and explained difficulties and was at hand to help if required; thus putting an end to the ingrained idea of so many, indeed the vast majority, of teachers of the old method, that for both master and pupil a terrible amount of "drudgery" was inevitable.

I have visited these Bradford Schools more than once, and also a very fine group of Gloucestershire Schools, in and about Stroud, and a notable and very large School at Brixton in the London Area.

All show similar results, and the results are astonishingly good, and in all of them the teachers declare their indebtedness to Miss Mason's guidance and say that nothing could induce any of them to go back to the old methods.

Miss Mason started with the conviction that the brains of all normal children are of the same calibre, and only require a constant supply of food, which children of all classes, if the supply is good and sufficient, readily assimilate.

Further, that each child was a person, and had its own points of view and its own ways of dealing with the matters that interested it, and was to be treated by the teachers as an individual, not simply as one of a class. Some were quicker than others, but all in time—and there was to be no hurry— would arrive; and each term would bring them increased intelligence and power.

The method was being used throughout each school I visited, beginning with the youngest: and the very first steps were, I think, the most interesting. All school teachers will agree that the great difficulty in teaching a class is to get and keep their attention.

This is the first thing our new method sets itself to do; and this, once obtained in the lowest class, is never lost; the children being eager to listen and to prove that they have done so.

The way this habit of close attention is acquired is really very simple. The teacher takes a subject which interests the children and reads part of a page in a clear and interesting manner. All listen, for they know that the next step will be that one of them will be called on to stand up and narrate to the others what all have just heard read. Everyone follows the narration, keen to correct if the narrator goes wrong, and with their help but with none from the teacher, the class gets through the piece and begins on another. But herein is the secret, all know that the teacher will only read the bit once, so if they don't give their close attention they will have no chance to join in the game.

In the next class the bit read is longer, and the accuracy and spirit with which a child of 8 or 10 remembers and repeats a whole page almost word for word is only less astonishing than the power the children show of retaining for weeks and months, again almost word for word, what they have once assimilated. And the powers thus derived from a habit of attention extends to all their work and they are found to have mastered and retained the subjects they have read to themselves.

This reading to themselves is their education. The books have always been chosen for each term by Miss Mason herself and the child is expected to labour and will in the course of a term have read two or three thousand pages of really good literature, gaining thereby not only information but a keen interest in many subjects, and imperceptibly a greatly enlarged vocabulary and a power of clear expression which raises them at once to a level they could under the old methods never even have dreamt of.

The first essential for working this wonderful new mode of education is a plentiful supply of the right sort of literature. It is books and more books that the children must have, both prose and poetry by good authors who have the power of writing clearly and in good English and have something interesting to say.

When once the children are well on their way they find a real delight in their work as is testified by the universal look of brightness on the faces of a whole class; and the increased intelligence, which is a marked consequence of their reading, shows itself in the quick way in which they master all the subjects put before them including, as one of the Head teachers told me, even their needlework.

From Literature we pass to the Arts.

Music has long been acknowledged as an elevating and refining power and a graceful handmaid of education. Miss Mason saw that besides music and poetry there was a potency in painting.

That great headmaster, Edward Thring, made drawing a necessary part of education, something to teach boys to observe and to assist the imagination. Miss Mason had good photographs of the work of the best painters both ancient and modern exhibited to her elementary school children, who were quick to follow the details and to notice the essential beauties and the means by which the painter had got his effects, and they could write an account, after studying these reproductions of famous pictures, which almost always showed what a hold a fine work of art is able to get on a child's imagination. Now here is, I cannot but think, a powerful aid to the educating of children to see what is

beautiful in nature and to give them a proper feeling of
disgust at the defacement and want of sympathy with those
natural beauties which is everywhere today exhibited by the
papers, tins and bottles left littering the ground after a picnic
in any lovely spot which English men, women and children
visit in their summer excursions.

We shall not get rid of these horrors until education has
brought to our people a proper love of beauty and reverence
for Nature; and this process must begin as Miss Mason
wisely saw, in our elementary schools.

I have spoken of only the latest development of Miss
Mason's method; all children interested her, and she had the
real lake-dweller's love of the beauties of natural scenery, and
the greatest reverence for the Lake poets and for all the
eminent Victorians, and her enthusiastic nature
communicated an impetus to her friends for all that was best
worth living for, so that one felt how, from that invalid couch
we all knew so well, a benign influence radiated from her
gracious presence, which will light the way for many
hundreds of her friends and pupils in the future, and cause
all the present generation to keep her forever in their most
affectionate remembrance.

I should like to add a word about the PARENTS' REVIEW,
which Miss Mason edited and in which she from time to time
expounded her views, whilst others who witnessed the result
of her work often bore testimony in its pages; the frequent
papers on Natural History were a very pleasant feature which
we all looked forward to and followed with enjoyment. But
what is perhaps most remarkable is that the REVIEW has had
so long a life—it began in 1890—and except at the first
starting it has been maintained entirely by voluntary
contributions. May its life be still prolonged!

Willingham F. Rawnsley

Memories

It was in the year 1887 that the nucleus of the P.N.E.U. was
formed by a small committee of members who had known
Miss Mason's work in Bradford. It is now nearly 30 years ago
that I attended my first meeting in London at a house in
Grosvenor Square and there decided to join at once. I hardly

know what it was that attracted me so strongly to the
movement; whether the honoured names of educational
pioneers included in the list of officers of the Council, or the
Programme with its offer of the best classics on the subject in
the lending library, the lectures, discussions, cooperation in
securing teachers, and forming classes; or was it the
PARENTS' REVIEW—a magazine of Home Training and
"*Culture,*" magic word! Anyhow I resolved to seek the earliest
opportunity of making Miss Mason's acquaintance and this
fortunately happened in the autumn of the same year. She
was staying at Highfield, Ilkley, a house which was a
favourite resort for intellectual and poetic natures in holiday
time, high up on the edge of the moor, and as I was in the
neighbourhood I ventured to write and ask her to allow me to
go over one afternoon, and met with her usual kind response.
Accordingly I climbed up from the station at Ben Rhydding
one hot August day and there in the sunshine and the
heather I spent a happy and memorable hour with the sweet
and gentle person for whom I had acquired such an inward
respect and veneration.

Her encouraging manner and quiet simple talk disarmed
all nervousness and made me entirely at ease; her
understanding and sympathy, her love of children and
confidence in the good in them, her ideas of developing their
tastes and talents, of avoiding the stumbling blocks put in
their way by injudicious elders, her respect for the efforts of
well-meaning parents ignorant of their own inefficiency, and
her earnest desire to help them, her estimate of the value of
early environment, example and training, the formation of
habits, the love of Nature, the freedom of leisure, the
atmosphere of truth that should surround these tender little
ones whom none may despise, the ultimate goal of character,
all these and many other ideals inspired me with noble
ambitions, though with a despairing sense of shortcoming;
for what mother could suffice for these things? Later
glimpses, all too short, but always a privilege, came in
meetings at Bad Nauheim, where the grave heart trouble that
affected her for so many years, caused her to spend several
weeks each summer following the cure, which happily
brought invariable benefit. The wonderful patience and
cheerfulness with which she bore her physical frailty and

limitations were a living testimony to that Faith which was her 'sure foundation' and inspired the optimism and calmness of spirit, the wise and steadfast philosophy that made her such an unfailing counsellor to others in difficult ways, and gave pause to realise she tapped the Source that makes "quietness and confidence your strength."

I have often thought that the initials which form the familiar title of the UNION are a fortuitous combination for a work which the Founder so ardently yet humbly regarded as a channel for the manifestation of the Spirit τό '' Αλιοσ Πνεῦμα.[18] The HOUSE OF EDUCATION was to those who knew its true inwardness, a dedicated Temple of the Holy Ghost and surely no one ever more adequately expresses the sevenfold gifts in her sphere of influence than Charlotte Mason, the spirit of Wisdom and Understanding, of Counsel and Might, of Knowledge and true Godliness and of Holy Fear; none more truly illustrated the charge of St. Paul "If ye live in the Spirit walk in the Spirit." May we not apply to her the 'Old Lament of Ephraem Syrus' in the *Times* of February 8th:

> From her home is borne a Woman
>   Whose dear Presence was its guide;
> Those now left there mourn in common,
>   As men wept when Rachel died.
>   Strong Upholder
>   In that House do Thou abide.
>   I.B.S. Whitaker-Thompson

A Few Recollections

It was at a drawing room meeting at the London house of the Duchess of Portland, in the year 1892, that I first met Miss Mason and heard her speak. I have always remembered the impression then made upon me by her gracious personality, and great charm of voice and manner.

The title of the address is forgotten, but it concerned her gospel of education and from that day others, besides myself, must have realised that they had seen a new vision. That was

---

[18] The Holy Spirit.

the beginning, too, of a friendship which has been for 30 years one of the greatest privileges and pleasures of my life.

A little later in Florence I came upon Miss Mason and her friend, Mrs. Firth, standing by Giotto's Tower, and together we studied his beautiful medallions. I shall always especially associate with them that of the woman weaving on the loom which Ruskin copied when he revived hand-weaving in the Lake country.

In September 1894 I paid my first never-to-be-forgotten visit to Miss Mason at AMBLESIDE. At that time she and Miss Kitching[19] lived at Springfield, down in the valley, which was one branch of the HOUSE OF EDUCATION in the early days. The day after my arrival Miss Mason took me across the road to view the big house on the hill which she thought of moving into, so as to have all her students under one roof, and make a worthy home for the HOUSE OF EDUCATION. As we walked up the drive the sun shone brightly, and in front of the house we stopped and turned round to gaze on Loughrigg and Wansfell, with Windermere between and said to each other, "Just think, Wordsworth stood here and looked at all that!" for his niece Mrs. Harrison (née Wordsworth) had lived at SCALE HOW in his lifetime and till 1892. We went all over the house, up and down and into every corner, and decided with Mr. Curwen, the architect, who met us there, about the few alterations and improvements which would be needed. Altogether we planned for a beautiful future, nearly 29 years of which, with its fine record, now belong to the past.

Another day Miss Mason took me to Keswick on the top of the mail coach. It was a good old fashioned coach with four horses, a leisurely vehicle from which one had plenty of time to see everything. That day I had a wonderful lesson in "sight-seeing," as Miss Mason understood it. And what delightful fun we had, and how much enjoyment out of all kinds of little everyday trifles!

Shortly after this time when Miss Mason had to realise the physical limitations due to ill health, she had the great wisdom to order her life in such a way that every available grain of energy could be given to the work which was so dear to her, so that in the many future visits which I paid to her

---

[19] See pages 67 and 120.

our excursions did not go beyond the beautiful daily drives in the near neighbourhood.

These were taken in her little Victoria, driven by her faithful man, Barrow.[20] Here we looked for red-starts, and there to see if the daffodils were in flower, and some days we went round by Grasmere and bought gingerbread from old Sarah Nelson.

I wish I could give a clearer picture of it all. Those who were at that delightful Conference at AMBLESIDE last May will always carry with them some idea of the charm of SCALE HOW under its dear Mistress.

Helen Webb

Our Leader Still

Our teacher and leader is gone from us. For a moment we look back to gather up the memories that are to be our inspiration for the future. But she would not have us look back for long, nor at all with purposeless regret. Our work, her work, is before us. And the loss of the leader is a stage that must be passed in the progress of the cause. She sows the seed, but she cannot reap the harvest. For its ripening there must be time, and many suns: for its garnering a multitude of helpers.

We have leaned upon her hitherto: now we must take up the mission she has left us. There is no room for any loss of heart or vain regret. Rather, it is the time for a great thankfulness—thankfulness that the long rich years of that full life have been lived fully to the end, that to the end she worked with mind undimmed; her last book lately finished, still to publish. She has taught us what to do. The rest is our task. We shall go forward, for she leads us still.

I never saw her until the summer of 1919. Not until the end of 1917 (I say it to my shame) had I knowledge of her work. There were three short visits to AMBLESIDE, one of them most brief for the memorable Conference last summer, and an hour one afternoon at Gloucester, when she had come down to meet the teachers who were working with her (they always felt that it was *with* her) in the Gloucestershire

---

[20] See page 79.

Schools. Those schools were very dear to her. She loved all children, and all teachers were her fellow workers; but these had shown the world how truly she had gauged the powers of the child's mind (the mind of the worker's child does not differ from the mind of the rich man's), and had divined and provided for its needs in those generous programmes that ask so much of it, and in asking, give.

When you first saw her, knowing that she had been an invalid for many years, and must have suffered much, you looked perhaps for marks of pain and weariness and weakness. But there were none. After an hour you never thought of that again. Years had written many lines upon her face, but they were not those lines. They spoke perhaps of the passage of time, but not of age; unless age is what gives and does not take away. You no more felt that she was old than that she was frail and weak of body. She had quietly (for she was always quiet) put pain and weakness and age away from her, and you were conscious only of what she had—of her surpassing gifts; it did not seem to you that she lacked anything. Her face was full of light, of wide sympathy and understanding, of delicate humour and gentleness and love. She always knew. From the first moment, the first word, the first letter, you had no doubt. She knew; she always would know; you could put your whole trust there.

When she talked with you she brought out the best that was in you, something that you did not know was there. That is a rare gift. The learned and the wise are seldom so endowed. We admire from afar—and remain afar. I have known only her and one other, who had that generous and princely way with their rich store. She and Sidney Irwin of Clifton College were alike in this. They would both of them take it for granted, or appear to do so (but I think it was natural and unaffected in them) that you had read and thought what they had read and thought; that you knew what they knew, and could do what they did. They caught you up to their level, and for the time you stayed there; and you never quite fell back again. They had given you new light, new power.

She expected much of you, more sometimes than you knew that you had to give. But, as always, she was right; you had it and you gave, and of course gained by giving, for exercise gives strength.

Her gift for inspiring deep personal affection in the hearts of many who never saw her was rare, if not unique.

Though she taught a new thing, a new way, and in teaching had to show the old things and the old ways for what they really are, her criticism left no sting. She could not be anything but generous, and the ways of her mind were wide. So she did not make you feel small and foolish. You did not bite your lip or flush with vexation. She lifted and inspired. She did not drive: she led, and you went with her by happy choice.

In any difficulty she always saw the right way. With few words, always perfectly chosen, yet coming naturally and without trace of effort, she said what you knew at once to be the right thing, though you had groped long and had not found it. The right thought and the right word were always there.

It is not yet the time to measure up her whole achievement. The full harvest is not yet. But there is enough to justify the confidence that posterity will see in her a great reformer, who led the children of the nation out of a barren wilderness into a rich inheritance. The old bidding prayers of our homes of learning rise to our lips. The children of many generations will thank God for Charlotte Mason and her work.

H. W. Household[21]

A Father's Part in the Home Schoolroom

I feel it is a great privilege, as the father of children brought up in a PARENTS' UNION SCHOOLROOM, to bear testimony to the joy which this training brings to both parents and children.

In following Miss Mason's method the early work of the children is full of interest; every faculty has the opportunity of development, and the powers of observation and appreciation are stimulated, so that in later life the mind is

---

[21] See also page 185.

prepared to receive intelligently fresh impressions as they present themselves.

In the days of our home schoolroom there was great pleasure at the end of each term in hearing the oral examination, and noting with keen interest the progress that had been made and the intelligent appreciation of the various subjects shewn by the children. Then there were the country walks, which for me, owing to my professional engagements, were few and far between; but when they could be indulged in, were a source of great delight, as the children showed their knowledge of the surrounding villages, of every lane and turning, of every field path leading to some well known meadow, wood, or stream, and were able to point out where the earliest primrose or wild daffodil was to be found, to tell me when the herons had returned to their nests in the lofty trees above the lake, or note the scent of the fox that had passed that morning.

As time went on and new interests developed, a real appreciation of architecture shewed itself, and I was struck with the way in which the children were able to compare the details of a church which I explained to them with others about which they had read or which they had visited. When I took them to the National Gallery there was great pleasure in picking out the original pictures, the copies of which they had studied in their schoolroom.

One remembers so well the Winchester gathering of 1912, when on reaching the city the children knew their way about the town, having mapped it out aforetime, and when they met their fellow pupils in the school to note, how, though having come from places far apart and never having met before, they fell into their classes at once, so that onlookers would think they must have worked together for many weeks, so harmonious was the atmosphere. At the same gathering also, one was impressed with the intelligent way in which all the children showed their appreciation of the Cathedral, St. Cross, and other places of interest about which they had read during the previous term.

The work of the P.U. SCHOOL led up naturally, and without any real break, to the larger life of the public school, for which the children by their early training were well fitted, as it seemed merely the stepping from one classroom to another, so comprehensive and intelligent had been the previous preparation.

The whole training seems to invite a close companionship between parents and children through common interests and opportunities for nature study and the discussion of the problems of their own life history; thus the interest which parents and children take in each other's lives is largely due to Miss Mason's influence in teaching us as parents to realize that our children, from earliest babyhood, are persons with an individuality of their own, and are to be treated as such, not looked upon as mere playthings.

One cannot but feel what an enormous influence for good Miss Mason has bestowed upon the children of the country, now that not only home schoolrooms, but also large numbers of elementary and secondary schools have adopted her teaching and ideas, and that the work commenced at AMBLESIDE has spread throughout the English speaking world, and how helpful it has been to our colonial brethren, my own knowledge of the work done in New Zealand testifies.

Though the Founder has gone her influence remains and her work will continue.

J. W. Walker
O.B.E., F.S.A.

The P.U.S. from a Mother's Point of View

The obituary account of Miss Mason's work in the *Times* took me back to the days when, as a young mother, I started to teach my small boys with the help of the P.N.E.U. school. Now I am asked to write a short appreciation from the mother's point of view. I will try and put the clock back 18 or 19 years to the days when I first started to teach our children; two boys who began their school life in 1A and 1B. The years went on and I went on teaching, the family increased, five boys and one girl; gradually the elder boys went off to school, but the younger ones took their places; my one girl I taught till she went to school at 16 and then at last, when the two youngest boys went to school about three years ago, my teaching days came to an end. How little I thought when the first P.U.S. papers came, for how many years I should go on with the work—I who knew nothing of teaching and who had forgotten much of what I had learnt at school; how could I accomplish such an impossible task? Only by the arrival of the P.U.S. syllabus term by term.

As I look at some of the old books the intervening years are forgotten. I am back once more in thought to the days gone by when the children and I were learning together. History was a fascinating subject when taught by Arnold Forster. Magna Charta meant something with the story of the sewing machine. Elizabeth became a real person as one read *Kenilworth* and *Westward Ho*; French History, and later on as they grew older, European History added different points of view. Geography—such a dull subject in my day—lists of capes and bays, imports and exports—quite another thing, as one wandered through Northern Italy or took part in lion hunting in Africa; so too Nature Study by the help of Mrs. Brightwen and her delightful pets or Gilbert White, or that old friend *Life and Her Children*. Arithmetic was certainly the hardest subject when one had forgotten all but the four rules; however, by means of keeping just a little ahead, teaching myself by means of the examples, even this difficulty was negotiated. Housekeeping had to be done by 10 o'clock, for my bell rang then and my small people had to leave the garden for their work till one, with a short break in the middle of the morning. Scripture was always taken first and my mind goes back with gratitude to Dr. Paterson Smyth's books which helped to make the Bible stories so vivid—one could almost see Joshua and his men starting off for the long night march from Gilgal to the relief of Gibeon. Literature we generally took after lunch, I had old-fashioned ideas of the value of a rest then for the children, and I wish I had kept a list of books that I read aloud to them then. How many subjects we took and what a good library we gathered together and how exciting it was to see the new books that arrived each term. Picture talks, with the reproductions of artists of bygone days or modern times, Tales of St. Paul's Cathedral, and Westminster Abbey, Shakespeare plays that we read together—what a wide world we lived in, though we worked in the depths of the country! Then the end of the term with the examination, I as secretary taking down what my small people happened to remember (as days went on it was rather a comfort when they were able to write down their own answers), at the end of the week the big envelope went off—what excitement when the report came back, always with the kindly and encouraging criticisms, how interesting to see what marks were given and what fortunate person could take a step up into another form! Much water has flowed under the bridge since those days, and the scholars are scattered far and wide; some of the picture reproductions went to an Indian College where one of them is now teaching.

I have been living in the past as I write, realising how much happiness I owe to the vision of one woman. My case no doubt is similar to many others, scattered all over the world. Others will write of Miss Mason's work from the point of view of the trained teacher, but how much greater is the debt of the mother who without any training at all, could teach her children through the method that Miss Mason had worked out. It was she who made the impossible possible, who shewed us term by term what books to use and how to use them, who taught us to take the children straight to the fountain head and let them learn from the books themselves. It was she who realised what home education might become, who changed the whole atmosphere of the home schoolroom, who inspired us for our work and gave us the power to carry it out; a pioneer who blazed the trail that many of us followed with keen enjoyment and grateful hearts.

Gone are the schoolroom days—I am back again in the present,—the Indian mail is just in; for the two long letters, both so different yet telling so much of lives lived in that far off land; for that power of expression which means so much to those at home, how much we owe again to the lessons learnt long ago in P.U.S. days.

E. M. Capron

A Mother's Tribute

Would it not be true to say of Mothers that "some are born mothers; some achieve motherhood; and some have motherhood thrust upon them?" There are some women who although they are not called to marriage and human motherhood, have yet begotten spiritual children who "rise up and call them blessed." And of such surely was Charlotte Mason. Endured with powers of vision, of love, of courage, and of patience, such as are given to few, she has been the designer, the chief engineer and the foremost labourer of a road which now is trodden by many feet—both young and older—with hope and joyfulness.

The task God has given to mothers must always be the most responsible committed to any human being. It is nothing less than the training for His Service of His own children—children whose bodies must be sound and healthy, whose minds must be disciplined and alert, whose souls must learn to grow in the knowledge and love of their Father, if they are to fulfil the purpose for which He has sent them here. It was this vision which Miss Mason saw and which she gave her life to make real, this ideal which she ever held before the eyes of those who in the dusty ways of daily life were apt to rest content with a lower, a more material standard.

And so we mothers owe her a debt of gratitude which it is hard to put into words, for her wonderful help and inspiration in this great work of child training. As one who during the past eight years has had five members of her family in the P.U.S. I am grateful for the privilege of being allowed to try—ever so feebly—to voice this gratitude. It is difficult to single out special points, but I shall always remember with thankfulness how the Principal of one of our best known and largest girls' schools commented on my daughters' "power of concentration," and this I consider they owe almost entirely to their P.U.S. training. I have been asked whether this education was a good preparation for public schools run on somewhat different lines and I have no hesitation is answering "yes," an opinion which is amply justified by personal experience. The habit of concentration already mentioned, the love of good books for their own sake, the encouragement of wide and varied interests, all these are to my mind the best possible equipment for a boy or girl not only in public school life but in the wider life which follows, whatever its particular channel may be. One other point stands out clearly—the unvarying *personal* interest taken by Miss Mason in all her work; the little note in her own handwriting on every examination mark sheet was an eagerly looked for joy even to those of us who had never been privileged to see or know her more intimately.

We parents then would offer our tribute of gratitude to a loved and honoured name in firm faith that the road so nobly planned shall lead many travellers "on to the City of God." For though our leader has passed into the fuller light, her work lives and grows.

> No work begun shall ever pause for death!
> ... Through such souls alone
> God stooping shows sufficient of His light
> For us i' the dark to rise by.
>
> M. H. Swingler

Secondary Schools

It is no easy task to attempt to estimate the work and influence of Miss Mason in Secondary Schools. The greatness of that influence must be felt and acknowledged by all those who have watched with interest the development and progress of education during the last 30 years, and who have at the same time followed the teaching and studied the methods of one who by her entire lack of self-advertisement, her steady adherence to principles now acknowledged to be sound by the best thinkers, must surely take a leading place among the educational pioneers of our generation.

It is a comparatively easy task to recognise and appraise her work in those schools which profess to follow the principles of the UNION which she founded, but her influence has been far-reaching and it is in schools that have "tacitly adopted" her ideals without recognition or even realisation of her leadership that the greatest progress has been made, the most striking triumphs won. So great is the leavening power of a noble and forceful personality.

It is hardly an exaggeration to say that there is scarcely a Girls' School in the country that has not been directly or indirectly affected by her teaching, and it is interesting to find some of her firmly held principles embodied in the recently published Report of the Committee appointed to inquire into the Differentiation of Curricula between the sexes in Secondary Schools.

First and foremost of the gifts which Miss Mason brought to secondary schools is the gift of Freedom,—the taking of the child back to nature and reality and leading him into the realms of knowledge not only through the glories of our great literature, but by showing him his heritage in the world around him.

Let us go back to the year 1890 when Miss Mason came forward publicly as an educationist.

There are many of us who remember well the conditions in the great High Schools in the early 1890's. We realise as we look back how much gratitude we owe to the Headmistresses of those days for the firm stand they made in their demand for equal opportunities in education for boys and for girls. But we realise, too, the mistake that was then made by the majority of teachers. They aimed at fitting the girl to compete in all points with the boy, with too little regard for her social wellbeing and physical fitness. The pressure of homework came heavily upon the girl after her strenuous work at school, too seldom relieved by games, drill or any form of handwork. The approaching shadow of Public Examinations in which Art, Music, and other aesthetic subjects had no place cut her off from all pleasure in these subjects. Time would not permit her indulging in them.

The study of English Literature, apart from the books and periods set for examination purposes in the higher forms, was in some well known High Schools excluded from the curriculum. I, myself, remember being introduced to some of the glories of English poetry by a mathematical teacher who snatched moments in the intervals between examinations to fire the imagination of her pupils and to make them realise the beauties of their own language.

To how rich a heritage of books has Miss Mason introduced her children;—with what abundance of intellectual food she has supplied them to their lasting benefit! Shakespeare is now read by children of 10 years with enjoyment and intelligence, and annotated texts are becoming the exception and not the rule.

Again, in those early days the History lesson with its dry textbook, and short question and answer test gave little opportunity for training in thought and judgment. The affairs of the mother country were studied with little or no attention to the contemporary history of Europe, and for World History no time could be allowed. The teacher who realised a better way would seize moments to read short extracts from the great historical writers. One remembers being introduced in this way to Lecky, Tolstoi and others, and those moments remain fresh in the mind when much besides is forgotten.

For the giving to the child a wider knowledge of history—a subject which she believed was the most important in the training of good citizens—Miss Mason makes ample provision, and there are few schools to be found now where some teaching in World History as well as in European and English History is not given.

In quite recent years similar conditions might have been found prevailing in many of our large Boarding Schools, and even in the Government Training Colleges,—the same imprisonment of spirit—and sometimes of body, too—the same starvation diet, the same narrowly academic outlook.

But, thanks to the work of Miss Mason and others zealous in the cause of education, light has come into many dark places. The Girl Guide movement has been most helpful in this respect. The Heads of many schools now realise that the movement is a valuable aid, not a hindrance to the ordinary work, and are giving Guiding an honourable place in the Time Table. It must not be forgotten in this connection that the Scout movement may be said to owe its origin to Miss Mason.

But though progress in the schools has been steady much still remains to be done, and this no one realised better than Miss Mason herself. Those who were privileged to attend the P.N.E.U. Conference held last May at AMBLESIDE will remember well the inspiring words with which she closed her second address—

Let us be up and doing. Let us do battle with the schools for 'a liberal education.'

P. S. Goode, B.A.

Elementary Schools

Every member of the PARENTS' NATIONAL EDUCATIONAL UNION is realising the burden of a great loss in the death of its Founder, Miss Mason. Each has the knowledge that a great organiser and leader has been lost. Each feels that a dear friend has gone; one whose friendship was sweet because of its understanding, its sympathy, its largeness. Her spirit went abroad in her letters and books. And when one met her for the first time, it seemed like the renewal of an old friendship, and one picked up the conversation of yesterday without the poignant reminder of a break which "yesterday" often conveys.

One was conscious of the strength and urge of her spirit, of her enthusiasm for the cause of education, her faith in it, her will to pursue it. She expressed herself completely in the motto of all P.U. SCHOOLS: I AM, I CAN, I OUGHT, I WILL.

In forming the P.N.E.U. and establishing P.U. SCHOOLS, Miss Mason did the supposedly impossible. She blended the democratic and the aristocratic. By a seeming paradox she demonstrated a great truth. The "demos" were to be the "aristos." All were to have liberal opportunities of development, full and complete, so that the State she contemplated should not contain the self-destructive elements of a blind democracy and a selfish aristocracy. The best for all, that from the all would come, by Nature's logic, the best. Miss Mason promised no pre-natal change in the nature of the inhabitants of her "Utopia." The change would come as the fruit from the culture and care of the growing child. Humanity was not to be shipwrecked before it could reach her "New Atlantis."

Miss Mason had all the qualities of a great reformer; clear thinking, intelligent continued effort, high ideals, and faith. Faith she had abundantly. None who had the honour and privilege of meeting her in the Shire Hall, Gloucester, and the pleasure of listening to her address to the Heads of Schools in Gloucestershire working as P.U. SCHOOLS, will doubt her abundant faith. Its rays shone through all her words. She began by a confession of her own faith in children, in human nature, in the work of education. She ended by exhorting her audience to hold fast by faith.

The founding of the PARENTS' UNION SCHOOL in 1891 was followed by a steady growth of its influence on education in the home countries and the colonies, a growth springing from healthy root principles.

But if the extension of the UNION'S sphere was gratifying, it satisfied neither Miss Mason nor the helpers she had trained and imbued with her enthusiasm. The millions of children attending the State Primary Schools were not touched, the hunger of their "perfect but immature" minds unsatisfied because the rich and ample fare of mental food provided in the programmes of the P.U.S. was not given them.

The opportunity to extend the operations of the UNION to the field of state education came in the wonderful years between 1916 and 1919. The times were favourable. The world witnessed the rebirth of spiritual interest in education and a demand from civilised peoples for the best that could be obtained from education. There was divine discontent with the character and amount of education given in all types of school.

The success which followed the experiment at Drighlington proved the practicability of the system in a new type of school; and the pamphlet written by Miss Ambler, the head of the school and the pioneer of the P.U.S. in State primary schools, made available to all interested in education the results of the experiment.

The growth in the number of State schools which adopted P.U.S. syllabuses and methods became rapid. Interest was awakened, and inquiries from education authorities came from many and widely separated areas. Miss Mason was happily spared to live long enough to see a wonderful fruition to her labours.

Thousands of children are today receiving the education urged by the UNION, in schools provided and maintained by the State, and local education authorities, and the name of Miss Mason must surely be one heard in hundreds of homes where a few years ago she was unknown.

The county of Gloucester has more schools affiliated to the P.N.E.U. than any other county.* The pity is that the rest of England is not so conscious of its loss as Gloucestershire is awake to its gain.

The number is increasing, every term marking an addition to the roll of names of those schools joined to the P.N.E.U.

It is as the Head of a P.U. SCHOOL (elementary), that I would pay a due but inadequate tribute to the genius of a great educational reformer and organiser; would try to express a measure of thanks, which must always fall short,

---

* Over 100 now. -Ed

for the example of a lifelong devotion and sacrifice to education of the nation's childhood, here and throughout the English-speaking world. And I know that what is said here will have willing assent from my colleagues, who will feel, like myself, that "the half has not been told."

We remember Miss Mason because she taught us to regard the children as "perfect but immature"; that their minds were each an indivisible whole, with the dignity of a personality we must not outrage. She saved us from the growing belief that man might be greater than his Maker.

We remember Miss Mason because she showed us how practice in school might be natural and simple, natural because it used the inherent element of interest which the child brought to our schools. We knew this, but she showed us how to use and retain it. Natural, too, because those conditions of attention and concentration were always present with interest, and could not be cultivated from adventitious roots. Simple, because their application did not involve a peculiar or elaborate training. The educated mother, fortunate in having the leisure, may well and successfully educate her child at home.

We reverence the memory of Miss Mason because she showed us how happiness might permeate our classrooms; how there might be joy in learning, joy which grew from the "team" spirit in the class room. She made it possible for sympathy to be a constant bond between teacher and taught.

We are thankful to Miss Mason for the wisdom and choice with which she built up her programmes. By them our scholars were led from a land of locusts and wild honey to a fertile plain of rich and varied food. By them she made it no longer possible to describe our schools as "elementary."

For these few reasons only we pay this valedictory tribute to Miss Mason who did so much for the scholars and teachers in the nation's schools.

We mourn her death, but in our mourning we remember she lived.

G. H. Smith
(a Gloucestershire Headmaster)

Some Reminiscences

I think that it may interest some readers of the PARENTS'
REVIEW to know something about dear Miss Mason's early
professional life, but I must state at the outset that the
following account is necessarily fragmentary. I have no
memoranda to guide me and my memory (at 73½) fails me
sometimes. Moreover, dear Miss Mason was so much
absorbed in her work that she spoke but little of her own life.
For many years before her death those who lived with her
tried to save her as much as possible from the fatigue of
conversation; we always read to her in her few leisure hours.
Both Miss Mason's parents died when she was comparatively
young, and as her father was ruined by the American Civil
War it was necessary for her to work. She seems to have
made up her mind at once to devote herself to the cause of
education. There were no High Schools, or Secondary Schools
for girls in those days, and no women's colleges; it was only
the teachers in Elementary Schools who were supposed to
need training for their work. Training Colleges in those days
were not generally very well managed, but Miss Mason was
determined to avail herself of any advantage that was to be
had and took a short course of training at the Home and
Colonial Training College in order to qualify herself for
teaching in an Elementary School. Then, as in later life, she
thoroughly believed in children; she respected them and was
always confident that in every class of life children would
respond to proper treatment. In fact she took up the
profession of teaching as work for God and for the country,
and as she says in the preface to her books,

> each article of the educational faith I offer has been
> arrived at by inductive processes; and has, I think, been
> verified by a long and wide series of experiments.

If I mistake not, it was about this time in her life that Miss
Mason made the acquaintance of two ladies, teachers like
herself with high aims who became dear and lifelong friends.
I am not sure whether Miss Mason took more than one
school after finishing the short course of training, but I know
that about this time she became Headmistress of a Church
School at Worthing, and held this post for some years. Under

her management the school became quite famous in the neighbourhood; perfect order was maintained without any severity and the pupils worked with intelligence and eagerness. It was not surprising that Miss Mason made many friends in Worthing and was recognised as an authority on education. At that time there was a movement among earnest people to induce educated women of the professional classes to take up teaching in elementary schools, and in order to further the cause The Bishop Otter Memorial College at Chichester was set apart for training such women as mistresses for Elementary Schools. Miss Trevor was appointed Lady Principal, and Miss Mason had become so well known in the neighbourhood that she was appointed Lecturer on Education and Teacher of Human Physiology. In 1876 I went to Otter College as a student and thus came under dear Miss Mason's influence. Unlike her, I was not a born teacher, I was simply anxious to do some useful work and help my family (my father was a clergyman and an invalid and I wished to help him to retire.) Under dear Miss Mason's teaching, my views of life changed; I saw that teaching might be a noble profession instead of a mere trade, and I too longed to put her theories into practice. I am sure that many old "Otters" would gladly testify to the help and enlightenment they received from Miss Mason's lectures on Education. I remember she told us that the true teacher must be prepared to lay down her life for her pupils. At the end of my two years' training Miss Mason left the College and I remained for two years on the staff to qualify myself for my certificate. Miss Mason went to Bradford to teach in a school kept by one of the friends I have mentioned, and also to get some time for writing on education. It was at Bradford that she gave a course of lectures to ladies on "Home Education"; these lectures were afterwards published under the title of the book we know so well. I decided not to remain at Otter College after I had gained my certificate as I wished to teach in a school, and through Miss Mason's influence I was appointed Headmistress of a Higher Grade Board School in Bradford. I did not succeed very well in this position; the little success I did achieve was due to Miss Mason's advice. She wished me to remain and work for complete success, but I was comparatively young and thought I should do better elsewhere and left.

Then a little later Miss Mason went to AMBLESIDE to be with the other of the old friends I have mentioned. Miss Mason taught in her school and then gradually evolved and carried out the scheme of the HOUSE OF EDUCATION which has been such a wonderful success. Miss Mason began with four students in a small house. I need scarcely say that it was with great joy and gratitude that I accepted dear Miss Mason's invitation to join her in 1898 as Vice Principal of the HOUSE OF EDUCATION. The 22 years I spent there were the happiest years of my life and I can only thank God for His goodness in allowing me to be there.

F. C. A. Williams

Miss Mason's Message

A s we think of Miss Mason's long and beautiful life spent in ceaseless happy toil FOR THE CHILDREN'S SAKE, we ask ourselves what it was she strove to win for them, why it was that she was always happy no matter how weary. Was it a method of education all summed up in one word, narration? Was it the use of books? Was it love of Nature? Was it the power of self-expression in words, in material, in music? Was it happiness? Was it goodness? Was it worldly success? One may say that the good which Miss Mason sought included all these, but it went beyond, it reached out till it became fullness of living. One of life's problems is to see people whose learning is a byword and whose companionship is so dull, no joy issues to them from their fountain of knowledge; rather, it seems that these learned people carry a heavy burden. This problem has yet to be solved and may be considered later; we are more tempted to rest our thoughts upon the sun-bathed path of those who, following Miss Mason's teaching, know less but understand more, understanding because of the fullness of life that is theirs.

Our beloved teacher has passed away from us. We may no longer take to her our every perplexity; we may no longer look for her next article in the PARENTS' REVIEW which will clear up some fresh difficulty for us; we may no longer hope for the talk that will give us fresh insight into that full life which she lived and which her disciples recognised without necessarily being conscious of its source.

Longing as we do for comfort, let us hear her speaking to us from the book she prized more than any of her works, basing on it all her teaching philosophy.

Day by day we are taught to pray, by way of summing up all our requirements in this life, for 'knowledge of Thy truth'—the prayer in the Liturgy which seems to summarise most fully our Lord's teaching. But our practice hardly keeps pace with our prayer; we are apt to put two or three legitimate desires before what should be our primary inspiration; to *have* good—the cult of prosperity—is the prayer and effort of the natural man; to *be* good—the cult of sanctity—is the desire of the spiritually minded; to *do* good—the cult of philanthropy— sums up the religion of humanity: these things we should have, be and do, but we are becoming aware that there is a further duty which we may not leave undone. Our Lord's promise concerning the teaching of the Holy Spirit implies this further obligation: 'He shall bring all things to your remembrance, whatsoever I have said unto you.'

'All,' 'whatsoever,' double superlative, lays upon us the duty of detailed devout study of each one of the divine sayings; for, how can we remember that which we have not fully known. (Vol. V)[*]

Nor knowledge good for man can mankind know,
But He vouchsafes it; He is all our light. (Vol. I)

Accordingly Miss Mason pondered on the words and the life of our Lord and as the light came to her she used it as she used all she had, in the service of others.

Think ye that knowledge is a little thing
A man may hide in casket sure,
Certain its worth a beauty shall endure,
Nor, like a timid bird, take sudden wing?

---

[*] All the extracts given here are from THE SAVIOUR OF THE WORLD.

Think ye that none against you count may bring
For that ye know, for 'tis your very own?
I tell you that your knowledge is a loan
For all men's use; ye shall not hide, nor fling

Into the dustbin of your memory,
That knowledge ye with pains have got of me;
Who knows and teaches not shall feel the sting
Of guilt intolerable when before
The Judge he stands: for him, hath little love,
A lighter chastisement decrees the King...

He that hath much must needs impart the more,
And each shall give according to his store. (Vol. I)

Six precious volumes of this work remain for us to study,
rather should we say, for us to use in our endeavour to
achieve the fullness of life. Miss Mason's intention was to
produce eight volumes. The first appeared at Christmastide,
1908. Afterwards a volume appeared regularly every
Christmas till 1914. None of them were very generally
appreciated, chiefly because many of us would have preferred
the thought expressed in prose as we had heard her speak,
but that was because we did not find all at once how closely
packed with thought is every page of the verses, nor see that
no other form was possible. In the summer of 1915 Miss
Mason saw the beginning of the movement in the Elementary
Schools which was from that time onward to engross all her
time and strength, and in 1917 she told us that the last two
volumes of THE SAVIOUR OF THE WORLD would never be
written. The six existing volumes are in constant use in the
PARENTS' UNION SCHOOL where the work of the children proves
their worth. The passage to be studied is read in the Gospels
and then narrated. The children then set to work to
understand the passage more fully by comparing the different
accounts and by bringing all they know to bear upon it;
sometimes the teacher asks questions or points out some
new aspect but more often she learns a great deal from the
children. When the teacher and the children have found out
all they can, the verses referring to it in THE SAVIOUR OF THE
WORLD are read by the teacher and narrated by the

children—"The intellectual labour we have given makes the conception our own, and we have gained some fragment of that knowledge which is eternal life." (Vol. V)

Searching for the source of Miss Mason's teaching, let us begin with the P.N.E.U. Motto and see how far the adoption of it is warranted by the study of the Life of Jesus. We must read carefully and take time to give the intellectual labour necessary to show us how Miss Mason's teaching philosophy grew and by the few examples given we shall see how those of us who did not know our Founder personally may get into closest touch with her thought and teaching:

Education is an atmosphere.
How fair thou art, O soul! how still a grace
                                        Mantles thy face!
What pure cool chambers do thine eyes reveal!
Sure dwells in thee some luminous mystery?
As you dull orb that yet so shines to thee,
                I do but stand
                        In the Light.

What seest thou, O soul, where thou dost stand?
                                        A shifting sand
Where vile things stir and live—pride, envy, strife,
Malice and anger, all that prey on love—
Lo, these within me doth the Light reprove!
                Yet fain I stand
                        In the light.
This the whole cheer, poor soul, light brings to Thee?
                                Nay, *One* I see
In heaven, in earth, but One: none may rehearse,
Nor any comprehend save them who see,
The healing of the Vision: He shines on me;—
                Wherefore I stand
                        In the Light! (Vol. V)

Education is a discipline.
Only those valiant souls who choose
To take the good, the ill refuse,
        Nor pleasures seek, nor pains evade,

Are worthy to follow where He leads,
By waters cool, through flowery meads
    Where innocent voices fill the glade.

Thou cri'st that "nature fixes fate,
No man becomes or good or great,
    Save as his nature makes him strong:"
To will is all God asks of thee;
Impulse, strength, scope, He granteth free;
    But man must *choose*, or right, or wrong!

Else men were puppets in a play
Moved hither, thither, every way,
    Without or strength to strive, or choice;
Perchance for this, the Accuser's hour
To test the souls of men with power:—
    For good or evil, is *thy* voice? (Vol. I)

Education is a life.
So God hath made us, that for every man
Are many chances of being born anew
Into a life still higher than the first:
What if were one great chance for every soul
Of highest birth creature of dust may know?
What if were some amazing thought, compelling,
That no man could pass by were it once brought
Within the focus of his narrowed vision;
A thought for wise and foolish, vile and pure,
That sudden, certain, should transform a man,
Give him new birth, within an air unbreathed
In all his grovelling days! Why, here, a lever,
With arm to lift the world to higher plane!
To make this weary, travel-stained, poor Earth
A place for angels to go to and fro,
A paradise of God! (Vol. I)

Next in order of dearness to us comes the children's
Motto.

I am.

In the Kingdom are the children;
    You may read it in their eyes;
All the freedom of the Kingdom
    In their careless humour lies.

What do they to take the Kingdom?
    Only this leave they undone—
Suffering Christ the King within them,—
    They in nought invade His throne:

On the children's brows no witness
    That themselves do fill their thought;
In the children's hearts no strivings
That to them be honour brought.

Therefore finds the King an entrance;
    Freely goes He out and in;
Sheds the gladness of His presence;
    Doth for babes great victories win! (Vol. IV)

I can.

The Lord beheld the Seventy, simple men
To whom He had discoursed of mighty themes;
And, lifting up His eyes, to praise was fain
The righteous Father, Who th' unlearned deems

Worthy to know; the simple heart sincere,
The little child who few things apprehends
But brings discriminating vision clear,—
To such as these the Father condescends.

The Lord, discerning, lifted thankful heart,
Loving the Seventy, that it was God's will
To shew His mysteries where is no art
To darken counsel with man's subtle skill.

So is it still; The Lord's mind who should know,
With a child's heart shall wait for Him to show. (Vol. VI)

I ought.

>   To each man I say,—
> A task is set for thee, none else can do;
> A task, not of set labour with thy hands,
> But of true thinking with the mind thou hast. (Vol. V)

I will.

> Working the Work, willing the Will!—Thou art
> A Teacher of mysteries! 'tis of Thy might
> We're able, O our Lord, to get by heart
> These lessons of thy setting, in despite
>
> Of all that heavy dulness 'tis Thy task
> To lighten with Thy glorious countenance;
> Till th 'inert *will* drop from us as a mask,
> And, quickened, wake we, as man out of trance.
>
> For what the secret then, of willing well?
> To keep the single eye, to think on Thee—
> Till seeing Christ, our lightened heart shall swell
> To that vast measure, His Humility!—
>
> Then of Thy doctrine we in truth shall know
> When all our will is—in Thy way to go. (Vol. V)

There is no space to quote at greater length, but the source of that principle which brings such joy to every P.N.E.U. schoolroom, Education is the Science of Relations, is to be found in Vol. V, page 120, and IV, page 84.

When we come to P.N.E.U. method of which one of the outstanding features is the use of narration, we find our authority for it in Vol. I, pages 61 and 62; pages 84 and 85; page 88. Again the fallacy of explaining every difficulty is exposed in Vol. III, page 47 and Vol. III, page 85.

SCALE HOW students feel this work to be their special treasure, for all the thought it contains was given first to them during the precious hour on Sunday afternoons when they gathered round Miss Mason to hear her speak. Those who know SCALE HOW can picture the drawing room packed with students eagerly listening to the wonderful woman who from her couch, with gentle voice and quiet smile and loving eyes that read every face, would seem to have the word that each one needed, inconveniently so sometimes, for many of us who came in feeling something of saints would go out feeling sinners, so had she bared us to ourselves. Yet not despairing sinners, for the keynote of all her teaching was the ever readiness of divine love and forgiveness.

How vast the firmament! We lift our gaze
And search the heavens for a boundary line;
Stars upon stars confound us; we divine
Numerous orbs within the glorious maze!

So, would we track th' illimitable rays
Of the Divine Perfections, baffled we;
Outgazing further than weak eyes may see,
Efforts to focus too much glory daze

Our giddy sense! With what relief we rest
On one great star that dominates the sky!
A three-mooned planet, bright, diffusing light,
Divine Forgiveness glorifies our night—
For wilful souls, for those, neglected, lie,
For them who knew and loved, yet—left the Best!

E. A. Parish[22]

The Day's Work

A sweet attractive kind of grace
A full assurance given by looks
Continual comfort in a face,
The lineaments of Gospel books.

Did ever any spirit pass who could be claimed as a personal friend by so many people of all ages! The many letters that have come since January 16th, all testify to a sense of personal loss. Letters from her "bairns,"[23] as Miss Mason always called them, were the first to come, brought by the happy thought of Miss Parish in sending from AMBLESIDE notice of the "passing" to each of her "bairns" before a press

---

[22] See also page 201.
[23] Scottish for children.

notice could reach them. Then came letters from friends, grateful parents, Heads of schools, Secondary and Elementary, expressing, so many of them, a curious sense of nearness to the beloved spirit that has "passed." A letter from an Elementary school begs for more personal details, and so these few lines are written for those who never met Miss Mason except in spirit.

Up to the end of last term Miss Mason was living the College life as usual. She took her Sunday class, was present for the Criticism Lessons on Thursday mornings and at the "SCALE HOW Tuesday" Evenings. During the Inspector's visit in October she was down at 9:30am each day for three days and spent the day with the Inspector. She was present at the students' farewell party and at the Seniors' last talk in December and drove out as usual on December 16th. Even on January 11th, she listened to and decided about two articles offered for the REVIEW and on the 12th she heard the most important letters and approved, or not, of the answers suggested. Weary days and nights of pain were never referred to and she continued to enjoy reading aloud to the end and then she "fell on sleep."

In spite of frail health and much suffering for 30 years, Miss Mason led the life of a fully occupied woman. Only a week before she passed she said—"It is so difficult to get into invalid ways." She never thought of herself as an invalid and planned her life and work without thought of any personal handicap but that of physical inactivity. Her days passed with a regularity of employment, a fulness of joy in life and work that left no room for thoughts of self, no word of regret that she was unable to exercise the hospitality which she would so dearly have loved to do or to meet the many friends and acquaintances who would have been only too glad to come to see her. She had a genius for hospitality and for good talk, and during the summer holidays when she was less occupied, she often met distinguished men and women of affairs and the talk was brilliant. But the physical effort of talking was always a difficulty, and many a time has she had to decline the visit of a distinguished visitor lest the strain should incapacitate her for work that never ceased its claims upon her.

Every day brought a heavy post, editorial duties, housekeeping details, College business, the constant work of the PARENTS' UNION SCHOOL, and it was only by the utmost regularity of hours of work and times of leisure that work could be carried on.

But how to help anyone to realise the way in which Miss Mason answered the claims upon her! The details may sound so little. The output was so great.

The lines at the head of this paper give some idea of the aspect of our beloved Chief at all times, and especially when the day's work began. It might have been a sleepless night, or a night of pain, but always after her morning preparation for the day there was a radiance of countenance, that grew as the years passed, that made one hesitate in awe, a radiance that only 'gospel books' could bring. The day's work began with the post at 9:30am. Every letter, every card that came was considered, answers discussed, sometimes a letter dictated, though of late years Miss Mason wrote many letters herself. The letters were very varied; a mother wanting help with a difficult child, one student wanting advice, another changing her post, a father sending thanks for his son's successes at school, "due entirely to his preparation in the P.U.S.," a postcard asking for some special consideration in the date of sending in papers, letters asking for advice as to a school from parents returning from China or Madagascar, for example, with children who had up till then worked in the P.U. SCHOOL. These and many others were dealt with and always from the point of view that a child, or a grownup, is a *person*.

Letters sometimes required thinking over and Miss Mason would say,—"I will give you the answer to that tomorrow"; and tomorrow the answer would be ready without any reminder, and the letter would be answered in detail and without any further reference to its pages. She constantly said,—"Always remember that persons matter more than things. Don't say anything that will leave a sting."

Letters done, perhaps the house mistress would come for a short talk over household details, accounts, some repairs, a new maid, the students' meals. Then would come the work of the morning. If it was the first week of the month it would be the PARENTS' REVIEW that must be considered, articles

submitted, read and accepted or not, articles wanted—
many—where, indeed, could they be got from? "We want a
paper on this subject? Who shall be asked to do it?" Miss
Mason treated any paper as she would its author, with
unbounded respect. She would not alter or rearrange; she
had too much respect for the writer. She would often refuse a
paper which needed omissions on account of some of its
teaching lest she should spoil the author's creation, a living
product of his mind. Perhaps the work of two or three
mornings would be the reviewing of books. She dictated the
reviews without pause to a typewriter, having read the books
in her leisure hours. Conference papers were always dictated
in the same way and sent to the printer with hardly a
correction. At 11:00am, she would on bad days be sometimes
too tired to go on, "Give me *Punch*," she would say, if it were
Wednesday, or 'a Trollope,' "and come back in 20 minutes,"
and she would start again rested and refreshed at the end of
that time.

Perhaps the work for a fortnight or more would be the
children's written examination papers, each of which she
would consider before she signed the report, sometimes
modifying or adding to the report herself. How she loved the
papers! "I am always happy when I am reading these," she
would say, "Just see how these children take pleasure in
their work!" The preparation of the new programmes and the
examination questions was the morning work for weeks. The
choice of new books took much time. Miss Mason tested
them herself for narration, considered them, rejected them,
sent for more—for she followed all new book lists—and asked
for all books she thought likely to yield what she wanted. At
12:15pm she stopped work. Then would follow 10 minutes of
some favourite classic author and she would be ready at
1:00pm for dinner with the students. After dinner came
occasional interviews and the reading aloud of some book of
travel or biography. At 2:15pm whatever the weather (unless
it was raining heavily or there was a high wind) Miss Mason
drove out in her little victoria till 4:00pm. Her life was a
constant evidence of the joy of "the science of relations," her
relations with earth, with man, with bird, with beast and
flower, and with God. She never came back without some
"find," some fresh flower out, some new sound she had

heard, some new aspect of the beauty in the sky or on the fell. And she was ready with expectancy to hear of what others had to tell. After tea, at 4:00pm, came an hour with the Vice Principal considering posts, letters from ladies wanting students, letters from students wanting posts, all considered from the point of view of each side, the lady whose needs were so-and-so and the student who best could meet those needs and go to the post as to the "very place God meant for her." Then would come reading, or proof correcting, till 6:00pm and then some old favourite novel, Charlotte Brontë, George Eliot, Thackeray, Meredith, Jane Austen, till supper at 7:00pm. After supper came reading aloud, the *Times*, and books of travel, literary essays, memoirs. At 8:45pm came Miss Mason's carrying chair and, last of all, her evening reading and a Scott novel. She always had "some Scott" the last thing, and as one novel was finished another took its place and had done for 30 years.

How Miss Mason would enjoy any bit of humour or good story that came her way, how she loved to hear about the children's joy in their work, how she was always touched to tears by any bit of real understanding shown by anyone of the principles she was labouring to make known, or by any evidence of that wonderful insight a child will show when his mind has got what it needs to feed upon—these things would take pages to tell. Miss Mason had no personal "feelings," she could not be "hurt" by want of understanding; but, oh, how she was cheered and helped by any recognition of what she was trying to do in the face of so many vested interests! She did not care for possessions, she rarely permitted gifts, but any tribute of understanding, any recognition of the philosophy that was so dear to her was a gift to be treasured. She never hesitated as to the value of this philosophy. It had come to her much of it at 25, or even earlier, and she often said how strange it was that she *could* only repeat what she had said so often. Her answers dictated to letters were the same in thought as pages in HOME EDUCATION. Tiresome letters she answered with gentle graciousness, and she would say, "Remember, no one is made up of one fault, everyone is much greater than all his faults"; and then she would add with a smile, "I find it much easier to put up with people's faults than with their virtues!"

Miss Mason rarely touched upon controversial subjects, she read very little controversial matter, she steadily refused to enter the lists in condemnation of theories with which she had no sympathy. She prayed "Lead us not into temptation" in thought as in other things and she *would not* enter in and let her thoughts dwell in the many byways of modern thought when so much work was needed on the highways.

Miss Mason disliked any form of red tape or apparatus, and she dreaded organisation. "In proportion as a piece of work needs organisation it lacks life," she would often say. "Don't make schemes for arranging the school work ahead. It must be fresh term by term or it will get stale." "Things must be judged on their own merits, not by rule." "Don't waste time copying." Miss Mason would take a book out of the school if it was not doing good work for the children.

She never worked out of hours nor let herself think of problems at night. Hasty decisions were never made even when she was pressed to make them. She took time to consider the many problems that inevitably connected themselves with the vast work for which she alone was responsible. She had a wonderful power of estimating the value of anything, from a psychological problem in a book, a scientific discovery, a person's character, a builder's estimate, to a child's work, on paper or in handicrafts. She always saw the essential details, the trend of a line of thought, the fallacy in an argument, the weak place in an estimate, the testing place in a person's character. She did not talk of these things though she betrayed her knowledge of them when necessary. She never discussed the students or one member of the staff with another, or one person's work with another; she bore to the farthest limit her own responsibilities and tenderly shielded those who worked for her from any anxiety as to ways and means; and such times of difficulty were not infrequent for she bore the financial responsibility entirely alone and went on with faith and courage when many a lesser spirit with a life so frail would have quailed. She would never let herself be "anxious." She avoided expressions of personal opinion lest they should act like "suggestion" on those who loved her. She distrusted personal influence as limiting and belittling the person influenced and she steadily set her face against any form of personal influence over any with whom she came in contact. She laid down principles and waited for others to think along her lines of thought and find the right solution. She would not deliver those she loved from the growing pains of thinking for themselves, and sometimes those who did not understand took her silence for consent when they suggested things she did not wish. They little knew that she was only waiting for them to think clearly for themselves. Life was too full, she was too frail, it is true, to talk much, and also she did not think it wise to do so. She *thought* and acted and she wished others to *think* too. Her "masterly inactivity" was a thing to wonder at when she could so easily have set things, or thought, going in the way that she thought was right. A word from her, beloved as she was, would have done it: but, no, her work had to be done with the mind and heart of a person who must not be weakened by personal influence if the work was to be done by a mainspring and not a lever.

Her power of attention was equal to that which she laid claim to in the children. She gave her whole attention to whatever demanded it,—a book, a conversation, household details. Her perception of 'the way of the will' and of 'the way of reason' made her watchful lest the managing student or child should lose her way in wilfulness or in crooked thinking. It is surely a rare thing that a philosopher should translate his philosophy into practical life as Miss Mason did. Many philosophers are content with the supreme joy of intellectual effort, others are content with making experiments as well, but Miss Mason had put each dictum of her philosophy to the test of daily life and its needs. It lay behind all her actions, for she ever said that right thinking was the most important act in a man's life. If he thought right he would act right. She guarded the philosophy which was her Trust with a jealous care that made people sometimes wonder, even criticise, but it was a Trust so entirely apart from herself and from any personal considerations that she *could* speak of it, consider it, uphold it, maintain it. It is this that makes her disciples feel it also is a sacred Trust that they too must needs guard for the sake of the world.

E.K.[24]

---

[24] Miss Elsie Kitching. See also page 120.

Miss Mason of House of Education

It is an amazing thought when now it has pleased God to take from us our Head, full of years and honour, that when first I came to the HOUSE OF EDUCATION and fell under her influence, she was not more than five years older than I find myself today. She seemed to us then ageless and immortal, a completed being, because she had self-command and a power of standing aside and leaving the young to be young, which is the rarest of all gifts at any age.

Though of course we students did not realize it then, the training of teachers for home schoolrooms was still something new and experimental, and we were unconsciously taking part in a great movement which was to raise the status of the teacher, because behind us there was a central authority and control which could uphold our interests on the one hand, and give sage advice on the other, when foolish youth had not yet mastered "the art of living in other people's houses."

When I went as a student to AMBLESIDE it was from experiences of many different worlds. I had been dragged up by the worst types of governesses at home, I had spent a few years in what was then considered an excellent high school, and one year in a typical old-fashioned boarding school where English did not matter and French and Music did. I had had glimpses into the great world of people who mattered and who had every earthly advantage which might lead to culture and knowledge of the world, and all through my childhood I had had the constant companionship of an old godfather who knew every building of note and every person of distinction, and I had had glimpses into the merely frivolous narrow life of a social residential town, and into the poverty and restrictions and sheer vacuity of a small country commercial town. All this is detailed not from the biographical point of view but to show the standards of judgment and of living which I, as one type of student, brought with me to be revolutionized by that great influence. The first thing which struck me was Miss Mason's marvellous courtesy—she knew only the bare outlines of our previous lives, but she spoke to us all as 'persons,' and helped us to be dignified by treating us with dignity. Such varied experiences had given me the rather ugly cynicism of observant youth, and yet when in Psychology lectures our opinions were asked for and freely expressed and I rapped out some bitter half-truth, far from snubbing the distorted vision Miss Mason would always enlarge our perceptions by some word of wisdom or charity while not denying the half-truths which were all that we could see. Once, and once only in my student days, was she confronted with one of those examples of youth's foolish rebellion which were commonplaces of school life in those days—her method of dealing with the situation gave me a marvellous insight into what she meant by discipline—nothing was 'done to' the offenders—we were all simply left to talk over the situation and find a solution; the offenders having time to 'come to themselves' bitterly repented, and found, I think greatly to their surprise, that public opinion had been entirely against them.

The whole atmosphere of the house was so extraordinarily good—nothing ignoble seemed natural within its doors, and moreover the actual surroundings, the books, the pictures (reproductions of old masters), the simple furniture and the *wild* flowers for decoration everywhere were a revelation in themselves in those days when the world either lived in a crowd of ancestral treasures or in the unutterable hideousness of the Victorian Age when prosperity had to be apparent.

No one, I am afraid, will ever enshrine Miss Mason's 'Table Talk' in a book, but it was a marvellous training for young minds, her wit was so quick and her brain so trained and well-stored that ours had to take kangaroo leaps to keep up with her at all, and she had mastered the difficult art of eating *and talking*—in those days when heavy dinner parties were still frequent, most people either ate *or* talked and neither made for true enjoyment of any meal. She would often at meals repeat once some fragment of great poetry and ask us to say it to her on the following day at luncheon, and in that way we learnt more than one treasure such as Trench's Sonnet on Prayer. In those days too, we students received from her on Sunday afternoons the thoughts on the Gospels afterwards given a permanent form in verse in THE SAVIOUR OF THE WORLD. These too were a revelation of the *mental* side of our faith—young people are often dogmatic, often merely narrowly pious, more often one fears conventional and indifferent, but that hour in the crowded drawing room was an hour of thought in which we were brought suddenly to the point of asking ourselves 'What do I think?' 'How *do* I understand?' And very wise and helpful were the suggestions laid before us.

Life at the college with its many interests, in which she so marvellously shared, included, in those days, when the shadow of ill health was not lying so heavily upon Miss Mason, the constant joy and stimulus of guests. Then we would see what the play of mind upon mind really meant, then we would be made to realize that however distinguished and clever these personages might be, they were our guests as well as hers, and sudden calls would come upon us to whip up some *soufflé* of an entertainment for them on the spur of the moment!

It was that training in readiness and courage for which we could never be grateful enough in after years—again and again we would be asked to do something we had never dreamt of doing and be told to say "Oh, what a joke" and *do* it! Thus we learnt the humility which never thinks of self or fears to make a fool of 'self' when the call comes in the path of duty.

But for all the lofty heights pointed out to us it was the little human touches of understanding with our weaknesses which won our hearts—no scolding when there had been some wild ebullition of noise and high spirits at one of our revels, only the next morning, "My dears, weren't you a little wild last night?" No ignoring our natural love of pretty clothes (in which she always set us a delightfully good example) but, "Don't try to have *the* hat in church, my dears, but remember the neatness and care of Him who left the graves clothes 'folded together at the head' on Easter Morning." And I remember one of her very few personal anecdotes was a poignant little story of how she felt when one of her mother's white trousseau petticoats was made into a frock for her in childhood and she somehow felt that it was not 'new' and not 'right.' But it was the outlook on our future life which she gave us both by precept and example which was so marvellous—many of us came to our training as a professional necessity, anxious to teach, to use our own brains and good education, and to learn because we must, and because in those days the professions were not open to women but I think none of us left without the sense of a vocation, "I have a life to give." Teaching was to be a mission carrying the breath of life to God's children, going out 'two and two' with the mothers of our children to labour in God's vineyard—not looking for results or rewards or the praise of men but praying for our children that they 'might increase' even as we 'decreased.'

Many times since those long past years have I revisited the old scenes, and always found the same wonderful welcome and recollection of circumstances and people which made her interest so real and so living. She always looked ahead and so never belonged merely to any one 'present day,' for it is only the people whose opinions can be dated who ever really grow old.

We shall rejoice in later days to think that she was to the last living the ordered life of good habits which we so loved to remember and find still going on, working always, but having the self-control to rest at regular times (which few ardent workers have), reading enormously, and with extraordinary relish and width of selection, enjoying the marvellous country around her and loving her horse and her dog and her daily outing with them, which made it possible for her still to see the heron in the pool or the Globe Flower on the bank.

Only her 'bairns,' as she called her students, can piece together as in a precious mosaic her life of little personal kindnesses, of sage advice or admonition, of charity, and clarity of judgment—some lives are better written in the lives of those who come after them than in the pages of a biography—let us make it so with hers.

Let us now praise famous men
Men of little shewing
For their work continueth
Broad and deep continueth
Greater than their knowing.

R.A.P.

A Tribute from an Ex-Student

It has always seemed to me that the two years spent as a student in that beautiful spot among the mountains of Westmoreland, under the influence of that wonderful personality, whose passing has left us all to mourn, have been in my life, as in that of so great a number of students, as a mount of transfiguration, charging our common everyday life with a fulness of meaning and beauty unknown before. Perhaps the secret of Miss Mason's great influence—apart from the intellectual appeal of her genius—over those who, as students, came into daily contact with her was, firstly, her extraordinary power of seeing, and appealing to, the best in every individual. Somehow, in her presence, meanness and pettiness fell away, and one believed in and strove to reach the highest of which one was capable. And not only this—one learnt to believe in the goodness and joy of life. One felt that, at the back of all Miss Mason's teaching, was a philosophy of life based on an intense conviction of the personal relationship of every individual soul with God—a relationship that was the basis of all joy in living. One realised the power and joy of knowledge—the knowledge that is enshrined in all great literature, art and music, the knowledge of living creatures, of the goodness of sky and sea, of wind and cloud and of all the "green things upon the earth." Next to this power of vision—of seeing the *essential* goodness in everyone and everything—I would place her largeness of heart—a heart that was ready to embrace and make the most of whatever type came beneath her influence and care—a heart so full of understanding of human nature that, however greatly one's mind was impressed by her genius, one felt that no phase of human life—no joy, no difficulty, no weariness, no struggle—would be outside the pale of her sympathy. In that large heart she found room for hundreds of students—her "bairns" as she called us—and knew them with all their individual peculiarities, followed them as they went down from the mountain and "forth into the tumult and the shout," and was ever ready in after years to give counsel and sympathy in times of need or difficulty.

But perhaps it is only since one has become "a joyful mother of children" that one has fully realised what Miss Mason's life-work has done for the lives of thousands of children, not only in this country, but all over the world. It would be impossible, having been present at that gathering, ever to forget the Children's Conference at Whitby in May, 1920, with its extraordinary sense of uplifting power.

To see those eager children, from all parts of the country, hitherto unknown to each other, bound together by the joy of common interests and the enthusiasm of a common knowledge, was to realise what an extraordinary power lies in those educational principles to which Miss Mason gave all her life and brilliant powers of mind, and to make one long to see them spread among those who, though less blessed hitherto with opportunities than our own children, have the same thirst for knowledge which is the common heritage of our human and divine nature.

In those elementary schools where Miss Mason's educational principles and methods have been adopted the response of the children has been remarkable. Along this avenue it seems that a solution might come of many of those difficulties and troubles which beset the body politic, and cause such unhappy divisions among us.

In Miss Mason's philosophy, every child is a personality endowed with infinite possibilities, and to her vision—the true vision of the seer—the trail of the "clouds of glory" is ever visible even when the shades of the prison-house seem darkest.

The *power* of knowledge has been recognised through the ages, but to her it was given to tell of its joy and unifying power. For her life and work amongst us let us sing a glad *Te Deum*[25], and pray for wisdom and patience to carry on that work to the blessing of future generations.

E. Hughes-Jones

Miss Mason's Love of the Country Drives

Having served my late dear Mistress for 24 years, I should like to make known her love of, and interest in, all that moved or grew along the lanes or moors, for it was Miss Mason's delight to seek the quiet lanes and bits of moor away

---

[25] An ancient Christian hymn, the Latin title translated means "God, we praise You".

from the noisy motors, and only quite recently, using her own words, have they begun "to poach on our private drives."

From 1898 for a good many years Miss Mason would take the tea-basket on her drive, when with the late Miss Armitt, or the Hon. Mrs. Franklin[26] or others. If the weather was hot, in the woods by the lake towards the Ferry; if cool, Miss Mason enjoyed the hillside between Chapel Stile and High Close, where unrivalled views could be obtained of river, lake and mountain.

We could take at least 20 different drives, or circles, very rarely covering the same road on return except for a little distance from home. Each drive had its own peculiar charm. In September, the autumn tints were best on one. In October, another would be more brilliant. Then November brought the bracken on the mountains to the warm russet colour, Miss Mason's delight. A cold blast in December brought the Redwing to their favourite haunts for shelter, and then we knew a storm was brewing. In December, January and February, we usually saw the different species of wild duck on Elterwater, Loughrigg Tarn, or Rydal Water. The end of February and early March saw the Wild Goose going back to the breeding ground on the Scottish coast, Barngates being a favourite crossing place for them. It was on this drive in 1920 Miss Mason saw a pair of Waxwings quite close at hand and on a former occasion three Redpolls. Towards the latter end of March we saw the Curlew by Barngates come to look up his nesting ground. April brought Redstart and Wheatear. Though small birds, Miss Mason's watchful eye seldom missed them even in 1922.

Each drive seemed to yield something of its own. One snug corner produced Hazel Blossom, another Coltsfoot flowers; some drives were profuse in Wild Roses and Honeysuckle; another in Bog Bean and Bog Myrtle; another in Grass of Parnassus; and even the small Milkwort did not escape Miss Mason's keen eye.

Very often did we follow nature's ways in evading the storm. Sometimes, when quite calm at The HOUSE OF EDUCATION, (sheltered from North and East winds) on reaching the open we found a boisterous wind and it was then we had to follow the cunning of the fox and hug the

---

[26] See pages 33 and 113.

sheltered side of Loughrigg to Skelwith Bridge, thence to Barngates, and with back to wind could get our little circular drive without discomfort.

Miss Mason was fond of her horse, which was a great help in getting close to birds as they don't fear animals so much as persons. And it was always her first enquiry when staying at hotels during Easter Holidays,—Had I and her favourite little mare Duchess, been made comfortable and well fed? To her friends who asked why she did not have a motor, her answer was,—"I can talk to a horse but not to a motor." To illustrate her contention that it was so, I very well remember when once by Skelwith Falls on a stormy day, Miss Mason wished to return, not feeling well, and she had given me the word to turn again for home. Through the rush of water I had not heard Miss Mason's words, but Duchess had, and when I attempted to restrain her from turning, Miss Mason said it was quite right, Duchess had heard and knew all about it.

Miss Mason's nerve during these later years was marvellous, for we encountered all kinds of motorists, reckless and otherwise. We have even had horse's feet on the motor bonnet. Still she kept calm where many a younger person would have been panic-stricken, and probably by leaping out would have caused serious harm to herself.

Miss Mason was always punctual, never kept man and horse waiting and never left her carriage without the kindly, 'Good afternoon' and 'Thank you, Barrow.' And (had our drive been prolific in birds, etc.) "We've had a splendid bag." And I am proud of having had the honour and pleasure, for it was a pleasure, of driving such a kind and noble lady whose like none can excel. And her end was Peace.

T. H. Barrow
Coachman

A Personal Tribute from a Rydal Neighbour

By the death of Miss Charlotte Mason, AMBLESIDE has lost a great though unassuming personality. I do not speak of her works, which do, indeed, live after her, but of the character which produced them.

When I first had the privilege of knowing her—perhaps seven and twenty years ago—I was astonished, having regard to the position she already held, at the quietness of her manner, the gentleness of her speech, the absence of self-assertion in any form. She seemed rather like one who sought to know than one who was born to instruct. But presently, beneath all the courtesy and kindness that invited self-expression in others, one felt the strength of individual personality, of power, of knowledge, of purpose, and especially of patient persistence. To her the way she meant to go was plain before her; there was no need to hurry or struggle.

I think she dwells (in one of her works) on the theory that a child is a "person," an individual having a separate entity, not merely one of a crowd; and this theory pervaded the whole of her life and helped her to success. To her nobody was one of a crowd; and everybody was a person, requiring separate understanding and inviting individual treatment. "Big or little," she seemed to say, "you and I are each one. Let us treat each other as such."

Naturally, with this theory and practice, she became an expert in understanding character, in picking out at a glance the capabilities of those surrounding her, and putting him or her to the most appropriate task. She knew what to expect from each, made the opportunities, and reaped the results. She chose her friends in the same way, with her quick and far-seeing glance perceiving qualities and possibilities hidden from the casual eye. This particular power must have been of enormous use to her in the creation of her great organisation. It also was of service to everyone working with or under her. She expected from them the best they could do, and (so far as I know) she got it.

Seeing the best and expecting the best was not the least of her special gifts. We hear much of suggestion nowadays. The quiet suggestion of good made constantly by her own life and thought must have brought incalculable benefit to those working with her. It broke down the expectation of evil in those afflicted by difficult temperaments, and let in the sunshine of hope and of joy in many dark places.

Her great work (including the books she wrote) was, of course, directly educational. She introduced new ideals and methods of teaching, and these methods and ideals have spread far and wide. They have probed deep into the foundations of English institutions, and stretched over the ocean to take root in other lands. The wonderful statistics are recorded elsewhere.

I should like to add a word as to the generosity of her present dealings, her readiness to take the heavier share of financial transactions in which she was concerned with any other. Also her faithful friendship, which did not allow her own physical disabilities or the disabilities of a friend to make a barrier between them if there was any way out; her ingenuity in contriving meetings, her persistent kindness in keeping up private correspondence in spite of the almost impossible claims on her pen and time; her sense of humour which made hard things easy and dark things bright.

A great loss, indeed, to many people and places, but most of all to the HOUSE which she founded and the community among which she dwelt. She lived and worked at her fullest to the very end of a long life, and hers was a happy going away.

A. M. Harris

An Impression

I have been asked to try and recall any memories I may have of Miss Mason and I have attempted once or twice to write something adequate but have failed miserably. Time and events from the outside seem to have made a long leap from the days when I first worked for the P.N.E.U.

But a picture of a certain Sunday in Advent, though it must be 20 odd years ago, rises to my mind and is as fresh as if it had occurred yesterday. It was my first visit to AMBLESIDE as appointed, or provisionally appointed, Secretary to the London Office. I was horribly frightened (I had only arrived the night before) the students knew so much more than I did—I had no training—nothing but a hope that I might possibly be the right person for the job. Miss Mason I was told had talks with her students on Sunday afternoons. We assembled in the drawing room, it looked so countrified to my London eyes, and the trunk and branches of a cherry tree outside the window held my attention—as well as a portrait of Matthew Arnold on the wall. Trees and Arnold might help me I thought to keep my nervousness within bounds. I remember Miss Mason and her gentle smile and voice as she explained my presence to the others there. The actual words of her talk I have forgotten, but I hope not the spirit. "That thoughts out of many hearts may be revealed" was the stone upon which she built a complete "house of education" for us that afternoon—explaining how thoughts could be translated into action when revealed, and like young plants bear fruit in due season in the lives of the young children who were to carry on the work.

I have since looked up this text on which the little sermon was built and find I had underlined the words following: "There was one Anna a prophetess." Surely something then had moved me to connect the two ideas. Had I realised dimly at this first meeting that a prophetess was speaking, and that slowly and surely her prophecies would be fulfilled? That she was then revealing to a little handful of her followers something of that wealth of thought which she was depending upon us to translate into action? I know I hoped sincerely that I might bear my part in the good cause.

Miss Mason was gifted in many ways, but in none I think more than in her power of inspiring others with ideas, and ideas fundamentally so sound, that those who were able to work them out, felt that they must originate in truth—so often ideas are inspiring for a time, but having little actuality, little relation with facts—they do not live to bear fruit. We can all say of Miss Mason's work for children and true education that it dealt with those primary conceptions of the intense value of every human soul that nothing of God's gifts given direct by God Himself, or through the instrument of his creatures could be too good for it. I think I had the impression that this was the thought in her heart that Sunday that she was revealing to us, and that we on our part were earnestly desiring that it might be the spirit in which the work could be accomplished and the *only* way in which it could ever be accomplished. This must have been so for I find marked with the same date, "Out of the mouths of babes and sucklings." Whether I elaborated the idea for myself, or whether Miss Mason did for me, I am after this long stretch of years unable to tell. The train of thought was continued somehow to its conclusion. If we were able to reveal the thoughts in our hearts to the children, they would so express themselves that we could not fail to recognise the source from which all inspiration and good thoughts come, that are only truly revealed in "that perfected praise" which is the inherited gift of the children of God.

This little sermon, if I may call it so, has recurred to my mind over and over again and I have written it out as best I may—as a very small tribute to the memory of one for whom I had and have a very profound admiration.

Frances Chesterton[27]
Top Meadow, Beaconsfield

For The Children's Sake
In Memoriam

Her children shall rise up and bless her name.
Oh, glorious epitaph!—and meet indeed
For such a soul. These laurels ne'er shall fade,
Nor vanish as the fame of some short hour.
Hers was the living sympathy and love
Truly to see and feel her brethren's needs;
With vision clear behold the childlike soul
And know it greatest in the eyes of God,
Secure in this her faith, that from above
Was given her Trust, she guarded it with care;
And gave her life that thus might be supplied
Her children's many wants. Nay, all the world
Hath share in her great love: and we who work,—
Though small, or great our part,—may surely feel
That the Spirit by the Greatest Teacher given
To comfort those, who, mourning, and abashed
At thought of the great tasks were theirs to do,
Will be our Strength and Guide. Thus may we all,
With childlike trust, and purity of aim,
Fulfil the trust bequeathed and work with her,
"Our Leader still."

D.J.
(Ex-Student, H.O.E.)

---

[27] Wife of G.K. Chesterton.

PART III
From the P.U.S.A. Magazine

PART III

Table of Contents

The Children's Tribute

PART III
The Children's Tribute

I

I suppose the thoughts uppermost in our minds are of gratitude for the great and loving friend who has left us— for a serene and joyous spirit, a wonderful intellect, her effectiveness and great achievements, the beauty of her soul and the gracious beauty of her person.

Miss Mason had been ill a few weeks and, on her birthday, her bed was brought down to the drawing room where, surrounded by books and beautiful pictures, she had been want to see friends and students at work, lying on a couch near French windows that looked on to the garden with its lawns and trees and birds and mountain views. There was always a coconut hanging from the window for the tits.

She was 81 on New Year's Day, but, in spite of a frail body—which, indeed, had grown a little stronger of late years—she seemed to have perennial youth, and the keenness and vigour of her mind were unimpaired. She was at work on Friday and had lately drawn up the term's programmes for the P.U.S. Early Saturday morning, after speaking of the beauty of the starlit sky, with a jesting word to the nurse, she fell into a quiet sleep which lasted until she died, very peacefully, at noon on Tuesday, January 16th. She was buried yesterday (January 19th) in the quiet churchyard at AMBLESIDE. The Rev. H. Costley-White, chairman of the P.N.E.U. Executive, read the service and was assisted by her friend,[28] the Rev. F. Lewis and the Rev. J. Bolland, the vicar of AMBLESIDE. The sky was leaden and it rained during the funeral—some think the Lake District looks its best under a grey sky. The coffin was covered with flowers, and flowers (including those sent by the Students' Association) were carried in procession by her friends and colleagues, the staff at SCALE HOW, past and present students and the children of the practising school. One felt that thousands, all over the world, were thinking of her that day, and tributes of love and

---

[28] Mrs. Whitaker-Thompson. See pages 40 and 225.

gratitude were sent by hundreds, including many who had never seen her but whom she had helped and inspired—such as children of an elementary school, a preparatory school for boys "in the name of all who have passed through the school," pupils of girls secondary and private schools and home schoolrooms.

Miss Mason achieved great fame. Her writings and the P.N.E.U., which she founded 36 years ago, have spread far and wide, she trained some 400 students, and (including those in about 200 elementary and 100 secondary schools) there are some 40,000 children—many of them living in distant lands—actually working in the P.U.S. at the present time, her pupils, whose work she followed with the greatest interest.

Besides her own organizations, she inspired the work of others. Even where her work is not known the influence of her ideas has permeated modern education, and much that was new when she first taught it is now accepted everywhere. But in many things she is still far ahead and it is only when used as a balanced whole that P.N.E.U. methods give their best results.

Miss Mason was loved by all who saw her and had many dear and intimate friends. She had the power of seeing and bringing out the good in everyone, but I think she loved little children best of all. FOR THE CHILDREN'S SAKE is the motto of the HOUSE OF EDUCATION, and it was FOR THE CHILDREN'S SAKE that she lived and worked. She provided them with an education which is "an atmosphere, a discipline, a life," she reverenced them as "persons" and recognised their need for mental food in order that they might grow. She gave them living books, a love of literature, art, nature, craftsmanship, joy in learning and full lives. She never allowed the methods which she evolved or, as she preferred to say, "chanced to find"—to be called by her name; they were always "P.N.E.U." Her work will go on, not only because it is to be administered by those whom she has chosen and trained for this high responsibility, but because of its intrinsic vitality and truth.

By an old pupil

II

My first impression of Miss Mason was when I used to see her out driving. She had a smile and a wave for everyone whom she knew, and it was with a feeling of pleasure and exultation that one passed on after her greeting.

How wonderful to think that the great Founder of the P.U.S. and P.N.E.U. had actually waved and smiled at an insignificant person like oneself. For nearly a year I used to see her in this way, as I was fortunate enough to have lessons in the P.N.E.U. system near AMBLESIDE.

One summer I had the great privilege of being asked to a party at SCALE HOW. All the guests were greeted by Miss Mason in her beautiful drawing room. She made one feel at home straight away by her sweet and gentle welcome. She watched all the games and races which were part of the afternoon's entertainment, and when teatime came she went to a table where the little ones were sitting and had her tea with them.

It had been arranged that I was to go to the Practising School of the H.O.E. the following term.

That term began on a Saturday in late September. On the Sunday we went up to see Miss Mason. I can remember how sweetly she kissed us all as one by one we filed into the drawing room where she was lying on her couch. She then spoke to us about our work for the term and dismissed us with a nod and smile.

After that we saw her out constantly driving, at Criticism lessons or on our visits to College. One thing I shall always remember was when, after the Members' Conference, we were summoned to Miss Mason, who thanked us for our part in the Conference. Little had she to thank us for. It was our part to thank her for the liberal education and books she had put before us.

At our drawing room evening when we had to play to Miss Mason, there was always a charming smile and a few words to encourage us.

Whenever I think of Miss Mason, I always see that same beautiful smile which made one love and respect her more each time one saw her.

E. da Fonseca

III

I am sensible of the honour of being asked to write a few of my personal remembrances of Miss Mason; and I know that what I write will have been the experiences of many others beside myself. When at the age of 12, I first came to the Practising School and saw Miss Mason, I had had it carefully explained to me by the other girls that she was a very great and wonderful person; and I was very much awed at seeing a person of such great wisdom and learning, and very surprised to find that she was the sweetest, kindest-looking old lady instead of the learned-looking person whom I had expected to see. And that, I think, was one of the chief charms of Miss Mason—she was so gentle, so quiet, so unassuming, and yet her personality was so dominating that everyone felt when they were with her that they were in the presence of a truly wonderful spirit.

Some of my happiest remembrances of Miss Mason are the almost daily pictures of her that we used to see as she came down the drive when going out in her carriage. One half of the gate was usually closed, and while Barrow[29] got down to open it, we used to flock to the window to wave to Miss Mason, for she always waved and smiled at us whenever we saw her.

There were certain memorable occasions upon which we used to see Miss Mason, and these were the musical drawing room evenings which we gave up at college once a term. Arrayed in our best frocks we used to go up to SCALE HOW and play the piece we had practised for a whole term before Miss Mason, the staff, and a roomful of students, and it was to us a terrible ordeal.

But how much worse it might have been!

Miss Mason was the gentlest and kindest of critics to us poor nervous children, and she never failed to make some encouraging remark to each of us as we left the piano.

At the beginning of every term we used to go up to College to greet Miss Mason, and she would talk to us of the coming term and ask about our holidays; she knew each of us by name, and very often would inquire after various relatives of ours whom she had met. At the end of every term we used to

---

[29] See page 79.

go up to say "good-bye" to her, and she would ask us whether we had liked the exams, and if we thought we had done well, and what we were going to do in the holidays, and many other such questions.

I was specially privileged in being prepared for Confirmation at AMBLESIDE, and once a week the two other candidates from the Practising School and myself used to go up to Miss Mason for a quiet talk. I doubt if we realised the extent of the honour done to us.

At the end of every summer and autumn term Miss Mason gave a party for us, at which, if her health permitted, she was always present. During the tea she would come round and sit for a while at each table, talking and smiling with us all, and presently there would be peals of laughter— Miss Mason had asked a new riddle! She was very fond of riddles and funny stories and always asked for some at the parties, and great was the joy of the girl who could ask Miss Mason a new riddle that she had never heard before.

During last year—my first year at College—I came into a much more personal touch with Miss Mason and I marvelled more and more at her wonderful mind, her wonderful personality, and her wonderful vitality. Everybody who knew her, loved her; and all who came in contact with her realised how great her influence was, and when they went from her presence they felt uplifted and inspired to nobler things.

When looking at that sweet, grey-haired old lady, it was strange to think that she held in her hands the workings of schools all over the world and that she had brought parents, teachers and children into one happy band of love, work and service.

It has often been said by ex-students of the HOUSE OF EDUCATION that the two years spent there were two of the happiest years of their lives, and it is true—I know I shall say it when I leave—and it is mainly because of the spirit of the place, everyone is happy and loves everybody else, and this will always be so because Miss Mason's spirit will always be there and her memory faithfully and lovingly cherished.

Olive Marchington

IV

Miss Mason was one of the great ones of this earth, and so I feel most unworthy to write about her, but as I have had the great privilege of having known her as a student, I think some of those who never saw her may like to hear a few personal recollections.

Miss Mason was not only the beloved Founder and benefactor but also the friend of every child brought up in the P.U.S. Those of us who came up to AMBLESIDE as students after our P.U.S. training had the honour of knowing her in a very special way, but all those thousands of P.U.S. children she never saw were her friends. I shall never forget the first time I saw her and what she said to me. I went up to AMBLESIDE a fortnight after term had begun and felt most shy and forlorn, not knowing a single soul. When I went into the drawing room to see her, she held out both hands and said: "Isn't it funny to think we are such old friends and yet this is the first time we have seen each other!"

We did not see very much of Miss Mason during the day, but her influence was felt in a most remarkable way throughout the house, whether she were actually in the room or not. That influence must have been entirely spiritual so we may assuredly believe and know that it still reigns throughout SCALE HOW, perhaps in a more real way than it ever did before. And not only is it felt at SCALE HOW, but throughout the world wherever her teaching has spread.

Miss Mason always used to have luncheon with us when she felt well enough, and it was one of the senior students' privileges to sit at her table—and it was a privilege to sit next her and talk with her. She always tried to get our thoughts and views on subjects before she gave us her own. If our views did not quite coincide with hers, she simply gently told us what she thought about it and left us to think it over. And after thinking it over somehow we always realised that she was right and we were wrong.

How she loved books! That is to say real living books. She used to talk to us about them in such a loving way as if they were personal friends. Often as not, I fear, we students had not read the particular books, but she always left us with a desire to read them.

What a sense of humour she had too! *Punch* was such a favourite with her, and at lunch time on Wednesdays she was generally full of choice little anecdotes from him.

At 4:15 on Sunday afternoons we used to go into the drawing room for "meditations" with Miss Mason. We used to read passages of the Bible to her and then she would discuss the passage, giving her thoughts and trying to get ours on the subject. The various volumes of THE SAVIOUR OF THE WORLD were really the outcome of "meditations" with former students. It was during that hour that we saw more clearly than at any other time how closely she lived with God. Yet withal she was so human and humble, one of her favourite quotations being, "how very hard it is to be a Christian." I think of all the "meditations" at which I was present, I appreciated her talks at Whitsuntide most of all. She was so full of the Holy Ghost herself that her very words seemed to have been inspired.

Her parting present to leaving students was always *The Cloud of Witness*, edited by Mrs. Gell. This makes one of the many bonds which bind all ex-students together. It is good to think of her now as one of the "Cloud of Witness" herself.

M.H.
Ex-Student and P.U.S. Pupil

V

Miss Mason gave her whole life to children, both rich and poor, in fact she took for her motto FOR THE CHILDREN'S SAKE, and this idea she kept before her through her whole lifetime. Everyone loved her, especially the children, and no one could help being affected by her influence although they did not always realize it. Although she was so clever I don't think that anyone could feel uncomfortable in her presence, and there was not one of us who would mind telling her anything if we were in trouble of any kind.

She always took an interest in everyone and everything, however small or insignificant, and she took a great pride in knowing how all the children in the PARENTS' UNION SCHOOL were progressing even when she was so very ill.

Many people knew her by correspondence, and others by reading her books, but whether one only saw her once or twice, or perhaps not at all, one could not help knowing and admiring her.

Although she was all this, she was very human and could sympathise and understand anybody, in fact I have never known anyone who could understand the feelings of everyone so thoroughly.

But I am quite sure that all who knew Miss Mason, although perhaps they never saw her, will continue and carry on her work in the way she would have wished.

Veronica Whitwell

VI

I have been asked to write something of my early recollections of Miss Mason because it has been my privilege to have known her since I was quite young. It is difficult to separate childhood memories from those of later life, and I recall a clear picture of her very vivid personality rather than outstanding incidents.

She used to stay at our home on her way to her annual journey to Nauheim, and her visits were delightful for us, although, as an invalid, she had to be spared fatigue and noise and we could only visit her bedroom separately and at special times. I can, however, recall one occasion when she was well enough to stay with us in the country and to take part in family life and country drives. It was here that Rudyard Kipling came to see her—probably to hear about her methods—and the *Jungle Book* was a great favourite with us. It must have been then, or soon after, that I read "Mowgli" to Miss Mason, most likely sitting by her bed, but that I cannot quite remember.

Reading to Miss Mason was a great pleasure, for she entered so genuinely into the spirit of the book, even if it was only a children's story, provided it had some literary value.

Once at school (not P.N.E.U.) a companion laid a challenge that she and I should each read the whole of Wordworth's *Prelude* during the weekend. It took all one's spare time, but Miss Mason was staying in the house and in reading it to her and listening to her occasional comments, I soon forgot in enjoyment of the poem the urgency of the self-imposed "task." I felt quite sorry when my friend, who had to read to herself and had less time, confessed that she felt too hurried to appreciate it.

Miss Mason had a nice sense of precision in the use of words and did not like them to be applied loosely or incorrectly or to be mispronounced. She seldom interrupted the child reader by criticism, but she had a keen sense of how a passage should be rendered, and gave us a most valuable course of reading lessons when I was a student. Her fine literary judgment has been diffused through her choice of books for the school.

Miss Mason had, of course, great sympathy with children, and she always seemed genuinely pleased to see one and never preoccupied. She radiated affection and gaiety and showed a quick interest in many things such as nature, plants and flowers, people, books, household and school affairs, and (I nearly said most of all!) in anything amusing. She had a splendid sense of fun and loved to hear or tell a good story. She often invented special names for her friends and liked to chaff the "dear people" around her, but never in a way that left the least sting.

I think children appreciated the serene happiness of her temperament. She never seemed to have "moods" and, although her cares and responsibilities must have been great, one never saw her in the least depressed.

I am afraid I have said very little—there is much that cannot be written down and other things that seem trivial on paper when separated from the atmosphere in which they occurred. Like thousands of others I owe a great debt to Miss Mason's teaching, although I was but a few years in the P.U.S.

Miss Mason has shown her love, respect and understanding of children in her work. The seclusion which her health exacted prevented her from seeing them as much as she would have liked, but she always took pleasure in contact with a child and read the children's examination papers with real enjoyment. The spread of her pupils from the home schoolrooms to private and secondary schools and especially to the public elementary schools brought her great happiness. She took a warm interest in the recently formed Association of old pupils, and herself set the syllabus for the reading course and gave a cordial welcome to the magazine the Association has started for the children of the school.

VII

*In as much, as ye have done it unto one of the
least of these my children, ye have done it unto Me.*

A great heart has ceased to beat, a great spirit has gone on, the memory remains.

I have been privileged to know Miss Mason. All of us in the P.U.S. were her "friends," yet I enjoyed the thing I account one of the greatest of my possessions, the special joy of being personally known to her. Every year nearly, she used to send me a book—"From his AMBLESIDE Friend, C.M.M." Even this last Christmas, when her health was declining, she remembered and ordered a Wordsworth to be sent to me. Therefore anything I can add to the beautiful words that have been said about her must be of a very personal nature.

She was always so thoughtful of everyone near her. When I last had the joy of staying under her roof, she saw me a boy, just in for his Oxford examination, and said, "Now would not he like to dance, all young men like dancing," and in a few minutes she was able to see her students dancing in the classroom with desks pushed back, and she was glad we were amusing ourselves. How many elderly people are annoyed by noise of any kind, especially when they are ill!

She was such a perfect hostess. On the same occasion she had arranged for us to drive to see the Langdale Pikes, and as we went she stopped the carriage at good viewpoints, pointed out gardens, showed us birds, asking Barrow's[30] opinion of their names. Arrived beneath the Pikes, she made Barrow and me climb up to look at the falls, and when we came back there was tea waiting in a private room at an inn, and the window was wide open, "So that we can think we are outside."

My mother read to her I remember, but what remains fixed is her shining face, lit up by the sun from within and the sun from without, and the joy of nature in her and the

---

[30] See page 79.

kindness of soul. Like Henley, her infirmity counted as so little; her personality, the poetry of her mind, for so much.

She seemed to me always to be smiling. Just as when one looks at the Mona Lisa in the Louvre, perhaps the greatest picture of a smile ever painted, one begins to smile oneself, one felt in her presence constrained to smile—her smile was indeed infectious. She had a huge sense of humour and fun. I had made a few verses upon the P.N.E.U. at a Students' Conference in London. Miss Mason had heard about it and made me repeat them to her, and she laughed right merrily at the jokes. Truly she might be called *"La Joconde."*[31]

One little book she gave me has been a real and great joy; a little anthology called *English Landscape*. It is small enough to go into my waistcoat pocket, yet in it are all one's favourite poems. I have read from it in Venice in a gondola and on the top of mountains in the Savoyan Alps with the snow around me and the sun shining on the wild rhododendrons and soldanella and gentians, and through the pages came the vision always of its donor—a frail little lady with the biggest heart in the world and the finest brain and the most marvellous energy that has ever come into my life.

From her teaching I have got—everything. I found in France lately that the keenness for flowers which had been received in the P.U.S. but had not been cultivated since my leaving it, was a possession for always, and I kept a flower list and a nature note book in the Alps. The same with pictures in Italy and with literature. Nothing I have intellectually has not its roots in the P.U.S. teaching.

One might say that one would have got this from any other method. I believe that one might have got the one thing or the other, but I do not believe that any other method has all that men could want in its teaching; it is an anthology of the best in education. Miss Mason used to say that everything that was good in itself should be given to children.

Her machinery was so perfect that I imagine—and this is very beautiful—that those of us who have not known her, yet have come under her influence, will hardly realise that she has gone. This means that the thing Miss Mason discovered was good in itself and was not only efficient because of a

---

[31] This is another name for Mona Lisa which literally means 'the happy one.'

dominating personality behind it. The machine has been set in motion; it is for each one of us to keep it going.

In Miss Mason's letters she had the art of appearing to understand and be in sympathy with one, a kindred spirit, a sharer in one's joys and interests. When I was going in for an Oxford examination, she wrote so encouragingly, so helpfully, so *personally*. "Yes, MacKail's *William Morris*," she writes, "is deeply interesting. I hope not just too much so for your ardent mind just now when you are so anxious to concentrate on that "key" to Oxford. I hope you will conquer all obstacles in March and make your friends happy—Do!" Such sweet and helpful sympathy; and then when I managed to pass the examination, "The good news of your success has made me very happy this lovely morning."

Then the desire, "I wish I could be with you and your beloved Mother to drink in Florence and much besides,"—in her own handwriting and it must have been a great trouble for her to write.

I always felt that Miss Mason had something of the fairy, of the Robin Goodfellow, of "Lob" in *Dear Brutus*. She was so young and so whimsical in her (to me) never changed body of the elderly lady.

There is much in the letter to me at the time of my confirmation too private to quote but such a phrase as "I think it is a happy thing to be a boy at a time when the air is full of great thoughts and great purposes" is such a beautiful thought and gives one an insight into her character.

I have had the great privilege of seeing elementary school children doing the same work as we did at school, loving the same books, the same pictures; here indeed is an example of the "good that she did to little children," here indeed are those whose lives have been brightened by the light of her wisdom, here indeed is the visible result of her service to mankind and to God.

I should like here to pay my tribute to those who have so long helped Miss Mason, each according to their might, in her work and its interpretation. It is, of course, to them that her loss comes as the greatest sorrow. I should like them to feel that we are grateful to them; both those at AMBLESIDE who tended her and helped her, and those in London who made her work and the spreading of it possible. Just as God could not have made Stradivarius' violins without Stradivarius, so Charlotte Mason could not have made the P.N.E.U. without her helpers and disciples.

Miss Mason, as is known, was responsible for much that today is in almost every educational system: script writing, musical appreciation, scouting, literary evenings. She has made thousands of homes happier, thousands of children brighter. To her students she seemed to impart something of herself. I have always said that we pupils could invariably tell a P.N.E.U. governess; she has always something that others have not.

I AM, I CAN, I OUGHT, I WILL. This was the motto she gave us. I am a human being, one of God's children; I can do right by my fellowmen and by myself; I ought so to do and God help me, I will so do. Is this not a great message she has given us?

Her students chose for the badge of her teaching, showing the humbleness of mind diffused through the College and Miss Mason's desire for no honour for herself, the "Humble Plant" or "L'humile Pianta."

She herself was a "humble plant." She was frail and the wind passed over her and she was gone, but her spirit lives, today and while her children live, so shall her spirit be green and fresh and so shall her word go forth from mouth to mouth.

And as she was humble, let us be humble—for she never thought her way was *the* way, but only *a* way—as she was strong and upright, so let us be strong and upright and let us remember her as a teacher, a philosopher and a friend.

Michael A. E. Franklin[32]

VIII

Hers was a Beauty rare and comforting—
A strength to stem the tide of discontent
And yet to sow new seed.
Give us, O Time, to learn what she would teach;
To stay upon the instant, there to find
God's measure of our need.

---

[32] Son of the Honorary Mrs. Henrietta Franklin. See also page 215.

PART IV

From the Memorial Conference

PART IV
Table of Contents

PART IV

The Memorial Conference

Held at Mortimer Hall, London
March 26th – 29th, 1923

"For a great door and an effectual is opened unto me."
—1 Corinthians 16:9

SOME IMPRESSIONS OF THE HOUSE OF EDUCATION

A summary of the address given
by Professor W. G. de Burgh, M.A.[*]

A.

It is a privilege, though a sad one, to be here this afternoon. Yet I feel that the dominant thought in our minds should be, not sorrow, but thankfulness. We are thankful for the gift of Miss Mason's personal friendship and personal influence. I do not think that Miss Mason would have altogether liked to have been told that she exercised influence. She would say that she set ideas in people's way and let them work in people's minds. But, however we express it, the fact remains for three generations of human life she gave herself, her wise and stimulating counsel, and the stores of her rich mind with lavish generosity to hundreds, thousands of individuals, both in personal intercourse and in correspondence. I am not thinking mainly of her published writings, books and articles addressed to a wider and more general public, valuable as these are. I was reading only the other day OURSELVES, which has been described as "the one manual of practical psychology" for the young. I am thinking rather, as is fitting on this occasion, of the untold gain derived by those who had the privilege of personal relationship with her.

We are thankful again that she was spared so long so that she could herself see much of her ideal accomplished, and know before she died that her work had taken firm root in an organisation with manifold activities. She would have disliked

---

[*] Professor of Philosophy, University College, Reading.

the term "organization"—"confraternity" is a more fitting word. It comprises the HOUSE OF EDUCATION, the PARENTS' REVIEW, the PARENTS' UNION SCHOOL and its schemes of teaching now adopted in many elementary and secondary schools, the support of educational authorities (e.g. of Gloucestershire); she often spoke of this to me, the thousands of children educated privately on her methods (altogether some 40,000) in the PARENTS' UNION SCHOOL. She lived for her work, and her work is known and its value recognised throughout the empire. It is truly a wonderful thing that she should have lived to see these fruits and to know that she left those behind her who would carry on the work in the spirit with which she had inspired it.

We are thankful, lastly, for this—that the end when it came was so peaceful—that she kept her astonishing intellectual vitality to the last. The eye of her mind was not dimmed, nor its natural force abated. In my visit late last November, I found Miss Mason with as keen an interest and knowledge of detail as ever. I feel bound to mention too (for she would most certainly have wished it mentioned) that our gratitude is due to those who in the last years surrounded her in her beautiful Westmorland home with such loving care and devoted service.

B.

I have entitled this address: "Some Impressions of the HOUSE OF EDUCATION." I am conscious how slight a claim I have to speak of her life's work. I only knew her by acquaintance in recent years, through my annual visits to the HOUSE OF EDUCATION. We had previously exchanged some correspondence, in reference to certain papers of mine published in the PARENTS' REVIEW, which showed her that I was likely to be sympathetic to her work and methods. As a result, she asked me to act as Examiner. I felt this to be an exceptional mark of confidence, for she disliked inspections and always kept clear of subjection to officialdom.

I well remember my first visit in 1916; the kindness I received from her, from Miss Williams,[33] and the staff; and the thoroughness of the arrangements that enabled me to see

---

[33] See page 58.

the work and life as a whole. I remember too how I went there with two questions in my mind:—

I wondered, first, whether Miss Mason's very definite convictions and methods in education led to a cut and dried, stereotyped imitation on the students' part, restricting their freedom and individuality. And, secondly, whether the wide range of subjects studied during the two years led to superficiality.

I need not say that my fears were groundless on both counts. In fact, it was the answers I got to these questions that impressed me most on my first visit. For I found (1) liberty of individual development. The very variety of the curriculum enabled students to show their distinctive talent, e.g. in languages, or in craft work, or in physical exercises. Miss Drury[34] is to speak presently on Nature Study; but I must remark in passing on the high quality and enthusiasm of the students at the HOUSE OF EDUCATION in this field. Their work was always intelligent and individual; they took full advantage of the unique opportunities of the district, and in vacations correlated their observations in their various home localities with the beautiful scenes that they became familiar with at AMBLESIDE.

I found (2) that the wide range of subjects, so far from conducing to superficiality, was the product of a sound and reasoned principle. Of course, no student can be equally proficient all around. Time hampers the teaching of many subjects, but Miss Mason's aim has been avowedly twofold:

(a) to equip students with such an interest in and knowledge of the main subjects, that they may be qualified to teach them on leaving, and

(b) in regard to auxiliary subjects, to awake interest so that, while the students are not necessarily qualified to teach them on leaving, they are started on new lines and enabled to pursue these interests afterwards for themselves. This is the case, e.g. with Italian and with Greek, a subject which I induced Miss Mason to add to the curriculum. Miss Mason ever looked ahead. One of the striking characteristics of teachers trained by her is that they too move forward on their own in after life;

---

[34] See page 108.

> realising that they must teach from a flowing stream,
> not from a stagnant pool.

I must add another impression which has been confirmed on each succeeding visit. The students teach *naturally*. Even in the unsatisfactory and artificial atmosphere of criticism lessons, there is a notable absence of self-consciousness. Both to the students who give the lessons and to the girls in the Practising School, my presence in the room as Inspector made little difference. I believe that this is due in no small measure to the system of narration and to the wise insistence by Miss Mason that the teacher must never impose her personality from without upon the child.

C.

Before I close, I must say a few words of a more general nature about Miss Mason's work in education.

In the first place, though no one was more critical of defects in educational theory and practice, her criticism was always *constructive*. It was based on personal experience (in a training college and in schools, as Miss Williams has told us in her all too brief retrospect of Miss Mason's early life in the PARENTS' REVIEW for March) and on an intense faith that education was a power—a power either for immense good or for disaster. She realised the point of Plato's startling question in the *Republic*; how can the State foster the study of philosophy without being ruined by it? To the solution of this problem she brought a rare sobriety of judgment and the sense of proportion which was one of the most striking qualities of her intellect. She loathed faddists and cranks in education. She united a sane conservatism with a passion for reform and a spirit of bold adventure. She grasped an ideal of education that was veritably democratic; uniting the children of the rich and the poor, the aristocrat and the labourer, in one comprehensive scheme of training. She brought to bear on her work both speculative insight into problems of philosophy and a typical North-country sense of what was practical. For instance, by her firm insistence on adequate salaries and conditions of service, she raised single-handed the status of the private governess throughout England.

Miss Mason stood, firm as a rock in a Utilitarian age, for the essentials of a humanist education. She grew up in an atmosphere of materialism in education; that this is no longer dominant is due largely to her efforts. The fact that she had to fight for her humanist ideal braced her and called forth her full powers. I sometimes wonder how it was that the Victorian age produced women leaders of such distinction compared with their successors of today. We recall Miss Buss, Miss Beale, Dr. Garrett Anderson, Dr. Emily Davies, and many others besides Miss Mason in women's education; Mrs. Fawcett, Miss Octavia Hill, Florence Nightingale in other fields. Was it not that they had to fight for their causes against strong opposition? Miss Mason's life was one long struggle against mechanism. She distrusted organisation and standardisation. For this reason, she would have no truck with government departments or municipal control. Again, she set little store by the results of public examinations. It is noteworthy that these great Victorian reformers had no University degrees. The admission of women to degrees is, assuredly, a great onward step, but we go wrong if we regard them as essential to the good teacher. Many of the best teachers at the HOUSE OF EDUCATION are Miss Mason's own products and show that first-rate teaching by no means depends on University qualifications. I should like all sticklers for such things to hear, as I have often had the pleasure of hearing, Miss Drury take a class in Science or Miss Millar (if I may call her by her maiden name) in Mathematics.

I need not dwell at length on what is known to all—how Miss Mason stood for freedom for the child. She held that the teacher must not impress her personality on the child but let the child's personality grow freely. Thus both teacher and child are freed from strain and bondage. This does not mean that the teacher's task is thereby rendered easy; the teacher is no cipher, nor is her personality suppressed. It means that for an external relationship is substituted one of inward sympathy and insight. The result has been that Miss Mason's students learn to love teaching. She taught the teacher to love teaching and the child to love learning. Her students learnt too that education is not, as in some universities, a departmental subject; rather, that all life is education and all education that deserves the name is life. Plato taught, in the *Republic*, that the theory of education is the theory of life

(Philosophy) and its message the message of life (Religion). So likewise taught the wise and noble teacher whose life-work we commemorate, in reverence and thankfulness, today.

THE NATURE WORK AT THE HOUSE OF EDUCATION
by A. C. Drury

The character of the Nature Work at the HOUSE OF EDUCATION is largely determined by Miss Mason's choice of AMBLESIDE as her training centre.

Besides being in the midst of beautiful scenery with literary associations, AMBLESIDE is rich in having a great variety and profusion of flowers within easy walking distance. There are plants of the meadow, mountain, bogwood and water, northern species, rare and characteristically mountain species—to be climbed for on special occasions.

The extremely complicated but interesting geological formation affects the flora, which is remarkably different from that on a contrasting rock, the mountain limestone, near enough to be reached on half-term holidays. The soil of the valleys shows the effect of past glacial action which limits vegetation and farming operations, sheep-farming being the most lucrative on the fells.

Some of the cornfield weeds which are conspicuous by their absence were introduced by war-time cultivation and at least one had established itself.

The climate of the Lakes favours the growth of very beautiful trees, particularly of the Coniferae, and some of these are specially fine in gardens near AMBLESIDE. The autumn colours are often glorious beyond description, and so are the fungi until the frosts begin. To my mind, the English mountains are never more beautiful than when covered with snow and in winter they are often white when rain alone has been falling on the lower ground. The rain supports a wealth of mosses and liverworts, rare ferns are not unattainable, and some of the rarest may be seen by climbers.

Though very seldom detected, such scarce animals as the badger and the pine marten, dwell in the Lake District, and I have heard from visitors that the otter is to be seen by following the hunt in the early morning.

The head of Windermere is a station for migrating birds. They land there for a few hours or days on their journeys north in spring, they come to Rydal for open water from the frozen north in winter, or linger on their way to feast on our beech mast or berries. The redwing and the brambling come to SCALE HOW garden for this purpose.

In founding the HOUSE OF EDUCATION in AMBLESIDE, it was Miss Mason's intention that her students should become familiar with these beauties of Nature; and the Nature Note Book, which she designed, is the symbol of their knowledge: that precious green book with its red title, "House of Education, Students' Nature Note Book," which is the peculiar privilege of the student.

The inside of the book is nothing more than good drawing paper (for painting, without pencil outlines) until the possessor begins to make it the record of her own observations.

Every fine day (except on half-holidays) one or two small parties of students go out with members of the staff for Nature Walks and Bird Walks, or the whole number start off occasionally for a Geology Walk to find fossils or ice scratches, or in summer for weekly Geography Walks.

Miss Mason loved to see what "finds" the students brought back from their expeditions and to hear what birds they had seen or to tell what she had seen.

I remember how she talked about the cock-redstart at table and made us eager to notice the patch of intensely white feathers on his head contrasting with his black throat.

Out of doors the students learn to look and to watch that they may know creatures and plants by sight as they know friends; to recognise the birds by their song, flight, feathers and nesting places, and their time of arrival and departure; to observe the flowering seasons of all trees and herbs and the ripening of common spore-bearing plants such as horsetails and large liverworts; to note the reappearance of butterflies and dragonflies, stone, caddis and mayflies, and to know some of their eggs and larvae.

Each one records in her own Nature Note Book that which has interested her, and takes home something to paint. The effort of attention during the time given to painting the twig, flower or fruit, chrysalis, shell or egg, fixes its form and colour in the memory. This is the way to get to know "its position as it grows, its trick of holding its head, the grace of its profile" (as Ruskin says of a flower in words quoted in the PARENTS' REVIEW for February, 1923). The Nature Note Book becomes increasingly valuable when the records of one year and one locality can be compared with another; and a student generally feels that she is making more progress in her second year though she was unconsciously storing up first impressions in the early days of her training.

There is a delightfully casual element in Nature Walks. We simply choose which way to go and then "Nature" does the rest because AMBLESIDE is an unrivalled spot to learn in. We like to be teased when the Nature Walk lingers to watch a dipper or a grey wagtail, or the Bird Walk finds the yellow Gagea or the marsh Cinquefoil, as if we were poaching on each other's preserves! For the fact is that we take whatever comes, and the unexpected almost always happens.

The Rev. Alfred Thornley, who examines the Seniors' Nature Note Books, testifies to the freshness and pleasure which this mode of Nature Study secures, and this spontaneous enjoyment was provided by Miss Mason when she taught us to gather the materials for science by studying Nature out of doors for ourselves and adding to our knowledge year after year.

We get a tremendous stimulus and answers to many of our queries when Mr. Thornley comes for his annual visit. A day spent out of doors with him acquaints us with many kinds of insects, their haunts, their food. We see an astonishing "number of things" in a few hundred yards of wood or of lakeside, and time passes like magic. To arouse wonder and admiration must be one of the teacher's principal aims.

Two years is but a short time to spend in preparing to read intelligently with PARENTS' UNION SCHOOL pupils. So the Nature Walks are supplemented by lectures, the average time allotted to scientific subjects being three to four hours a week.

There are Natural History lectures on British wild animals, birds and their feathers, British insects, forest trees, spore-bearing plants, seed dispersion, autumn colours and the fall of the leaf.

A course of Human Physiology in the first year gives a knowledge of the skeleton and vital organs, very useful for comparison in studying the animal kingdom, which is the special subject of the second year's Biology class.

Botany is taken by the first and second year students separately and concerns the detailed study and classification of flowering plants. So the Biology hour is chiefly devoted to Miss Arabella Buckley's wonderful books on the animal kingdom: *Life and Her Children* and *Winners in Life's Race*. The books are illustrated in class by as many specimens as possible, fossils or shells from the museum, and such living species as the earthworm, snails and woodlice.

We note in passing comparisons and contrasts between animals and plants, and attention is drawn to examples of laws common to the two organic kingdoms.

Blackboard summaries and classifications have not yet been dispensed with, although we seek to use the book as the principal part of the lesson and to approach the ideal set in the PARENTS' UNION SCHOOL. It is impossible to read *Life and Her Children* through in two terms when three years is the time taken over it in Form II. Lord Avebury's *Flowers, Fruits and Leaves* is the kind of book that cultivates a scientific spirit of enquiry, but time forbids the Natural History lecturer to use more than a chapter of it. Books we should like to depend on: Scott Elliot's *Nature Studies*, for example, go out of print, and in other cases, the right book for our use has never been written. So we still lecture at the HOUSE OF EDUCATION, and some of the science books of the PARENTS' UNION SCHOOL are unsatisfactory.

Half a dozen lectures on Sound, Light and Electricity with simple experiments are given to introduce the group of books: *The Sciences, First Year of Scientific Knowledge, Some Wonders of Matter*, and *Scientific Ideas of Today*. The least acquaintance with these mighty mysteries makes us grateful for an occasional scientific lecture from an expert who opens up new lines of thought and subjects for wonder.

I think that the stupendous facts with which Geology and Astronomy deal, educate a scientific habit of mind most effectively. There must be a study of the reasons which lead Geologists and Astronomers to their conclusions, conflicting arguments must be faced, inferences drawn from geological

maps or from astronomical diagrams representing the
movements of the heavenly bodies. In Astronomy we rely on
Sir Robert Ball's *Story of the Heavens*, which students who
have been in Forms V & VI possess, although we can only
take extracts in a course of about 15 lectures. Our object is
to lead students to know the stars and to follow the
movements of the moon and planets. Odd half-hours are
seized on fine nights for learning the names of the stars and
constellations, the monthly star maps in the *Times* being
found useful.

Geology replaces Astronomy in alternate years, and
begins with local Geology from the maps and papers of the
Geological Survey and from Professor Marr's comprehensive
book on *The Geology of the Lake District*. As Miss Mason often
said of all the science teaching, the most we can do in these
lectures is to aim at arousing interest.

The peculiar fitness of AMBLESIDE for the studies which
Miss Mason initiated and developed there, is realised best of
all in connection with Out-of-Door Geography. On all sides
are the mountains, water-sheds, rivers, tributaries and lakes
themselves, neither miniatures nor models. Distance is learnt
by pacing, and direction, from the sun and the compass, in
order to appreciate the making of maps to scale. The height
of a tree or spire is measured by triangles, the ordnance map
is used, contours explained, and bench marks found on an
up-hill road and checked by the aneroid barometer. This
occupies six weeks of the summer term one year, and the
next year we follow the more delightful of the two courses for
Geography Walks worked out by Miss Williams (late Vice-
Principal): that on the history of the Lake District,
Westmorland, and AMBLESIDE. Boundaries, old routes, places
with significant names, old houses or sites of mills, famous
remains like the Roman Camp at Waterhead and the Rydal
Thing-mound,[35] are visited or viewed from Loughrigg, and
from them we learn of the different peoples who entered the
country and the traces left of their occupation.

It is frequently said by students that their two years'
training opened many windows for them. The windows that
open on to Nature Study admit us to endless sources of

---

[35] Also known as Rydal-Mount.

happiness, explored at AMBLESIDE if not first known to us there.

Most of us look back upon this result of our training, together with the practice of taking walks which it implies, as among the greatest of the benefits we owe to Miss Mason. And the pages of our old Nature Note Books recall, as nothing else can, the choicest walks we have had and our most cherished memories of birds and flowers.

THE PARENTS' UNION SCHOOL AND ITS FOUNDER[*]
by the Honorary Mrs. Franklin[36]

Mrs. Franklin said: I have given myself a difficult task—it is to give the pupils of Miss Mason's School a little idea of what she was and of what she expected of you. You will all feel that you have known Miss Mason since you joined the School: that she has given you ideas and ideals.

Miss Mason has passed on, but her spirit is with us—especially at this moment, because she loved everyone of the children in the School so much. She gave her life and her work to you.

I have had the honour of being her friend for nearly 30 years: the friendship began when I was not much older than some of the members of the P.U.S. It has meant more to me that I can express: it was the greatest privilege to be allowed as a young mother to help Miss Mason in her great work. Besides all the great things she taught me she taught me so many little things—for instance to love open windows, to go out in all weathers and she taught me, and you through the P.U.S., though you may not realise that you are learning this lesson, to try and see the best in everyone. It was because she saw the best in us that we did our best, and when you are tempted to dwell on some little thing in anyone which is not the best, remember that in doing so you are not being loyal to Miss Mason.

Another thing that little people, as well as old people, need to learn is that when anyone has done a thing wrongly, don't go and tell them so but wait until they are going to do

---

[*] From notes taken of an address to P.U.S. children.
[36] See also page 33.

the thing again and then just remind them to do it right. Perhaps you could remember this when you are dealing with your little brothers and sisters or with school fellows.

Miss Mason—you can see it in her face (pointing to Mr. Yates' beautiful portrait which was on the platform)—not only saw the best in everyone, but she loved human beings. The consequence was that everyone who came in touch with her felt her influence.

Someone who knew her 60 years ago says he has never forgotten the things she told him then, and one of her maids told me she will always remember the few words Miss Mason said to her when she left to be married 14 years ago after only two years in her house. This was because Miss Mason when she talked to us was able to imagine herself in our place and to say what would be helpful to us. Her own conversation was witty and delightful, but she also made even the shyest person talk, and talk well.

I hope you in the P.U.S. will be good conversationalists: I do not think you will be afraid of hearing your own voices. Some of you little ones will remember that you were at first afraid to narrate; that you did it very softly and slowly. Now I expect it goes quickly and distinctly. We have heard two of the P.U.S. speak today and judging by how they did it, I think you will all be able to speak and to talk well.

Miss Mason was remarkable for her courteous manners. She always received her dearest, oldest and her newest and youngest friend in the same way. People felt that it was a privilege to meet her and they felt at ease with her.

She worked very hard, but she never appeared rushed; hers was an inward peace. One often hears people say that they can only do this or that "when the spirit moves them." She on the other hand got through her huge amount of work by working to a timetable up to the end of her days. She was a great, good and God-fearing woman and she was allowed to keep her powers until the last and now that she is gone, she leaves us not sad, but full of thankfulness for her and her work and profoundly grateful that she was with us, working for us in the world for so long.

Her work had many sides. She edited a magazine, she wrote books, she founded the HOUSE OF EDUCATION, the P.N.E.U. and the P.U.S. which now has 40,000 pupils. Some

of the pupils live at home and work there, but they are in the
P.U.S., some go to classes and schools—elementary or
secondary schools—and all are in the P.U.S. When we met at
the Children's Conference at Winchester and again at
Whitby, the children attending the Conference received
letters from their school fellows from almost every part of the
world; from children who were doing the same lessons and
caring for the same things.

Why is the P.U.S. different from other schools? Do you
ever ask children from other schools if they like their lessons
as you do yours? I fear many say they do not because they
have not learnt as you do in the P.U.S. the joy of getting
knowledge on which the mind can live. Lewis Carroll, who
wrote *Alice in Wonderland,* says in a serious essay on
knowledge that we are very careful to feed the body on
various foods—we do not give it nothing but dry bread or
nothing but chocolate, but we are not so careful of the mind.
Miss Mason felt that the mind needed food to make it grow
and in the P.U.S. she gives just what will make it do so.
When you feel a joy in working it is because your hungry
mind is being fed.

Miss Mason when she was a little girl had a geography
book from which she had to learn long lists of towns, rivers,
export, imports, etc., and she did not like it, but she *did*
enjoy reading some little notes at the bottom of the page
which were quoted from what people who had lived in the
foreign country had to say of it. When she grew up she
remembered this and decided that she would make a
geography book something like these notes so that children
while they were learning about the country might feel as if
they were living in it.

I think you know that Miss Mason was very fond of
nature, and when she went out for her drives she was always
looking for the first flower or bird of the season. Then she
would come home and compare notes with her students.

She knew too the joy of making things for oneself—not
only in handicrafts, but in other ways, too, for instance of
making a Nature Note Book or a Book of Centuries—and
helped us all to this joy.

She also felt that in order really to enjoy going to a picture
gallery one must know something of the pictures beforehand,

so she arranged Picture Talk and showed children in the School reproductions of the great pictures so that when they went to a gallery they would understand the artist's message. She did the same with music: through Musical Appreciation she prepared children to understand and enjoy concerts.

She gave each child working in the School a library of his own. All the books you use in the School are worthwhile— even the books used in IA are worth keeping. I expect you find when you have read Scott and Kingsley, for example, you do not much care for rubbishy books. This is a good thing because rubbish is badly written and spoils our knowledge of English and also it does not give us a true picture of life. Good books on the other hand help us to understand life, as great writers make their characters act as human beings do act and so help us to know something of life from different aspects.

I AM, I CAN, I OUGHT, I WILL. Miss Mason chose your inspiring motto. You can say,

I AM the greatest thing in God's creation: a human being with a spark of God's divine spirit in my body. Because I belong to the human family I can do the great things that other human beings have done: I have powers of doing, thinking and loving.

I CAN use these powers. I can change my thoughts from things that harm me and that worry me to the beautiful things I have learnt in my School: I can know the joys of activity, I can think kindly thoughts of God's creatures in the past and in the present, in this and other countries, of people who do not think as I do in religion and politics.

I OUGHT to do these things: I owe it to my God, my parents and my School.

I WILL forget myself, and live up to the ideals of my School.

God is on the side of those who will, and with His help we will all go on working as Miss Mason hoped we would."

Mrs. Franklin at the end of her address quoted from letters written by Miss Mason to children attending the Gatherings at Winchester and Whitby. To those at Winchester Miss Mason wrote:—

It is a delightful thing about this School of yours that the Scholars love their books; I know, because every post brings me a letter from someone to say so, and besides, I can tell by the way you answer your examination questions. When all the papers reach me I often say, 'this is a very happy week for me'; I am happy because your papers show me that you have had a delightful term's work and that you LOVE KNOWLEDGE.

I think that is a joyful thing to be said about anybody, that he loves knowledge; there are so many interesting and delightful things to be known and the person who loves knowledge cannot very well be dull; indoors and out of doors there are a thousand interesting things to know and to know better.

There is a saying of King Alfred's that I like to apply to our School,—'I have found a door,' he says. That is just what I hope your School is to you—a door opening into a great palace of art and knowledge in which there are many chambers all opening into gardens or field paths, forest or hills. One chamber, entered through a beautiful Gothic archway, is labelled Bible Knowledge, and there the Scholar finds goodness as well as knowledge, as indeed he does in many others of the fair chambers. You see that doorway with much curious lettering? History is within, and that is, I think, an especially delightful chamber. But it would take too long to investigate all these pleasant places and indeed you could label a good many of the doorways from the headings in your term's programme.

But you will remember that the School is only a 'Door' to let you in to the goodly House of Knowledge, but I hope you will go in and out and live there all your lives—in one pleasant chamber and another; for the really rich people are they who have the entry to this goodly House, and who never let King Alfred's 'Door' rust on its hinges, no, not all through their lives, even when they are very old people.

I have a great hope for all you dear Scholars of the P.U.S.; other people always know what we care about, and I hope the world will be a little the better because you love knowledge, and have learnt to think fair, just thoughts about things, and to seek first the Kingdom of Heaven in which is all that is beautiful, good and happy-making. I

must not take up any more of the time in which there are
so many things to be done, so, wish you the very happiest
week in all your happy lives.

To those at Whitby she wrote:—

My dear Children,
    It is eight years since I had an opportunity of writing
to each of you and to all of you as a body. Let me repeat
the welcome that you received at Winchester in the words
of Isaak Walton, that wise fisherman who gathered
wisdom while he waited for the trout to rise :—
    'I will tell you, Scholar, I have heard a grave Divine say
that God has two dwellings; one in Heaven and the other
in a meek and thankful heart. Which Almighty God grant
to me, and to my honest Scholar; and so you are
welcome.'
    Some of you may still have the card with this motto
among your treasures, but all of you, I know, have
brought the meek and thankful heart that Isaak Walton
desired for himself and his Scholar; meek, because we
shall be thinking about great persons in a place touched
with the magic of holy and serviceable lives; about the
work in stone and on parchment of famous men and
women of old, and of the wonders of sea and sky and
earth; of tales told by the very rocks, all uniting in a
chorus:—
    'The merciful and gracious Lord hath so done his
marvellous works that they ought to be had in
remembrance.'
    Let us remember that the works of men indirectly, and
the work of Nature, directly, are the great and marvellous
works of God. Thinking of these things, we shall be meek
and very ready to learn, and so we shall find out that 'the
meek shall inherit the earth,' for those things that we love
and delight in are far more truly ours than the things so
easily spoilt, which money can buy.
    A famous schoolmaster was asked by his boys to
explain that saying of our Lord's about the meek, and he
said—

'Napoleon thought he inherited the earth by force of arms, and he died on Elba. Wordsworth had no such proud thoughts, but he *did* inherit the earth; all the Lake country and much of the world besides belongs to him still.'

Being rich in these great things we shall be gentle and generous, and I am very sure you all have thankful hearts, thankful for Whitby and all that it means and will mean for all your lives; very thankful that God has set us in a world so full of beauty and joy; thankful to our kind and hospitable Whitby friends; thankful to the beloved friends who have brought you here, and tenderly thankful, I know, to those other kind friends, who have taken great delight in planning and arranging for this wonderful week. That is how people writing to me about Whitby describe the Winchester Gathering, 'that wonderful week.'

How I wish I could be with you to share all your joys and to see your dear faces!—the more so, because you have made me quite intimate with you in those examination papers which give me happy weeks, because I can see how happy you were in writing them, and what great joy you have in that knowledge, some of which you pour out in your papers. I have news to tell you which will, I think, give you a great deal of pleasure. Nobody can enjoy a treat by himself; he wants other boys and girls to share it with him, and the bigger the treat the more friends he would have to share it. I know you think of the P.U.S. work as a treat. I get letters every day to tell me how much so-and-so *enjoys* his or her lessons, and, though I cannot see you today, I know what happy faces you carry. I wonder do you know what gives happy faces to children and grownups? Just this, people look happy when they have nice things to think about, and you have so many delightfully interesting things to occupy your minds that I have never seen an unhappy looking P.U.S. scholar.

When we are happy we long to make other people so too; therefore I know you will be delighted to know that thousands and thousands of children have joined the school since Winchester days, and what is better than all, many of them are in elementary schools; these dear children, too, wander in the woods with Titania and Oberon, pitch their tents on the plains of Palestine with King Richard, see the wonders of the Parthenon, and lift up their eyes to the hills and to the stars. Some of them, with their teachers, are, you know, present at this Gathering, sharing in the generous welcome given to us by all our kind friends in Whitby, and all of you together have your thoughts full of great and beautiful things, and mean to learn and be of use in God's wonderful world.

I wonder, would you like to add to your prayers at night, 'God bless all children, parents and teachers in the P.U.S.'

THE BEGINNING OF THINGS
by E. Kitching*

We are met here to think of the work that has been done and of the worker who did it in a long life of 81 years, and it is a privilege to be allowed to speak of the beginning of that work. Its author spoke little of her early life, less of its difficulties, but of her mind on education she has told us much. Miss Mason was entirely without any thought of herself, she never dwelt upon details that concerned herself alone. When asked if she would not dictate some notes of her life her only reply was,—

My dear, my life does not matter. I have no desire that it should ever be written. It is the work that matters and, I say it with all reverence, it will some day (not in my lifetime) be seen to be one of the greatest things that has happened in the world.

It was a startling thing to say, but those who know Miss Mason's quiet confidence in the work that was given her to do, in her resolute patience that could wait, years if need be, till the right moment came, who could plan and wait for the means to come when no means were there, who could say, as she did only last year,—"We do not attempt things, we do

---

* Director of the P.U.S. and Secretary to Miss Mason from 1892. See also page 67.

them," those, and those only will understand that it was said with no tinge of egoism but with the passion of a great idea. Frail as she was, Miss Mason had faith to live, not ignoring difficulties, not denying pain, but facing both with courage and with a sure and certain hope that workers, strength, and means would come in so far as the work was 'the very work God meant for her' for she loved to say to her 'Bairns,' "Thou cam'st not to thy place by accident."

There was another reason why Miss Mason never talked of herself. It was a matter of principle. Her first thought was always for those who were to carry on her work and she practised in her daily life all that she put before their consideration in the ordering of their lives. She never said,— "Do this because I do it," even in thought. It was always— "The laws of life and conduct are laid down for us by our Lord and we do well to ponder every hint that the Gospel story gives us." On this particular point she would, as that part of the Gospel came in its natural sequence, dwell on the words "If I bear witness of myself, my witness is *not* true," and she would say to the students,—"My dear friends, think of this. Do not dwell upon yourselves, your belongings, even your families unduly, in talking to others. This saying is literally true. 'If I bear witness of myself my witness is not true.'"

Miss Mason was an only child of only children, a precious child, sharing the sheltered life of a rather delicate and much-loved mother and a devoted father. She learned at home and she once or twice mentioned her earliest recollection, that of her mother lying on a couch with a little brown leather Homer's *Odyssey* in her hand. One other recollection she mentioned in 1916 (in connection with the coming in of the Elementary Schools) and this must have been of the time when her vocation came to her. An only child, she was lonely, her mother being too delicate to entertain much and she had no child friends. She was probably about 8 when her parents moved and she became aware that children, lots of children, might be watched passing the window every day at certain times. From that time she was always there to watch them go by. She wondered where they went and if she might ever speak to them? There was a tall lady who went by too and how happy the children seemed when they saw her and away they would

run after her! How happy the lady must be with those
children! Later the opportunity came and the little girl was
taken to the school by friends and allowed to see the children
at work and she wondered what sort of books they had and if
they liked them as much as she did the books her father read
to her, *Anne of Geierstein* being at the moment the supreme
favourite. On page 322 of the first volume of the PARENTS'
REVIEW we read what must be a biographical touch, "We
wonder does any little girl in these days of many books
experience the joy of the girl of 11 we can recall crouching by
the fireside clasping her knees and listening as she has never
listened since to the reading of *Anne of Geierstein*? Then
came long, long thoughts about those children and then
came great sorrow and the cherished little daughter was left
alone in the world without means, for the American war had
ruined her father and he never recovered the shock of his
wife's premature death.

But the thought of the children came to fill her bereaved
heart and her one idea was how she could get into touch with
children. As Miss Williams[37] has told us in the March
REVIEW, an elementary Training College was the only open
sesame in those days to the teaching profession and so a
short course of training took Miss Mason in 1863 to a church
school in Worthing. Here she had some opportunity for
finding out what was in children but she had even more
intimate intercourse with some Anglo-Indian children who
lived with their aunt, a very dear friend. Miss Mason was able
to watch these children to see what and how they thought,
how they worked, what sort of knowledge appealed to them.
She came early to one or two conclusions. First, that children
had an unlimited power of attention; secondly, that mere
information did not call out that power; thirdly, that they had
an unlimited hunger for knowledge; fourthly, that their
minds always worked by the question put to themselves,—
what next? The years passed and at Bishop Otter College,
Chichester, Miss Mason came into touch with the minds of
young women and she found them very little different from
those of the children except that their powers were not so
fresh. Here Miss Mason lectured on Education and Human
Physiology. But the teaching of Geography, its possibilities,

---

[37] See page 58.

its life-giving interests, its delights, also took hold of her and she tramped county after county, Hampshire especially, visiting every spot of interest, reading local records, going to London and reading in the British Museum books of first-hand travel. Then in order to show how Geography could be made a living study, Miss Mason gave up her work at Chichester and went to Bradford where she gave much time to writing geography books and some to her beloved work of teaching in a school kept by a friend. The first book published was THE FORTY SHIRES: THEIR HISTORY, SCENERY, ARTS AND LEGENDS, (1880). Then followed in quick succession THE LONDON GEOGRAPHICAL READERS (now THE AMBLESIDE GEOGRAPHY BOOKS) published from 1880 onwards and dedicated to teachers trained at the Otter Memorial College. Another friend of Miss Mason's had a school in AMBLESIDE left to her by Miss Clough when she went to Newnham and here Miss Mason spent many a holiday and learned to know and love the place which was to be her home for the rest of her life. I was talking only the other day to the father of a student who remembers being taught there by Miss Mason 60 years ago.

THE WORLD TO COME (quoted in the March REVIEW) and a number of other poems were written about 1865.

In 1885 a parish room was wanted for the church in Bradford which Miss Mason attended and she offered lectures in lieu of money. These were delivered in the winter of 1885-1886 and HOME EDUCATION was published in the autumn of 1886. In the Preface to HOME EDUCATION, Miss Mason says,—"In venturing to speak on the subject of home education I do so with the sincerest deference to mothers, believing that in the words of a wise teacher of men the woman receives from the Spirit of God himself the intuitions into the child's character ... but just in proportion as a mother has this peculiar insight ... she will feel the need of a knowledge of the general principles of education ... and this knowledge not the best of mothers will get from above seeing that we do not often receive as a gift that which we have the means of getting by our own efforts." HOME EDUCATION contains in essence all that Miss Mason developed in her further writings and activities. In the first lecture we get the child's estate, a belief in which led to what has been called

the Children's Magna Charta, the PARENTS' UNION SCHOOL;
this belief also runs through every detail of the work set in
the programmes. Lecture II takes up out-of-door life and this
has led to the awakening of the world to the bliss of nature
study, a subject now learned in most schools though
nowhere with so much simple joy as in the PARENTS' UNION
schoolrooms where an academic or utilitarian aspect does
not creep in. The study of nature is a very different thing
from the study of science and this fact was brought home to
me only the other day in talking to a friend who has taken
high scientific honours and done scientific research work in
museums but her joy at finding a moss *in situ*,[38] for she had
studied mosses only in cabinets, of finding a beetle and
wanting to know its name, of watching a dipper on the beck
was good to see. Lecture III takes up moral training and
Lecture IV mental training. Miss Mason always dreaded lest
the P.N.E.U. should suffer by the repetition of shibboleths
and it is well to consider the position she gives to Attention in
mental training lest the method of narration should become a
shibboleth whereas it is only the outward and audible sign of
that inward and spiritual grace, the power of attention, by
which the mind feeds upon the food convenient for it. Lecture
V deals with Lessons, worked out later and more fully in
SCHOOL EDUCATION: Lecture VI, with the moral and spiritual
powers of a child. This was worked out later in detail in
OURSELVES, while in PARENTS AND CHILDREN we get moral
training from the parents' point of view. In Lecture VII[*]
literary evenings are taken up, also the study of pictures,
music and poetry. "It is a pity," says Miss Mason, "that we
like our music as our pictures and our poetry mixed, so that
there are few opportunities of going through as a listener a
course of the works of a single composer. Let young people
study as far as possible under one master until they have
received some of his teaching and know his style."

A class of children ranging in age from 5 to 7 voted
"Industry and Greed" as their favourite out of six pictures by
Watts they had been studying and next "The People that Sat
in Darkness," not "Una" or "Sir Galahad" as one might have
expected. A girl (Form III, aged 13) in an Elementary School

---

[38] In its natural environment.
[*] Now published in Vol. V Some Studies in the Formation of Character.

wrote the following in her Christmas examination paper in
answer to a question on Brahms' music.

Brahms made the Interezzo, (sic)
A song of slumber deep,
That every mother, sweet and low,
Should sing her babe to sleep.

He also composed the waltzes,
Of tones both great and small,
And some of Russian dances,
And some to be danced by all.

And unto Christ our heavenly king,
He made a carol light,
That people upon earth should sing,
To God each Christmas night.

The principles contained in HOME EDUCATION had been
further brought home to Miss Mason while lecturing to ladies
preparing to teach in Elementary Schools in Bishop Otter
College and during the years that followed, years of
educational work, literary and other, a single idea was
gradually taking shape and forcing itself into prominence,
becoming, in fact, a life purpose,—how to approach parents
without appearance of presumption and offer to them a few
principles which seemed a very gospel of education. The
interest roused in the lectures in Bradford paved the way,
and at the end of 1886 Miss Mason begs that she may have
"sea-room amongst all the vessels laden with gifts for the
Jubilee for a vessel laden with a gift meet for a queen."
Colleagues gathered, among the first and most inspiring the
late Mrs. Petrie Steinthal and the late T. G. Rooper, H.M.I.,
the late Dr. Mrs. Keeling and in the drawing room of Mrs.
Steinthal, just before the holidays in 1887, a syllabus, which
Miss Mason had drawn up for a PARENTS' EDUCATIONAL UNION,
was discussed. The central principles and the objects are
there almost intact and the syllabus contains in germ almost
every detail of the work as now carried on.

It is now possible to quote from records for Volumes I, II
and III of the PARENTS' REVIEW, the first Report of the P.N.E.U.
(1892) and, above all, the original DRAFT PROOF of the SOCIETY

(1888) give the various steps by which the P.N.E.U. and its activities came into being.

Its "object" was the physical education, the moral training, the mental discipline and instruction, and the spiritual growth, of the child. Its constitution, parents *of whatever class*, and others interested in education. Its plan of work included arrangements for business meetings, lectures, field excursions, schoolroom and cottage lectures, cottage field excursions, the dissemination of literature, occasional lectures by well-known educationists, an examination scheme, a magazine for the UNION, a training college, and lectures on education under the headings of the 'Objects.'

Later in the year the first meeting of the PARENTS' EDUCATIONAL UNION was held in the hall of the Bradford Grammar School and 80 members were enrolled the first day. I quote a few paragraphs from Miss Mason's address:

Bearing in mind that our object is to bring common thought on the subject of education to the level of scientific research, the question is how to give parents grip of the enormous leverage offered by some half-dozen physiological and psychological truths.

To this end we propose to hold meetings—say four—during the winter session, with a definite programme of subjects for discussion: if the four parts of education—physical, mental, moral, and religious—can be taken up consecutively, so much the better; the topic for the day to be ventilated by means of an original paper or other reading to be followed by discussion. And because these are topics, in which everyone present will have a vivid personal interest, and upon which every thinking person must at some time have thought, we expect such discussion to be both lively and profitable. Here we have a modest programme of work for the winter meetings of the UNION.

A little PARENTS' EDUCATIONAL UNION work remains to be done in the summer months. Children under 9 should get the more valuable part of their education in the open air. They should be on speaking terms with every sort of natural object to be met within miles of their homes.

Scientific knowledge is not wanted at this stage, but what Professor Huxley calls 'common information,' which, by the way, is not too common. It is from his parents the child must get this *real* knowledge. We all know how eagerly every child takes to the lore of the fields—but how shall we tell what we don't know, and do we not all wish we knew more of this sort of thing? Here is more work for the society. A couple of field excursions every year under the lead of a naturalist, with opportunities for asking questions, and with a note book, should give us at least a score or two of new acquaintances every year, and, what is more, should initiate us into the art of seeing—both communicable possessions, to be passed on to the children. The programme for working men and their wives is the same in principle. We should have two winter schoolroom or cottage meetings. One or two mothers' cottage meetings will be arranged for.

This is, roughly, our programme for our first year. We may see our way to more work than we pledge ourselves to. For instance, we may set on foot work under an examination scheme, in the case of parents or others being found willing to undertake a definite course of reading in education and its kindred sciences with a view to examination. Further delightful visions loom in the distance—hardly yet within measurable distance. We may live as a society to see ourselves possessed of an educational lending library; may see the issue of an educational magazine, which should make our work easy; and who knows but what some mothers amongst us may live to engage ladies from a training college, where women of some cultivation are taught the natural laws in obedience to which a child grows up healthy, happy, intelligent, and good? More, may we hope to see the day when no mother will engage a governess, however 'nice,' or however accomplished, who has not been duly trained in the art and instructed in the science of education.

That such a society should be of use goes without saying—therefore we believe it will be fostered, for most of us are of Matthew Arnold's mind, that the best thing worth living for is 'to be of use.' No doubt the working of the society will demand some power, moral and intellectual, as well as good will; but, happily, there is no lack of power among us, so that need be no stumbling block.

May I propose to you two ideas to the working out of which it seems to me well worth while that our society should devote itself:

(a) That the forming of habits is a great part of education;

(b) that body, mind, soul, and spirit, equally, live upon food, and perish of famine; all four require daily bread; all thrive as they work, and degenerate in idleness. That I am using a popular rather than a scientific description of man does not matter; we all know that our needs and our activities are of four sorts and this is enough for our present purpose.

Whose we are and Whom we serve. Here we have at once the motive and the safeguard of parents. An attempt to bring up children on scientific principles alone may produce splendid results in literature, science, even in virtue; but by–and–by, there is evidence of a leak somewhere, threatening to sink the ship. Startling illustrations will occur to us all. On the other hand, he who wilfully ignores the laws which regulate activity and development in every part of our being, is like him who puts to sea without rudder or compass, trusting to the winds of heaven to carry him where he would go. *Whose we are*—let us make the most and best of our children: *Whom we serve*—in order that their service may be of the worthiest.

The Report of the meeting adds "the idea of the establishment of the society has jumped with popular feeling and, though the scope and methods of the UNION remain practically as in the original forecast, the society is already deeply indebted to the judgment and earnest efforts of men and women of thought and culture."

In August 1887, Miss Mason lectured before the British Association and it is a significant fact that there was then no Education Section so that she spoke under the Section of Economic Science and Statistics.

In the second Session of the P.N.E.U. in Bradford the number of members was more than doubled. There were four meetings of members addressed by Mrs. Boyd Carpenter, The Countess of Aberdeen[39] and others, and the Countess of Aberdeen's question "Where shall I get a governess to carry out the principles of HOME EDUCATION?" gave impetus to working the scheme for a training College. There were also four mothers' meetings, two mixed parents' meetings, three meetings for nurses. Besides these, various parish mothers' meetings and women's guilds were also addressed on matters connected with moral and religious training and sanitation.

It was then felt that the society had justified itself locally and that it might be brought before a wider public. Before attempting to do this Miss Mason took counsel with a number of leaders of thought such as Dr. Butler (of Trinity) Dr. Temple, Dr. Welldon, Dr. Quick, Dr. Percival (Rugby), Professor Max Müller, Sir Joshua Fitch, Miss Buss, Miss Beale, Miss Clough, Canon Liddon, Professor Sully, Bishop Westcott, (some of whom she went to Cambridge to meet at the invitation of Miss Clough). Opinions and criticisms were freely invited and freely and cordially given and Miss Mason felt it was perhaps to this thorough thrashing out that we owe the fact that the P.N.E.U. has worked ever since with hardly a hitch. In 1888 the pamphlet oddly called the DRAFT PROOF was printed, and the following preliminary considerations were sown broadcast. I quote from them,—

No other part of the world's work is of such supreme difficulty, delicacy and importance, as that of parents in the right bringing up of their children. The first obligation of the present—that of passing forward a generation better than ourselves—rests with parents. As every child belongs to the Commonweal, so his bringing up is the concern of all. Yet parents, with the responsibility of the world's future resting upon them, are left to do their work, each father and mother alone, rarely getting so much as a word of sympathy, counsel, or encouragement. All other bodies of workers, whether of hand or brain, enjoy the help and profit of association; commonly, of co-operation. Thus the wisdom, the experience, the information of each is made profitable for all; enthusiasm is generated by the UNION of many for the advance of a cause, and every

---

[39] See page 32.

member is cheered by the sympathy of his fellow workers. More, association makes it possible to organise means of instruction—lectures, libraries, classes, journals, etc. It creates an ever higher public opinion, which puts down casual, uninstructed work, and sets a premium on good work, and it gives an impetus to steady progress as opposed to spasmodic efforts. But parents are outside of all this. They, who must do the vital part of the world's work, compare at a disadvantage with all other skilled workers, whether of hand or brain. There is a literature of its own for almost every craft and profession; while you may count on the fingers of one hand the scientific works on early training plain and practical enough to be of use to parents. There are no colleges, associations, classes, lectures for parents, or those of an age to become parents; no register of the discoveries—physical or psychological—in child nature, which should make education a light task; no record of successful treatment of the sullen, the heedless, the disobedient child; none of the experience of wise parents; there is hardly a standard of beautiful child-life (reduced to words, that is,) towards which parents can work. There is little means of raising public opinion on the subject of home training, or of bringing such opinion to bear. Every young mother must begin at the beginning to work out for herself the problems of education, with no more than often misleading traditions for her guidance. One reason for this anomaly is, that the home is a sanctuary, where prying and intermeddling from without would be intolerable; and, without doubt, the practices of each home are sacred; but the *principles* of early training are another matter, there is no more helpful work to be done than to bring these principles to the doors of parents of whatever degree.

How cordially parents welcome any effort in this direction one has but to try to be convinced. There is a feeling abroad that it does not do to bring up children casually; that there are certain natural laws—better named Divine laws—which must be worked out in order to produce human beings at their best, in body, mind, moral nature, and spiritual power. It is no easy matter to get at these laws, and here is where parents demand thorough ventilation, at least, of the questions that concern them. For people are beginning to perceive how lamentable and how universal are the miseries arising from *defective education*; the over active brain, the narrow chest, the sullen and resentful temper, the sluggish intellect are often, more or less, the results of faulty education: the tendency may have been born with the child, but education is able to deal with tendencies. Most of us are aware of some infirmity of flesh or spirit, a life-long stumbling-block, which might have been easily cured in our childhood. It is not too much to say that, in the light of advancing science, many of the infirmities that beset us, whether of heart, intellect, or temper, are the results of defective education.

This is, shortly, where we are today: the principle which underlies the *possibility* of all education is discovered to us: we are taught that the human frame, brain as well as muscle, *grows to the uses it is earliest put to*. It is hardly possible to get beyond the ground covered by this simple sounding axiom; that is, it is hardly open to us to overstate the possibilities of education. Almost anything may be made of a child by those who first get him into their hands. We find that we can work definitely towards the formation of character; that the *habits* of the good life, of the alert intelligence, which we take pains to form in the child, are, somehow, registered in the very substance of his brain; and that the habits of the child are, as it were, so many little hammers beating out by slow degrees the character of the man. Therefore we set ourselves to form a habit in the same matter-of-fact steady way that we set about teaching the multiplication table; expecting the thing to be done and done with for life. But fitful efforts after a habit—say, of tidiness, or of obedience—are of very little use, and are worrying to child and parents.

In 1892 the following was added:

But this doctrine of habit, all important as it is, includes no more than a third part of the ground covered by education. Parents are very jealous over the individuality of their children; they mistrust the tendency to develop all on the same plan, and this instinctive jealousy is right, for supposing that education really did consist in systematized effort to draw out every power that is in children, all must needs develop on the same lines. Some of us have an uneasy sense that things are tending towards this deadly sameness. But, indeed, the fear is groundless. We may rest assured that the personality, the individuality of each of us is too dear to God, and too necessary to a complete humanity, to be left at the mercy of empires.

The problem of education is more complex than it seems at first sight, and well for us and the world that it is so. 'Education is a life'; you may stunt, and starve, and kill, or you may cherish and sustain; but the beating of the heart, the movement of the lungs, and the development of the 'faculties' are only indirectly our care.

'Education is an atmosphere, a discipline, a life' covers the question from the three conceivable points of view. Subjectively, in the child, education is a life; objectively as affecting the child, education is a discipline; relatively, if we may introduce a third term, as regards the environment of the child, education is an atmosphere.

The whole subject is profound, but as practical as it is profound. We absolutely must disabuse our minds of the theory that the functions of education are, in the main, gymnastic. In the early years of the child's life it makes perhaps, little *apparent* difference whether his parents start with the notion that to educate is to fill a receptacle, inscribe a tablet, mould plastic matter, or, *nourish a life*; but in the end we shall find that only those *ideas* which have fed his life are taken into the being of the child; all else is thrown away, or worse, is an impediment and an injury to the vital processes.

This is, perhaps, how the educational formula should run; education is a life; all life must have its appropriate nourishment, as the bodily life is sustained on bread, so is the spiritual life on *ideas*; and it is the duty of parents to sustain a child's inner life with ideas as they sustain its body with food. The child is an eclectic; he may choose this or that; therefore, in the morning sow thy seed, and in the evening withhold not thy hand, for thou knowest not which shall prosper, whether this or that, or whether they both shall be alike good.

The child has affinities with evil as well as with good; therefore, hedge him about from any chance lodgment of evil suggestion.

The initial idea begets subsequent ideas; therefore, take care that children get right primary ideas on the great relations and duties of life.

Every study, every line of thought, has its 'guiding idea'; therefore the study of a child makes for living education as it is quickened by the guiding idea which 'stands at the head.'

In a word, our much boasted 'infallible reason'—is it not the involuntary thought which follows the initial idea upon necessary, logical lines? Given, the starting idea, and the conclusion may be predicated almost to a certainty. We get into the way of thinking such and such manner of thoughts, and of coming to such and such conclusions, ever further and further removed from the starting point, but on the same lines.

The DRAFT PROOF continues,—

It may be well to face at the outset the imperfectly understood attitude of education towards religion. Are we not claiming too much for education when we say that it can turn out a human being with every part and every function in vigorous play and in just proportion? Are we not trending on the transforming work of the Holy Spirit? This is a difficulty which confronts many earnest Christian parents. Perhaps the perplexity arises from our habit of limiting the operations of the laws of God to the region of man's spiritual nature. But as we cannot drop a pebble nor draw a breath save in conformity with certain divine laws, so every development and activity of body, soul and spirit is fenced about with its own laws. What the laws are, along the lines of which the child develops in every part of his most complex nature—that, it is the business of the parent to know that he may obey. There are few more intricate studies, but there are few so interesting in progress, so blessed in result, for these physical and metaphysical laws also are the laws of God in the keeping of which there is great reward. With deep reverence be it said that the Holy Spirit Himself, the Lord and Giver of Life, when He undertakes the education of a human being, operates according to law, works out those very principles of education which are proposed to parents, in fact, plays the part of parent to the willing and obedient soul. Is then education the whole? Does it cover everything? Is even the mystery of the Divine life no more than a result of education? By no means. Education is not creative, it acts upon that which is. For the life of the spirit it does no more than offer two or three helpful suggestions. For instance, reasoning from analogy the science of education teaches that if the spiritual life is to be vigorous it must be daily and duly nourished and daily and duly exercised, but it knows nothing of the "living bread" which is the sustenance of the spirit; nor yet of the spirit's functions of praise, prayer and adoration. Again, it is by revelation and not by education that man may know God; again, education hardly touches the sad mysteries of sin and temptation, nor the mystery of God manifest in the flesh—of the Birth of Bethlehem, the Sacrifice of Calvary. These things are spiritually discerned. Education can only water and dig about the garden of the soul and sow the seeds of the higher life.

The education the P.N.E.U. exists to further runs on two lines. The formation of habits: bodily, mental, moral and spiritual. The presentation of that Idea which is the all important step in the formation of every habit. As a corollary to these: the development of the faculties so much insisted upon by the earlier educationists takes a quite subordinate place in the educational thought as promulgated by the P.N.E.U.

The DRAFT PROOF concerns itself also with the Objects of the UNION and in view of recent developments the following are of special interest

(2) To bring before parents of *all classes* the best thought on education;

(3) To strengthen the hands of parents by association and co-operation and to stimulate parental enthusiasm by the sense that many are endeavouring in the same direction.

(5) To help to strengthen the social bond which unites parents of all classes and opinions.

In connection with (2) Members of the UNION have at different times given addresses on the teaching of the P.N.E.U. to other societies, to mothers' meetings, to teachers' meetings. One Branch of the P.N.E.U. worked through a Welfare Centre; we had also a working mothers' Branch at the Victoria Settlement, Manchester, but the most important development of this part of the work has been the PARENTS' ASSOCIATIONS started recently in connection with the Elementary P.U. SCHOOLS by the Hon. Mrs. Franklin,[40] the devoted Hon. Org. Secretary of the P.N.E.U. since 1897. I had the great privilege of being present at one of these meetings in October last when Mrs. Franklin addressed the ASSOCIATION of parents in connection with a P.U.S. County Council School in London. There are 70 members and the parents manage the working themselves. One or two took part in the discussions afterwards and one father enquired how it was that the P.U.S. system was not being carried out also in the boys' school, for he found his little girl was far ahead of her brothers.

To quote another instance, one amongst many: an ex-student of the College has spoken at mixed meetings in Gloucestershire where the children from her own P.U.S. class have had lessons in public with the children of the P.U.S. village school; she has also had 'picture talks' with working mothers, and has addressed the members of the W.E.A. All this work has brought parents and teachers of all classes and opinions together. The Conference at AMBLESIDE last year was yet another instance of this development.

The DRAFT PROOF which has been so largely quoted also takes into account the scope of the UNION. I quote a few of the considerations.

One object of the UNION is to insist that a child cannot be so well brought up all round by the best of mothers as by the co-operation of both parents;

---

[40] See page 33 and 113.

and again,

> the earnest mother is often hampered in her work by an
> inefficient governess.

> There is a near prospect that the UNION will be able to
> establish a HOUSE OF EDUCATION where young ladies who
> have left school, ladies proposing to teach in families,
> shall be taught,—the right ordering of a home
> schoolroom, the principles which underlie the moral and
> mental growth of a child and how to train him according
> to his nature, the most rapid and rational methods of
> teaching and how to train a child's senses by means of
> out of door work, by teaching him to know, name and
> delight in natural objects.

The possibilities of a Parents' Sunday, Local Education
Classes, Branch Libraries, Pamphlets for parents, are also
discussed in the DRAFT PROOF. Clause (6) refers to
Propaganda articles in Magazines and in that year, 1888,
Miss Mason had articles accepted in *Murray's Magazine*, the
Quiver, and *Cassell's Magazine* but the UNION soon had its
own magazine for its members and for propaganda work.
From time to time articles on the work are still appearing in
other organs. This present year (1923) there will be three in
The XIXth Century, and one in *The Hibbert Journal*, all by Mr.
Household.[41]

Lastly, the DRAFT PROOF considers the organisation of the
UNION. These considerations are much as we know them now
but two points are of interest.

> The P.N.E.U. desires to enter a protest against secular
> education and so the Council shall keep well to the front
> the four parts of education—physical, mental, moral and
> religious.

> Each Local Branch is a PARENTS' EDUCATIONAL UNION
> and pledges itself (1) to a religious basis of work, (2) that
> the number of addresses shall be equally distributed to
> the four parts of education, (3) that as much work be

---

[41] See pages 44 and 185.

done with the parents of the working as with those of the educated class.

Finally some valuable remarks sent by Miss Clough are quoted,—

The work should be done *locally* as much as possible. Different localities have to be approached in different ways. The smaller the area, the more quietly and effectually the work can be done.

On January 18th, 1890, the rules and constitution of the P.N.E.U. were drawn up by the Executive Committee at a meeting held in the Graham Street High School. The central principles and objects as originally drawn up were adopted, and on February 18th were finally discussed in a long and earnest debate in the presence of some leading educationists in the hall of the College of Preceptors, and the result was the principles and objects of the UNION in their present and final form.

Of the early days of the PARENTS' REVIEW Miss Mason writes,—

The SOCIETY struggled into birth without its own magazine, but it was felt, in very early days, that such a society, without an inspiring organ, would be a mere tool to the hand of every educational faddist who had a theory to advance. Now the P.N.E.U. owes its vitality to the fact that it is a propagandist society, existing to disseminate certain educational principles. Such a society must obviously have the means of communicating, month by month, with its scattered members, must guide the progress of the movement towards the end in view.

How to launch a worthy magazine was the question? We had amongst us but very few enthusiasts willing and able to risk capital in a costly and hazardous enterprise. A high-class educational magazine appealing to a public of parents, not in the least 'popular,' limited by the nature of its contents to educated and really earnest readers, would seem fore-doomed to failure. However, obstacles were overcome, personal friends came to the help of educational allies, a sufficient fund was raised to carry the PARENTS' REVIEW through over four years of its existence, during which the sales did not yet cover the costs of production. In these doubtful days friends made valiant efforts; the REVIEW was spread from hand to hand; a second small fund was raised at a distressful juncture; the publishers wondered at the enthusiasm of the subscribers; and now, the REVIEW is self-supporting and is in a position to help the SOCIETY. We take this opportunity of expressing our profound gratitude to those generous friends who supported what appeared to be a hopeless cause, and to those equally valuable friends among our subscribers who, from the very beginning, have laboured ceaselessly to spread the PARENTS' REVIEW, and with it the knowledge of our principles and our work.

A few words from the "Dedication" to the first number of the REVIEW, February 1890, will serve to indicate its original aim.

The PARENTS' REVIEW is dedicated, with great deference, and with a strong assurance of their warm sympathy and support, to parents. The aim of the PARENTS' REVIEW is to raise common thought on the subject of education to the level of scientific research, and to give parents grip of some half-dozen principles which should act as enormously powerful levers in the elevation of character.

Miss Mason writes later,—

How one remembers the 'fearful joy' of the first number of P.R., what it was to fetch it from the publishers at the moment of issue, to carry it to the nearest quiet place, to ponder its pages and its cover and the *tout ensemble*[42] of the (then) greeny-yellow magazine, now with joy, now with anxiety, now with doubt, again with rejoicing! Would it prove to be still born? Was there the least chance in the world that so new a venture in magazine literature would find a public? Those were intense moments, and not less intense were the months of incubation.

---

[42] General effect.

THE REVIEW went through troublous times but it has maintained its high level for 33 years, and Miss Mason used to say that it was a wonderful thing that the magazine could live without any fund for contributors. But it met a need and contributors have come forward generously to give their services to a cause which they felt to be worthwhile.

In March 1890, the first Annual Meeting was announced in the REVIEW, to take place on June 3rd, with the accompanying editorial note—:

We hope that many of our readers will make a point of attending, that they may hear the objects and methods of the PARENTS' NATIONAL EDUCATIONAL UNION fully set forth, and may learn how simple a matter it is to establish a 'Branch' in any neighbourhood.

The object of the promoters is to overspread the country with a great national educational league of parents of every condition; and thus testify that parents form an educational body, whose regard for the interests of the children is as intelligent as it is profound.

The strength of our position lies in the word *body*. The good and great amongst us show what great things individual parents have done and are doing. But the duty of even the best parents does not end with their own children; there are certain duties of fellowship of calling, recognized, perhaps, in every vocation but that of the parent. The clergyman owns responsibilities to his brother clergy; the doctor, the artist, the army man, above all, the teacher profits by free give and take with the members of his profession; the parent, alone, stands aloof, as one who should say, 'I have nothing to give and nothing to get; I am sufficient unto myself.' This aloofness of parents is hardly intentional; it is a mere relic of the sentiment of our barbarian days, the feeling we express in the saying, 'The Englishman's house is his castle.' We are waking up to the fact that, by his exclusion and seclusion we sustain a great national and personal loss; we lose much of the enthusiasm which kindles with the consciousness that many are striving together in a great cause.

It is no arbitrary reward which is attached to the assembling of two or three together; we warm ourselves at each others' fires, and glow with the heat we get. Let but the heads of two or three families meet together to talk over the bringing up of their children, and the best and wisest parents will go home with new insight, renewed purpose, and warmer zeal.

We shall learn by degrees that education is, like religion, a social principle as well as an individual duty; and, meeting on this higher ground, we shall find out the best of one another as we never should in the common intercourse of business or society.

On Tuesday, June 31st, 1890, the First Annual Meeting of the P.N.E.U. was held at London House, Dr. Temple presiding. The speakers included Bishop Boyd Carpenter, Canon Daniel, Dr. Gladstone, and the Rev. E. Wynne (for whose parish room, the HOME EDUCATION lectures were delivered). Today we are holding the 25th Annual Conference arranged, as always, by The Honorary Mrs. Franklin, who initiated the Conferences in 1897.

In September 1890, arrangements were made by Miss Mason for an organising tour beginning at Sheffield, working southward through Cambridge to the coast, crossing country by way of Cheltenham and working northwards again by Birmingham and Wolverhampton. By December, Branches at Belgravia, Forest Gate, Hampstead, and Bournemouth, Bradford, Cheltenham, Grantham were at work and by February 1891, Branches at Sheffield, Bowdon and Kendal were added. In September 1890, "suggestions" for Branch Secretaries were published in the REVIEW.

In October 1890, three courses of lectures were given by Miss Mason at Cheltenham to mothers, teachers and nurses.

In June 1891, New South Wales formed the first Dominion Branch, and Australia is still doing excellent P.N.E.U. work.

In November 1891, Miss Mason gave a course of lectures in London and in Lent 1892, she gave two courses, one at the Polytechnic and another at Hyde Park Court, Albert Gate, by invitation of the late Mrs. Dallas Yorke whose friendship was one of the great happinesses of Miss Mason's life: Mrs. Dallas

Yorke later became Visitor to the HOUSE OF EDUCATION where she inspired and encouraged the students by her presence and her talks to them.

During the year 1891 a number of lecturers came forward, one of whom, Dr. Helen Webb,[43] has continued for over 30 years to lecture for the UNION.

In January 1891 the scheme for a HOUSE OF EDUCATION was brought before the readers of the PARENTS' REVIEW and the notice says,—

We shall invite women of refinement and education to come to us for a year's training and they will leave us we hope with what we shall venture to call 'the enthusiasm of childhood.' In January 1892, the HOUSE OF EDUCATION was started in AMBLESIDE.

In December 1892, another scheme was brought forward. Of this Miss Mason says:—

The writer of an article in the REVIEW appealed to the students of the PARENTS' REVIEW. We find that the feeling is gaining ground, that 'Education' demands more than mere reading; many mothers feel that they would be the better in body and mind for the mental activity that nothing but definite study affords and the time seems ripe for the carrying out of another item of our original programme, and we have made arrangements for a course of study on Education—a three years' course—with questions.

In June 1892, the MOTHERS' EDUCATIONAL COURSE was started. It provided for a definite course of study, covering the principles of, and suggesting good methods for, the physical, mental, moral and religious training of children.

There were in (1899) about 80 mothers working in it, but after working for 23 years the M.E.C. was given up.

In June 1891, the PARENTS' REVIEW School was introduced to the readers of the PARENTS' REVIEW in an article from which the following is an extract:—

---

43 See page 42.

For lack of something analogous to school discipline in their early training children begin school at a disadvantage, they begin life at a disadvantage, and the world never gets the best of them. No school advantages can make to up a child for the scope for individual development he should find at home, under the direction of his parents, for the first 8 or 10 years of life. Later, sterner discipline, intellectual as well as physical, takes the field. The routine of the schoolroom and the virtues and habits of the communal life, the life of the citizen, are, perhaps, never so thoroughly acquired at home as at school. Exclusive home-training continued too long tends to exaggerated individuality, eccentricity; while school life, begun too soon, tends to loss of original power and individual character. But, theory apart, this is what actually happens. Most children of the educated classes, boys and girls, get their early 'schooling' at home. The children of parents who live in the country, where good day-schools are unattainable, have no alternative. Girls of the professional class, living in the country, commonly get the whole of their 'schooling' at home. Girls of the highest class are rarely sent to school. We have not found ourselves able to give this kind of help to parents through the pages of the PARENTS' REVIEW, because very mischievous results might follow from prescriptions of work being applied to children for whom they were totally unfitted. But we see a way, at last, to do what we have felt all along to be very important work. We propose to open a PARENTS' REVIEW SCHOOL. It shall be a unique school, for the pupils shall go to school and be taught at home at one and the same time and have the two-fold advantages of school discipline and home culture.

There is no waste more sad than the waste of those early years when the child's curiosity is keen and his memory retentive, and when he might lay up a great store of knowledge of the world he lives in with pure delight to himself.

The PARENTS' REVIEW SCHOOL opened on June 15th, 1891. The title was changed in 1907 to The PARENTS' UNION SCHOOL.

We have now issued the Programme of Work for the 96th term.

In July (1891) Miss Mason writes in the REVIEW,—

We have been asked to admit schools as well as families to the P.U.S. and we see no reason why not.

We have now, 1923, some 117 secondary schools and classes at work and 175 Elementary schools, while there are many hundreds of home schoolrooms all over the world.

The aims and objects of the SCHOOL are set forth in the article entitled "The PARENTS' REVIEW SCHOOL" (Vol. III of the PARENTS' REVIEW) and are just as we know them now. The variety of subjects and the limited times are also as in the original plan though the recent programmes shew much development in the way of books simply because the books wanted had not then been written; though we still use a few of the books first set, Mrs. Fisher's for instance, because none have ever been found better and for other books we are still waiting.

As we started with a vision of the children so let us end with one. I have with me a list of 103 schools in the county of Gloucester doing P.U.S. work (a wonderful tribute to Miss Mason's work raised by Mr. Household) and we must remember that it was Mrs. Petrie Steinthal's knowledge of, and faith in, the Elementary teacher which started the pioneer school at Drighlington and so made possible that vision of thousands of Elementary school children doing P.U.S. work which seemed to Miss Mason like a *Nunc Dimittis*[44] and which called forth in 1916 her recollections of that vision of the children which so filled her thoughts as a little girl.

In conclusion may I read a part of a letter which Miss Mason received from the Head of a Gloucester Elementary school on January 11th. It was almost the last letter read to her and gave her so much pleasure.

---

[44] The prayer recited by Simeon at the presentation of Jesus at the temple (Luke 2:29-31); used as a canticle in the Anglican liturgy.

May I be allowed to express my warm appreciation of your scheme. I have no desire to go back to the old methods, in fact, I do not think that I could teach in the old way now.

This was a very mediocre school, until we were allowed by Mr. Household to work your scheme, and although it is—the school—far from good, and has not nearly reached the mark which I have aimed at for it, yet I feel that the children are keener, more enthusiastic and interested and certainly decidedly happier in their work. Only today, some of the upper children asked me if they could come to my house this evening to read with me. Of course, I readily acceded to their request, and we have had a very pleasant evening together.

Parents too, have told me that they are amazed at the knowledge which their children have acquired during the last 18 months, and also that since we adopted the new method it is impossible for them to persuade their children to stay away, except in cases of real illness or extremely bad weather, for some of the children have to come from a considerable distance to school.

I felt that I would like to tell you these things to show you in perhaps a very feeble way, how much your work is appreciated in this isolated spot on the Cotswolds.

Here is an extract from a visitor to an Elementary school received just before the Conference,—

Miss —— is working so devotedly and loyally in Essex. She has only been there for a year, but the children love their work and quite understand that it is Miss Mason who had chosen such beautiful books for their study. The parents too are pleased with the children's interest and progress and the Inspectors, both H.M.I. and Diocesan, have made very good reports of the work.

And here are two notes which have also just come from the Heads of Elementary schools. One, in London, writes:

The programmes have brought much joy and interest into my school. The children are so encouraging—it is simply wonderful what they bring me. One girl brought me the other day a coloured print of Alexander receiving Darius' women-folk—really a most interesting picture, and the child brought a little framed picture of the Sistine Madonna, the "lodger upstairs" had lent it—wonderful people those lodgers!

I am more than grateful for the results of one term's work, it has made no end of difference to these girls. I have some very nice Books of Centuries, one is beautiful and the girl simply follows me about for books for drawings. Last Monday week I took 36 children to the British Museum.

Another in Warwickshire writes:

The Director visited our school last week, and was extremely interested in the progress the girls have made during the three years we have followed the Mason method. He asked for specimens of work to be sent to the Education Office, together with a short account of the introduction of the method into our particular school.

Finally, here is a glimpse into a home schoolroom,—

On hearing that I was writing to the lady who arranges the books, D has sent you a message, this is it, word for word:—
"Well, will you ask her please if 1B could have *Tales from Greece and Rome* next term? Because although T. always tells me what he has read I would like to have the real thing then p'raps I'd know who fought for Greece, and who for Troy." T. revels in it. Yesterday we spent the whole afternoon selecting suitable sticks for bows and arrows. This was splendid fun because we simply had to notice the difference between oak, ash, beech and hazel without any learning about it. Ash was finally chosen and the result was most successful. Today Ulysses (T.) and Hector (D.) have had a fierce fight outside Troy (the Hotel). "And we'll wear our yellow woolly caps, please Miss, because they are a bit like golden helmets, don't you think?"

In 1899 Miss Mason wrote words which may fitly close this brief survey of "The Beginning of Things."

> Life is more intense, more difficult, more exhausting for us than it was for our fathers; it will probably be more difficult still for our children than for ourselves. How timely, then, and how truly, as we say, providential, that just at this juncture of difficult living, certain simple, definite clues to the art of living should have been put into our hands. Is it presumptuous to hope that new life has been vouchsafed to us in these days, in response to our more earnest endeavour, our more passionate craving for "more light and fuller?" We look back at our small beginnings and thank God and take courage, for already we number our thousands. We have reason to congratulate ourselves and each other, but let us do so with diffidence. Success has its devils. May we each feel that we have a personal work to accomplish in connection with the UNION; that each of us is a propagandist, upon whom rests the duty of spreading the principles which seem to us so full of light.

MISS MASON'S IDEAL: ITS BREADTH AND BALANCE
By H. E. Wix[*]

Many of us here today must have known Miss Mason personally and probably the rest of us knew her so well through correspondence and various branches of her work that they too feel towards her as towards a personal friend. Perhaps there never has lived anyone who more speedily and lastingly won the friendship of persons she never saw. Teachers who had only known of her for a few months felt the blank of her loss with a curious intensity; so did parents whose knowledge of her was confined to gratitude for her teaching in HOME EDUCATION and PARENTS AND CHILDREN.

Breadth and balance are perhaps the main marks of Miss Mason's teaching, so that there are many standpoints from which we may try to study it. Surely few educationists have solved both a theory and a philosophy of education—in its

---

[*] Ex-student, House of Education.

broadest sense—and a practical concrete method of teaching as well. There are these two main sides of her ideal, often separated but not really separable. First, the upbringing of the child, the person; the teaching of habit, the training of the will, the gradual evolution of character. Founded on this and on much more, is Miss Mason's theory and practice of education in its narrower sense; how to teach children in their school days.

The training of the person is naturally a quieter affair than the imparting of knowledge; we can hold exhibitions of the work done by P.U. SCHOOL children or give demonstration lessons, but what we cannot do is to exhibit the character training of our children. This would seem to be one reason for the strangely mistaken idea that Miss Mason cared more for knowledge than for character. It is not however the whole reason.

Nowadays we hear much—perhaps too much—about freedom, individuality, sense-training and the importance of baby's earliest habits and so on. But these are no new things to members of the P.N.E.U. In HOME EDUCATION, written over 30 years ago, Miss Mason taught us that from the earliest days baby should learn the meaning of "must" and "must not," that we cannot too soon teach physical habits of regularity in sleep, food, etc. In her pamphlet CHILDREN AS PERSONS, we read that "liberty is the most sacred and inalienable right" of a child; that "public opinion is an insufferable bondage, depriving a person of his individual right to think for himself"; that "a mind that does not think and think its own thoughts, is as a paralysed arm or a blind eye." Much more could be quoted to show how important a place character, real character, held in Miss Mason's ideal, and how wonderfully this ideal has permeated educated thought. In fact some people who have seized this or that part of her teaching, not knowing whose it was, and have let it run away with them, have lost the balance and saneness which marks Miss Mason's teaching all through.

Indeed so much of what Miss Mason taught about the upbringing of children has passed into common possession of the thinking half of the nation that we forget to whom we owe it, which is just what she herself would have wished, what indeed she seems to have aimed at. And more than that, her teaching harmonises so well with the background of sane living, that when it is most there, we notice it least. Anyone taking up her book HOME EDUCATION and reading it for the first time is struck by the *sensibleness* of it all. "Of course" we say "that is just how we ought to do it, why didn't we think of it before? This is the help we have been hungering for for years; even what we knew already we probably owe to her too."

The following true story may serve as an illustration of this. There was a young mother who was wishful of joining the P.N.E.U. and so get help in the upbringing of her babies. But an older friend tried to dissuade her: "My dear, don't be so silly; all these societies are full of fads. Now just look at Mrs. So-and-so; do you know of a better or a more sensibly brought up family than hers? I never heard that she belonged to any new-fangled educational society."—"Oh, but," answered the young mother, "It was she who told me of the P.N.E.U. and she says she owes everything to it."

Indeed there could be no one more free from "fads" than Miss Mason. She used to tell us that we were not to try to *develop* individuality for that was the way cranks were made, we were to allow freedom to the "person," room for him to think his own thoughts.

Thus much of what was so new when Miss Mason first began to teach, is now part and parcel of common educational knowledge, and that being so, probably it no longer seemed necessary to Miss Mason that she should continually reiterate that which was already learnt. And so some people say: "Miss Mason cared more for knowledge than for character." But she held actually that the one was impossible without the other. Without knowledge there could be no character. Since character comes of thought and thoughts must come of what we know, knowledge makes character. This shows us what a sad fallacy underlies the argument that it does not matter what we learn but only how we learn it.

But Miss Mason did not mean quite the same as does the man in the street when she spoke of knowledge. In the BASIS OF NATIONAL STRENGTH, she gives us a most illuminating definition of knowledge. She says,

It is a state out of which persons may pass and into which they may return, but never a store upon which they may draw.

To her, knowledge was so bound up with "living" that the two were inseparable. Again, in the same pamphlet, Miss Mason gives us a negative definition of knowledge. "It is not" she says, "instruction, information, scholarship nor a well stored memory." "For too many of us," she says elsewhere, "knowledge is a thing of shreds and patches, knowledge of this and of that, with yawning gaps between." And again, "It is perhaps a beautiful whole, a great unity, embracing God and Man and the Universe, but having many parts ... all are necessary and each has its functions." "Knowledge is the science of the proportion of things." Yet one more quotation: "Fundamental knowledge is the knowledge of God and while we are ignorant of that principal knowledge, Science, Nature, Literature and History, all remain dumb."

So we see that knowledge to Miss Mason was a tremendous thing—indeed not a thing at all but a state, just as friendship is a state. It is a condition of happy friendship with God, with man and with nature, in which one's mind will grow and expand and blossom as happily as a plant in its native clime; the mind being in direct contact with other minds as a plant is surrounded by air; thus the mind drinks in from the Divine, from fellow men and from nature all that is needed for its complete sustenance.... It is interesting too to remember how Our Lord always taught people who came to Him; he did not criticise or find fault, but He enlightened their understanding; gave them truer knowledge for their guidance.

May I repeat that definition? It makes so clear how in Miss Mason's philosophy character cannot exist without knowledge. "Knowledge is a state out of which people may pass and into which they may return but never a store upon which they may draw." .... That is, real knowledge cannot be used as a servant, a crutch, a vaulting stick, to be thrown aside when we have passed that final examination and have "arrived." When so treated knowledge becomes mere information about some particular subject or subjects—and oh! how dull is a "well-informed" person and how untrustworthy are his opinions on people and on life! It is an obvious result, not because he is a specialist, not because he has passed examinations, but because of his attitude towards knowledge—something acquired solely to be made use of.

In Miss Mason herself we have the most wonderful example of her own teaching. We ourselves are mostly so far "outside knowledge" that we wonder and grope when decisions have to be made, but, as an article in the April REVIEW tells us, "she always knew without a second's hesitation what was the right thing" and afterwards the rightness of her decision was obvious to others.

But Miss Mason's idea of Education was not only that it was an atmosphere and a life, but also a discipline. "Without labour there is no profit" she said; but to emphasise this aspect hardly concerns this paper; though it must never be forgotten, since no one believed more strongly than she that knowledge is only for those who have the will to labour earnestly for it; it cannot be freely given by anyone.

Perhaps I have been able to show dimly the amazing breadth of Miss Mason's ideal. But as to balance there are some who seem to think that the scales of her favour were weighted on the side of letters rather than of things. Well, it may be so. She did believe that knowledge of God, of our fellow men, of living nature was more life-giving than knowledge of things. But she did not, as some people imagine, rule science, for example, out of her scheme of education. In fact, she says, "For our generation, science seems to me to be the way of intellectual advance," though, "For the most part science as she is taught leaves us cold. But the fault is not in the science, but in our presentation of it." And again, "Natural Science should be taught through fieldwork or other immediate channel. Huxley told us long ago that Science should be taught in schools as common information."

Physical Exercises and handicrafts she considered most important, but rather as adjuncts to education than as an integral part of education. She calls them "excellent training."

And mathematics and music she put together in a class by themselves, two branches of knowledge each with a speech of its own; a speech, as she put it, "of exquisite clarity."

As to methods of teaching these subjects, Miss Mason did not lay claim to any special knowledge. It is for this reason probably that some persons think they are not included in her ideal education, but when we remember, as she always did, that "knowledge is truth," we know at once that no part of truth can be omitted without wrecking the whole. And in some wonderful way, P.U. SCHOOL children do realise that knowledge is a balanced whole; that scripture, history, geography, botany and all the others are actually different facets of the same thing. Indeed it may be that herein lies the chief characteristic of a P.N.E.U. SCHOOL; for it is merely another way of saying that the children have a wide curriculum and that they get at knowledge for themselves and for its own sake. All this results in a real enjoyment and love of knowledge which is most delightful to witness, and certainly no P.N.E.U. children display boredom or are relieved when school days are over or give up learning or reading when they return home "for good" as we say.

What *is* the secret of this? I do not know. What we cannot do with Miss Mason's ideal is to reduce it to lowest terms, and just in so far as we try to, so far we misrepresent it, and misunderstand it. But some of the secret undoubtedly lies in the Programmes of Work; the longer we work from those wonderful programmes the more we realise how well balanced they are; how satisfying to the hungry mind; how the subjects dovetail; how difficult it is to teach history only in history time, how it will "flow over" into geography, literature, or even into such unexpected channels as arithmetic or botany.

We all know how delicate a matter is balance; such and such a change which seems so clearly sensible will sometimes seriously endanger it. Somehow even slight imperfections seem positively to help to maintain the balance; certainly constant little changes in the programme are necessary because otherwise they would stiffen and become rigid and lifeless. And so the programmes grow and change always; looking back through 20 years, it is amazing how they have developed—the sense of balance perhaps growing even in Miss Mason herself all the while. This may explain why as we read in the April REVIEW, Miss Mason so much disliked organisation, printed forms, stereotyped letters, card indexes and all the paraphernalia of a systematised business. Where the fulcrum is stiff there cannot be balance.

Looking through these old programmes it is most interesting to watch how subjects disappear and re-appear and are again displaced. Architecture for instance; and astronomy; geology and physiography. With a wonderful sense of fitness Miss Mason arranged and rearranged; chose this book, rejected that, tried such a one and removed it, either because it had not sufficient weight or because those unerring children refused to "take to it."

That is, they refused to "narrate" it. Narration is, as we all know, of enormous importance, not however because it is the sum total of Miss Mason's Methods, for very much more is included in her ideal, but because it looms so much larger in P.N.E.U. work than some teachers understand; because too its use is spreading to non-P.N.E.U. schools, where however its real significance as "food for the mind" is not yet fully understood.

Of late years, Miss Mason, in her far-seeing wisdom, laid more and more stress on narration, for she had discovered in it the foundation stone of learning, which provides, when the right books are used, the food without which the mind cannot grow or thrive. But we cannot reduce Miss Mason's method to lowest terms; we cannot say "P.N.E.U. teaching is narration"; for though it is not possible to do Miss Mason's work without it, it is eminently possible to practise narration of a sort and yet be far indeed from her ideal.

Perhaps the root of the matter is that narration includes so much more than mere re-telling of matter read.

We take our children for a Nature Walk. They talk, wonder, discuss, they paint little sketches of their finds, whether fossil, shell, insect or flower. They write notes; they keep lists. Is this narration? Surely. But they have not necessarily read anything, though probably they are now poring over some book to find out the name or habitat of one or other of their finds. But they have got at knowledge direct; no intervening wall of talk is there. Now in a non-P.N.E.U. school, each child, in nine cases out of 10 would be made to copy its notes from the blackboard where teacher had written up what were really her observations, cleverly and quite friendlily imposed on the children. That is one difference.

Take Science. There is a great change coming over the teaching of science. It used to be "If you take so-and-so and do thus-and-thus, such-and-such will happen." But now methods are changing.

In a boys' school not long ago, where there was a jolly Science room, hardly grand enough to be called a "Lab" the boys were learning the habit of things much as our P.U.S. children learn the habits of bird or flower. That is, through patient observation. Books were there to fill out the knowledge so gained and a teacher who knew both his subject and his place, and was inconspicuously giving help and advice as needed. The boys were very busy. Some were trying experiments, other were writing down exactly what they had done and seen, others were making drawings in their note books—"nature notes" if you like. Wasn't that "narration?" Surely it fulfilled Miss Mason's dictum that we must ourselves perform the labour of learning, the act of knowing; that we do not know a thing until we have ourselves and individually "given back." In fact here, where we might least expect it, we find a change which Miss Mason has helped to bring about. She hoped for more literary books on Science; they too seem to be coming.

As time goes on, we shall probably find it increasingly difficult always to remember this "Breadth and Balance" which is the subject of this paper. One might almost sum up Miss Mason's philosophy in those two words "Breadth and Balance"; "a pioneer of *sane* education" the *Times* called her. And just in proportion to the greatness and importance of these two characteristics, is the difficulty of carrying them out.

It is such a temptation to us ordinary folks to emphasise some part at the expense of the rest and so turn a strength into a weakness. There is only one way to avoid this danger. That is constantly to read and re-read Miss Mason's books, constantly to remind ourselves of her first principles—for from now onwards Miss Mason's work is in our hands; we dare not leave un-made any effort to keep the truth.

May I take Narration, the corner stone, as an example? In such a book subject as history, does P.N.E.U. teaching consist merely in reading a set portion once through and then allowing a certain number of children—out of perhaps a class of 50—to narrate as best they can? Is it not possible that such a lesson, repeated *ad infinitum* would result in a rigid system?

What is narration? Miss Mason tells us it is "the answer to a question put by the mind to itself." Then might there not be times when the narration might be a drawing or even a sketch map?

Are we perhaps in danger of systematising the method by insisting that reading and narration are in themselves forever all-sufficient? We know we may never omit that part of the lesson in which the child puts to his mind a question and answers it, in which he himself performs the definite act of knowing, in which his mind is fed. But should we, for example, never also set questions for the older children of a thought provoking type? Let us see what Miss Mason says. In SCHOOL EDUCATION after giving an account of narration she adds:

> But this is only *one* way to use books; others are to enumerate the statements in a given chapter, to analyse a chapter, to divide it into paragraphs under proper headings, to tabulate and classify series, to trace cause to consequence and consequence to cause, to discern character—and perceive how character and circumstance interact ... The teacher's part is, among other things, to set such questions and such tasks as shall give full scope to his pupil's mental activity ... Let the pupil write for himself half a dozen questions which cover the passage studied. These few hints by no means cover the disciplinary uses of a good school book.

So we evidently may require—at least from our older pupils—something more than narration. But, we must never forget that without narration the mind will starve; whatever disciplinary exercises we use, they should be *in addition to* and never *instead of* narration. Physical exercises of the mind are admirable, but will not take the place of food. On the other hand, a well fed mind does need a certain amount of disciplinary exercise at times, and the children lose something when they do not have it.

Miss Mason was an idealist; unperceiving persons might even call her a "mere visionary." All of us who try to follow in her steps are idealists too, and yet on every hand we hear that what the world wants is a sound, practical, useful education; it has "no use" for the idealist. But, looking back through history, it is inspiring and immensely cheering to notice who it is who have most greatly influenced the world. Is it not always the idealist? The man who attempts the impossible? What practical man of affairs or politics or war or commerce can stand alongside Plato, Socrates, Dante?

For Spirit is stronger than matter and we who know even but a little of Miss Mason's teaching, know that it rests on eternal truth.

A TRIBUTE

Mr. H.M. Richards, C.B., H.M.I.,[45] Chief Inspector, Board of Education, in introducing the next speaker, said:—

"We are to hear the distinguished Headmaster of a great Public School read a paper by one who believed in the reverend Study of great thoughts embodied in great language, the very spirit of that Renaissance from which our great Schools got their impulse and inspiration. It may strike us as a curious fact that the Headmaster of Westminster, one of the leaders of a great profession, should become the willing disciple of one who was not a professional teacher at all. The reason is, I think, that Miss Mason from her own powers of head and heart saw some of the obvious truths which we professional people are often so slow to see. The truth she saw was simply this, that all that is great and beautiful in literature, art, music, and nature can make an appeal not only to the well-to-do, but to the very poorest of our people. It seems so extremely easy to say this, but it required great courage and faith to do it, and I would like on behalf of the Board of Education to make this public acknowledgment of the debt we all owe to Miss Mason, who by her courage and

---

[45] Her Majesty's Inspector.

faith brought into the poorest schools of the country and to the most neglected children the opportunity of seeing and feeling and believing in beauty and in truth. There are very few people, who, like Miss Mason, can leave behind them such a work and such a message. To those people death has no sting and the grave is only a doorway to continued achievement."

EDUCATION IS A LIFE*
by C. M. Mason

We all know the P.N.E.U. motto, "Education is an atmosphere, a discipline, a life," especially well in the neat diagrammatic form in which it appears on the covers of our Library books. I am told that we, as a society, are destined to live by our motto. A notable educationalist writes to me, in connection with public education, "there is more need than ever for such a view of education as that embodied in the memorable words which are the motto of the PARENTS' REVIEW." An inspiring motto must always be a power, but to live *upon* the good repute of our motto, and to live *up* to it and *in* it are two different things, and I am afraid the PARENTS' UNION has much and continual thinking and strenuous living to face, if it proposes to stand before the world as interpreting and illustrating these "memorable words." But we are not a faint-hearted body, we *mean* and mean intensely; and to those who purpose the best, and endeavour after the best, the best arrives.

Meantime, we sometimes err, I think, in taking a part for the whole, and a part of a part for the whole of that part. Of the three lines of our definition, that which declares that "education is an atmosphere" pleases us most, perhaps, because it is the most inviting to the *laissez-aller*[46] principle of human nature. By the way, we lose something by substituting "environment" (that blessed word, Mesopotamia!) for atmosphere. The latter word is symbolic, it is true, but a symbol means more to us all than the name of the thing signified. We think of fresh air, pure, bracing, tonic,—of the

---

* Read by the Rev. H. Costley-White (Headmaster of Westminster and Chairman of the P.N.E.U. Executive Committee).
[46] Letting go.

definite act of breathing which must be fully accomplished, and we are incited to do more and mean more in the matter of our children's surroundings if we think of the whole as an atmosphere, than if we accept the more literal "environment."

But, supposing that "education is an atmosphere" brings a fresh and vigorous thought to our minds, suppose that it means to us, for our children, sunshine and green fields, pleasant rooms and good pictures, schools where learning is taken in by the gentle act of inspiration, followed by the expiration of all that which is not wanted, where charming teachers compose the children by a half mesmeric effluence which inclines them to do as others do, be as others are,— suppose that all this is included in our notion of "education is an atmosphere," may we not sit at our ease and believe that all is well, and that the whole of education has been accomplished? No; because though we cannot live *without* air, neither can we live *upon* air, and children brought up upon "environment" soon begin to show signs of inanition; they have little or no healthy curiosity, power of attention, or of effort; what is worse, they lose spontaneity and initiative; they expect life to drop into them like water into a rain-tub, without effort or intention on their part.

This notion, that education is included in environment, or, at the best, in atmosphere, has held the ground for a generation or two, and it seems to me that it has left its mark upon our public and our private lives. We are more ready to be done unto than to do; we do not care for the labour of ordering our own lives in this direction or in that; they must be conducted for us; a press of engagements must compel us into what next, and what next after. We crave for spectacular entertainment, whether in the way of pageants in the streets, or spectacles on the boards. Even Shakespeare has come to be so much the occasion for gorgeous spectacles that what the poet says is of little moment compared with the show a play affords. There is nothing intentionally vicious in all this; it is simply our effort to escape from the *ennui*[47] that results from a one-sided view of education, that education is an atmosphere only.

A still more consuming *ennui* set in at the end of the 18th century, and that also was the result of a partial view of

---

[47] Boredom.

education. "Education is a life" was the (unconscious) formula then; and a feverish chase after ideas was the outcome. It is pathetic to read how Madame de Stael and her coterie, or that "blue-stocking" coterie which met at the Hotel Rambouillet, for example, went little to bed, because they could not sleep; and spent long nights in making character sketches of each other, enigmas, anagrams, and other futilities of the intellect, and met again (some of them) at early breakfast to compose and sing little airs upon little themes. We may be as much inclined to yawn in each other's faces as they were, but, anyway, if we sin as they did by excess in one direction, there is less wear and tear in a succession of shows than in their restless pursuit of inviting notions. Still, the beginning of the 19th century has its lessons for the beginning of the 20th. They erred, as we do, because they did not understand the science of the proportion of things. We are inclined to say, "education is environment"; they would say, "education is ideas"; the truth includes both of these, and a third definition introducing another side, a third aspect of education.

The third conceivable view, "education is a discipline," has always had its votaries and has them still. That the discipline of the habits of the good life, both intellectual and moral, forms a good third of education, we all believe. The excess occurs when we imagine that certain qualities of character and conduct run out a prepared product, like carded wool, from this or that educational machine, mathematics or classics, science or athletics; that is, when the notion of the development of the so-called faculties takes the place of the more physiologically true notion of the formation of intellectual habits. The difference does not seem to be great; but two streams that rise within a foot of one another may water different countries and fall into different seas, and a broad divergence in practice often arises from what appears to be a small difference in conception in matters educational. The father of Plutarch had him learn his Homer that he might get heroic ideas of life. Had the boy been put through his Homer as a classical grind, as a machine for the development of faculty, a pedant would have come out, and not a man of the world in touch with life at many points, capable of bringing men and affairs to the touchstone of a sane and generous mind. It seems to me that this notion of the discipline which should develop "faculty" has tended to produce rather one-sided men with the limitations which belong to abnormal development. An artist told me once that the condition of successful art is absorption in art, that the painter must think pictures, paint pictures, nothing but pictures. But when art was great, men were not mere artists. Quentin Matsys wrought in iron and painted pictures and did many things besides. Michael Angelo wrote sonnets, designed buildings, painted pictures; marble was by no means his only vehicle of expression. Leonardo wrote treatises, planned canals, played instruments of music, did a hundred things and all exquisitely. But then, the idea of the development of faculty, and the consequent discipline, had not occurred to these great men or their guardians.

Having safe-guarded ourselves from the notion that education has only one face, we may go on to consider how "education is a life," without the risk of thinking that we are viewing more than one side of the subject.

It has been said that "man doth not live by bread alone, but by every word that proceedeth out of the mouth of God," and the augustness of the occasion on which the words were spoken, has caused us to confine their meaning to what we call the life of the soul; when, indeed, they include a great educational principle which was better understood by the medieval church than by ourselves. May I be allowed once again to describe a painting in which the creed of the HOUSE OF EDUCATION, and, I hope, that of the PARENTS' UNION, is visibly expressed. Many of us are familiar with the frescoes on the walls of the so-called Spanish Chapel of the church of S. Maria Novella. The philosophy of the Middle Ages dealt, as we know, with theology as its subject matter; and, while there is much ecclesiastical polity with which we have little sympathy pictured on the remaining walls, on one compartment of wall and roof we have a singularly satisfying scheme of educational thought. At the highest point of the picture we see the Holy Ghost descending in the likeness of a dove; immediately below, in the upper chamber are the disciples who first received his inspiration; below, again, is the promiscuous crowd of all nationalities who are brought indirectly under the influence of the first outpouring, and in the foreground are two or three dogs, shewing that the dumb creation was not excluded from benefiting by the new grace. In the lower compartment of the great design are angelic figures of the cardinal virtues, which we all trace more or less to divine inspiration, floating above the seated figures of apostles and prophets, of whom we know that they "spake as they were moved by the Holy Ghost." So far, this medieval scheme of philosophy reveals no new thought to persons instructed in the elements of Christian truth. But, below the prophets and apostles, are a series of pictured niches, those to the right being occupied by the captain figures, the ideal representations of the seven Liberal Arts, figures of singular grace and beauty representing such familiar matters as grammar, rhetoric, logic, music, astronomy, geometry and arithmetic, all of them under the outpouring of the Spirit of God. Still more liberal is the philosophy which places at the foot of each of these figures him who seemed to be, to the artist, the leader and representative of each several science,— Priscian, Cicero, Aristotle, Tubal Cain, Zoroaster, Euclid, Pythagoras; men whom a narrower and later theology would have placed beyond the pale of the Christian religion, and therefore of the teaching of the Spirit of God. But here all are represented as under the same divine outpouring which illuminated the disciples in the upper chamber.

Our nature craves after unity. The travail of thought, which is going on today and has gone as long as we have any record of men's thoughts, has been with a view to establishing some principle for the unification of life. Here we have the scheme of a magnificent unity. We are apt to think that piety is one thing, that our intellectual and artistic output are quite another matter, and that our moral virtues are pretty much matters of inheritance and environment, and have not much to do with our conscious religion. Hence, there come discords into our lives, discords especially trying to young and ardent souls who want to be good and religious, but who cannot escape from the overpowering drawings of art and intellect and mere physical enjoyment; they have been taught to consider that these things are, for the most part, alien to the religious life, and that they must choose one or the other; they do choose, and the choice does not always fall upon these things which, in our unscriptural and unphilosophical narrowness, we call the things of God. Let us bless Taddeo Gaddi and Simone Memmi for placing before our eyes a creed (copies* of which we might all hang upon our walls), which shows that our piety, our virtue, our intellectual activities, and, let us add, our physical perfections, are all fed from the same source, God Himself; are all inspired by the same Spirit, the Spirit of God. The ages which held this creed were ages of mighty production in every kind; the princely commerce of Venice was dignified and sobered by this thought of the divine inspiration of ideas,— ideas of trade, ideas of justice and fair balance and of utility; Columbus went out to discover a new world, informed by the divine idea, as our own philosopher, Coleridge, points out, adding that "great inventions and Ideas of Nature, presented to chosen minds by a higher power than nature herself, suddenly unfold as it were in prophetic succession systematic views destined to produce the most important revolutions in the state of man." When Columbus came back, his new world discovered, people and princes took it as from God and sang *Te Deum*.[48]

Michael Angelo writes to his friend Vittoria Colonna, that "good Christians always make good and beautiful figures. In order to represent the adored image of our Lord, it is not enough that a master should be great and able. I maintain that he must also be a man of good morals and conduct, if possible a saint, in order that the Holy Ghost may give him inspiration." In truth, a nation or a man becomes great upon one diet only, the diet of great ideas communicated to those already prepared to receive them by a higher Power than nature herself.

We are a small society, little talked about and little known, but I think we hold amongst us the little leaven which is able to leaven the whole lump. Let us set ourselves to labour with purpose and passion to restore to the world, enriched by the addition of later knowledge, that great work in the past. Nor need we fear that in endeavouring after some such doctrine of ideas as may help us in the work of education, that we are running counter to science. Many of

---

* La Discessa dello Spirito Santo & Ailegoria filosofica delta Religione Cattolica, to be had from Mansell, 405, Oxford Street, Nos. 4077 & 4093.
[48]An ancient Christian hymn, the Latin title translated means "God, we praise You."

us feel, and, I think, rightly, that the teaching of science is *the* new teaching which is being vouchsafed to mankind in our age. Some of us are triumphant and believe that the elements of moral and religious struggle are about to be eliminated from life, which shall run henceforth, whether happy or disastrous, on the easy plane of the inevitable; others are bewildered and look in vain for a middle way, a place of reconciliation for science and religion; while others of us again take refuge in repudiating "evolution" and all its works and nailing our colours to religion, interpreted on our own narrow lines. Whichever of these lines we take, we probably err through want of faith.

Let us first of all settle it with ourselves that science and religion cannot, to the believer in God, by any possibility be antagonistic. Having assured ourselves of this, we shall probably go on to perceive that the evolution of science is in fact a process of revelation, being brought about in every case, so far as I am aware, by the process which Coleridge has so justly described, that is, "that the *Ideas* of nature, presented to chosen minds by a higher power than nature herself, suddenly unfold as it were in prophetic succession systematic views destined to produce the most important revolutions in the state of man." Huxley defines the utility of Biology "as helping to give right ideas in this world which is, after all," he goes on to say, "absolutely governed by ideas, and very often by the wildest and most hypothetical ideas." Again, he writes, "those who refuse to go beyond the fact rarely get as far as the fact; and anyone who has studied the history of science knows that almost every great step therein has been made by the 'anticipation of nature,' that is by the invention of hypotheses." One cannot help thinking that scientific men would find the unifying principle they are in search of in the fine saying of Coleridge's which I have twice quoted; so would they stand revealed to themselves as the mouthpieces, not merely of *the truth*, for which they are so ready to combat and suffer, but also as the chosen and prepared servants of Him who is the Truth.

Few of us can forget Carlyle's incomparable picture of the *Tiers Etat*[49] waiting for organisation,—"Wise as serpents; harmless as doves: what a spectacle for France! Six hundred

---

[49] Third Estate.

inorganic individuals, essential for its regeneration and salvation, sit there, on their elliptic benches, longing passionately towards life." Less picturesque, but otherwise very much on a par with this, is Coleridge's description of Botany, as that science existed in his own day, waiting for the unifying idea which should give it organisation,—"What," he says, "is Botany at this present hour? Little more than an enormous nomenclature; a huge catalogue, *bien arrangé*,[50] yearly and monthly augmented, in various editions, each with its own scheme of technical memory and its own convenience of reference! The innocent amusement, the healthful occupation, the ornamental accomplishment of amateurs; it is yet to expect the devotion and energies of the philosopher." The keyword for the interpretation of life, both animal and vegetable, has been presented to our generation and we cannot make too much of it. We cannot overrate the enormous repose and satisfaction to the human mind contained in the idea of evolution. But it is well to remember that for three thousand years thinkers have been occupied with attempts to explain the world by means of a single principle, which should also furnish an explanation of reason and the human soul. Herakleitos and his age thought they had laid hold of the informing idea in the phrase, "the true Being is an eternal Becoming:" the "universal flux of things" explained all. Demokritos and his age cried—Eureka! solved the riddle of the universe, with the saying that "nothing exists except atoms moving in vacancy." Many times since, with each epoch-making discovery, has science cried— Eureka! over the one principle which should explain all things and eliminate Personality.

But some little knowledge of history and philosophy will give us pause. We shall see that each great discovery, each luminous idea of nature that the world has received hitherto, is like a bend in a tortuous lake which appears final until your boat approaches it, and then—behold an opening into further and still further reaches beyond! The knowledge of God will give us something more than the wider outlook of which comes a knowledge of history—the knowledge that there *is*, what Wordsworth calls, the "stream of tendency," a stream of immeasurable force in shaping character and

---

[50] Well arranged.

events: but there is also Personality, a power able to turn the "stream of tendency" to its uses, if also liable to be carried away in its current.

Forgive me if I appear to dwell on a subject which at first sight appears to have little to do with the bringing up of children; but I think that his attitude towards the great idea, great lesson, set for his age to grasp, is a vital part of a parent's preparation. If parents take no heed of the great thoughts which move their age, they cannot expect to retain influence over the minds of their children. If they fear and distrust the revelations of science, they introduce an element of distrust and discord into their children's lives. If, with the mere neophyte of science, they rush to the conclusion that the last revelation is final, accounts for all that is in man, and, to say the least, makes God unnecessary and unknowable, or negligible, they may lower the level of their children's living to that struggle for existence—without aspiration, consecration and sacrifice—of which we hear so much. If, lastly, parents recognise every great idea of nature as a new page in the progressive revelation made by God to men already prepared to receive such idea; if they realise that the new idea, however comprehensive, is not final nor all-inclusive, nor to be set in opposition with that personal knowledge of God which is the greatest knowledge, why then their children will grow up in the attitude of reverence for science, reverence for God, and openness of mind, which befits us for whom life is a probation and a continual education. So much for the nutriment of ideas laid on the table of the world during this particular course of its history.

Next, we may have poetry, or art, or philosophy; we cannot tell; but two things are incumbent upon us,— to keep ourselves and our children in touch with the great thoughts by which the world has been educated in the past, and to keep ourselves and them in the right attitude towards the great ideas of the present. It is our temptation to make too personal a matter of education, to lose sight of the fact that education is a world business, that the lessons of the ages have been duly set, and that each age is concerned, not only with its own particular page, but with every preceding page. For who feels that he has mastered a book with the last page of which only he is familiar? This brings me to a point I am anxious to lay before you. We do not sufficiently realise the need for unity of principle in education. We have no Captain Idea which shall marshal for us the fighting host of educational ideas which throng the air; so, in default of a guiding principle, a leading idea, we feel ourselves at liberty to pick and choose. This man thinks he is free to make science the sum of his son's education, the other chooses the classics, a third prefers a mechanical, a fourth, a commercial programme, a fifth makes bodily health his cult, and chooses a school which makes the care of health a special feature of its programme (not that we must allow health to be neglected, but that, given good general conditions, the less obvious attention their health receives the better for the boys and girls): and everyone feels himself at liberty to do that which is right in his own eyes with regard to the education of his children.

A negative purpose of our society is to discourage in every way we can the educational faddist, that is, the person who accepts a one-sided notion in place of a universal idea as his educational guide. Our positive purpose is to present, in season and out of season, one such universal idea, that is, that education is the science of relations.

A child should be brought up to have relations of force with earth and water, should run and ride, swim and skate, lift and carry; should know texture, and work in material; should know by name, and where, and how they live at any rate, the things of the earth about him, its birds and beasts and creeping things, its herbs and trees; should be in touch with the literature, art and thought of the past. I do not mean that he should *know* all these things; but he should feel, when he reads of it in the newspapers, the thrill which stirred the Cretan peasants when the frescoes in the palace of King Minos were disclosed to the labour of their spades. He should feel the thrill, not from mere contiguity, but because he has with the past the relationship of living pulsing thought; and, if blood be thicker than water, thought is more quickening than blood. He must have a living relationship with the present, its historic movement, its science, literature, art, social needs and aspirations. In fact, he must have a wide outlook, intimate relations all round; and force, virtue, must pass out of him, whether of hand, will, or sympathy, wherever he touches. This is no impossible programme. Indeed it can be pretty well filled in by the time an intelligent boy or girl has reached the age of thirteen or fourteen, for it depends, not upon *how much* is learned, but upon *how* things are learned.

Give children a wide range of subjects with the end in view of establishing in each case some one or more of the relations I have indicated. Let them learn from first hand sources of information—really good books, the best going, on the subject in hand. Let them get at the books themselves, and do not let them be flooded with a warm diluent at the lips of their teacher. The teacher's business is to indicate, stimulate, direct and constrain to the acquirement of knowledge, but by no means to be the fountain-head and source of all knowledge in his or her own person. The less parents and teachers talk-in and expound their rations of knowledge and thought to the children they are educating the better for the children. Peptonised food for a healthy stomach does not tend to a vigorous digestion. Children must be allowed to ruminate, must be left alone with their own thoughts. They will ask for help if they want it.

You will see at a glance, with this Captain Idea of establishing relationships as a guide, the unwisdom of choosing or rejecting this or that subject, as being more or less useful or necessary in view of a child's future. We decide, for example, that Tommy, who is 8, need not waste his time over the Latin Grammar. We intend him for commercial or scientific pursuits,—what good will it be to him? But we do not know how much we are shutting out from Tommy's range of thought besides the Latin Grammar. He has to translate, for example,—"*Pueri formosos equos vident.*"[51] He is a ruminant animal, and has been told something about that strong Roman people whose speech is now brought before him. How their boys catch hold of him! How he gloats over their horses! The Latin Grammar is not mere words to Tommy, or rather Tommy knows, as we have forgotten, that the epithet "mere" is the very last to apply to words. Of course it is only now and then that a notion catches the small boy, but when it does catch, it works wonders, and does more for his education than years of grind.

---

[51] The boys see the beautiful horses.

I would only add one word. Our own living function, our power as a society, and with our power, our endurance, will depend upon how far we lay hold of and carry out the living thought which our UNION is intended to embody and express. I venture to think that one proof that we are in this sense a living society, is the happy immunity of the P.N.E.U. from educational fads.

MISS MASON'S IDEAL IN SCHOOL LIFE
by Laura C. Faunce[*]

That "Education is the Science of Relations" is a phrase familiar to all those who have studied the works and principles of our Founder, Charlotte M. Mason, and it has a peculiar significance and vitalising force, as presented by her, which inspires the teacher and lifts the work to that high plane where truly it belongs. This great unifying principle, that Education is the Science of Relations, should be firmly held and acted upon as the only way to the attainment of that "true knowledge whereby a child may be put into touch with the great thoughts of the past, and be kept in a right attitude to the thoughts of the present, so that he may be prepared to meet new ideas" and come upon fresh avenues of thought in the future with an open mind, and be able to form his own opinions which will be the outcome of all the wide knowledge he has collected.

Among those liberties which we in this UNION claim for the child, due to him as a person, is freedom of thought, the function of right thinking,—the importance of which cannot be exaggerated. This is an article in his Bill of Rights which we should be most careful to safeguard and to establish for the child. All those who teach know how difficult it is not to violate this right. It is so easy to impose opinion, and so to create prejudice unless a careful watch be kept. All unawares we trespass on this right, and it is in this way that the world becomes filled with men and women whose minds run in grooves and work on conventional lines,—the stereotyped as opposed to the individual. Thought is, I suppose all will allow, the greatest force in the world, and of each world citizen is

---

[*] Principal, P.U.S. School, Queen's Gardens, W.2.

required this duty:—to contribute to the thought of the world, if not in actual original ideas, at least in the power of original thinking, for on thought all action depends and all achievements are based. It is by the friction of mind with mind that thought is produced. The illuminating idea, the vivid suggestion, quicken our minds and awaken our latent powers of thinking. We consider that this liberty of thought is best secured for the child by supplying to him all that is good and most helpful in the way of mental foodstuffs; that is through the use of books,—and those the best books,—as well as through things; that he should know great men through the books and works of art which they have given to the world. By this means the child is able to form opinions for himself, the outcome of his thoughts and knowledge: a knowledge gained by himself in his reading, a knowledge gained for *itself* and not for any ulterior motives. His mind, thus fed, grows: the power of vision increases, and ardent and close communion exists between himself and the spiritual forces that govern the world. Such growth, mental, moral and spiritual is, we all grant, the sole end of education. We in whose hands rests so high a life-service must see to it that we aid the children in the formation of those principles of conduct which shall guide the intellect, control the will and so govern action.

It is through the stages of this mysterious unfolding of the child that I want to take you, showing how from the age of 5, when he is a person incapable of expressing himself, after acquiring words he begins gradually to communicate with us, letting us into his thoughts, his ideas and his desires, and how eventually he attains to a whole world of knowledge, and all this in an amazingly short time.

We, who teach in schools, are indeed privileged in having so many and so varied characters and temperaments to study, and it is because I have had a school working on Miss Mason's methods for 17 years and have had some hundreds of children passing through my hands during that time that I venture to speak to you this afternoon.

We of the P.N.E.U. hold, and experience has proved to me over and over again, that all children are receptive of the right kind of knowledge rightly introduced, and no matter how despairing one may be of a child, one has always the joy of the sudden revelation, when the vital spark has been struck. No one knows so well as a teacher what a delight it is to see how the awakened mind, set aglow by the reception of a living idea, lights up the face, the quick recognition, the eager response; together the teacher and taught are sharing the same thrill of enthusiasm and enjoyment. I wish I could tell you of the countless moments of such pleasure that I have had and the bond of sympathy which this creates. Of course in order to arouse this eager receptivity there must be the love of knowledge and enthusiasm towards the acquiring of it for himself on the part of the teacher, for love is contagious and children do as we do. Not only is this love communicated by the teacher but in class-teaching by one member to another. An illustration of this point occurs to me which may interest you.

In a class in my school a child was anxious to keep a Nature Note Book and to have many beautiful paintings in it, but in London, as many of you will know, it is very difficult to get wild flowers to paint. As this child was a great lover of Nature and of flowers, she solved the problem for herself in the following way. She decided to paint garden flowers and to trace, where possible, the development from the wild flower. This inspired the class and we now have some quite delightful books. All unconsciously to themselves this atmosphere of delight in knowledge prevails amongst the children in the different classes, and this note is not confined to one class in itself, but communicates itself from one class to the other, the work being linked together and graded in the varying degrees of difficulty according to the age and requirements of the pupils. For example, we establish the relation with the glowing glories of Greece and Rome and all the inspiration of their Art, Legend, Literature and History in the excellent choice of books set on the programmes, from Andrew Lang's inimitable *Tales of Troy and Greece* (a true source of joy to the young children in Form I) on to Mrs. Beesley's *History of Rome* (as keen a delight to Form II) then to *Plutarch's Lives* in Classes III and IV, culminating in Classes V and VI with the reading of Professor de Burgh's[52] *Legacy of Greece and Rome* where again and again recognition and remembrance are due to the work done when

---

[52] See page 103.

in the lower forms. How living are the books is shown in the following instances:

The other day I heard of a little girl whose feelings were deeply aroused and whose opinion could not be altered by the comparison of present day standards with those pertaining to the time, by the incident of Ulysses' chastisement of Thersites (we are reading the story of Ulysses this term) in Form I. Again the story of Thomas a Becket, as told in *Our Island Story*, has appealed most deeply to the children. In *Plutarch's Lives* I often have spontaneous expressions of opinion or emotion. On one occasion a child whose sense of justice had been sharply wounded exclaimed aloud with head thrown back and with flashing eyes, "Oh, but Miss Faunce, how unfair!"

Again the following poem shows how sympathies had been touched and imagination fired:—

The form I think is interesting because it is significant of the impression which the child wished to convey which may have been that of a distant age, or we may suppose it to represent a free translation from the Persian; indeed we might almost call it "vers libres!"[53] I asked the children to write for me either in prose or verse on anything that had caught their fancy in the morning's lesson. This particular child, aged 13, wrote for me a poem expressing grief either of King Darius or his Court on hearing the news of the death of his Queen while in captivity under Alexander. It is entitled:—

MOURNING FOR THE DEATH OF THE PERSIAN QUEEN
    Let the light of the sun be hid;
    Let him shine no more.
    Do the little brooks laugh?
    Oh, let them be silent and still.
    Let the long grasses sigh
    When the wandering wind
    Stretches his hand to bow them;
    For he is the Master-Musician
    Let him join in the mourning-song,
    The song of the grief of man;
    Everlasting as he is the song,

---

[53] Hurling verse.

Everlasting the grief and the song.

Surely this is proof, if proof were needed, that the great book and the classic are a continual joy and a constant supply of mental food; that the teacher, even though she may have read the book again and again, always finds her enthusiasm rekindled, her inspiration refreshed in the appreciation of the children to whom the work comes in all its freshness and vigour.

How living this world of knowledge is to the children and how it becomes a very part of their life comes home to us in many pleasant byways. The children to whom the Book of Centuries means so much will often collect pictures to share with their classmates; others, perhaps, awakened by the studies at school become aware that certain possessions in the home, before meaningless to them, are now vested with a living interest. I know of children who have arranged Century Book teas, exchanging visits to each other's homes in order to enjoy the community of interest provided by the books. This year I have had an illustration which seems to affirm that indeed "dead bones can live," I have been teaching quite young children in Form II about the Stone Age, a very different study from any that they have done before, so dim and distant with the fascination of a word new to them, "Prehistoric"; but what an appeal it has made to them and how keen the response! One instance may suffice:—

After reading about the Stone Age from the book *The British Museum for Children*, I suggested (not as a set task but something to be done if they liked, and if they had the time) that they should write for me a story report on what they imagined would be the life of a family living in those distant ages of "stone weapons" and "cave dwellers." The results were delightful, and to shew how vividly their imaginations had been fired, I will read to you one of the stories which were given in to me.

A STORY OF THE STONE AGE

"No, sir, no, indeed—it is not a lie, sir, I swear it is not." "Really, Marcus, do you expect me to believe such fairy stories? You have been dreaming—or more likely drinking—besides, this isle is uninhabited." The Roman

Prætor surveyed the excited young soldier with contempt.
"But, sir, he struck me—a little dark pigmy—he appeared
out of the mountain side—and vanished again as quickly
as he came." "Struck you, you say? And where is the
mark, what did he strike with?" "A sort of stone hammer,
I think," said the young man, drawing aside his cloak as
he spake, "It hurt enough anyhow" and, sure enough he
revealed, on his arm, an ugly wound, bleeding freely. "My
dear man, why did you not show me this before? You
must have it seen to at once—Claudius, take him to the
doctor's tent, this moment."

When the soldier had been taken from the tent, the
Prætor turned to one of the consuls "What is your opinion
of this affair, sir," he asked—"It looks very much as if the
boy spake the truth, judging by the blow he has received,"
replied the consul—"Then you, Linus, and you, Sextus,
take half a dozen men, arm yourselves, and go and
explore the hillside—bring me word at once if you see any
more of these 'little dark pigmies.'" The two men saluted
and went off in high spirits to collect their little band. A
few moments later a small party of eight men stole up the
hillside, spear in hand. Suddenly a rustling was heard in
the grass—the soldiers swung round—it was only a wolf
darting over the hill. After about a quarter of an hour of
wandering—a man touched Linus on the arm—"See,
yonder," he whispered—A figure darted out of the
undergrowth, and, seeing the soldiers, vanished into the
hillside. The men stared at each other in silence... At last
Linus pulled himself together—"Run, Claudius, and tell
the Prætor, quick." Claudius vanished into the darkness.
When he had disappeared Linus gave a sharp order, and
the soldiers hastened towards the spot where the figure
had been seen to vanish—Sextus pushed and bent the
shrubs and creepers—and, with an exclamation of
astonishment revealed a small opening in the hillside. By
crouching to a crawling position the men were able to
creep—one by one—into the cave, for a cave it was.

Often in the 10 minutes playtime in the middle of the
morning, a class will arrange a tableau representing some
dramatic moment which has caught their fancy either from

History or Literature, or from some poem, and the excellent grouping, the gesture, play of expression shew how real a picture has been created in their minds. Out of many which ome back to my memory is the illustration (they gave) of the Crusaders falling on their knees when first viewing Jerusalem; of the death of James IV (that was really very effectively grouped); of Alexander receiving the cup of medicine from the hand of Philip the Arcarnanian while handing to him the letter of warning which Parmenio had sent to the King; of Perseus in the Garden of the Hesperides when the maidens playing with his shield revealed to him how he might slay the Gorgon without looking on her face (this last tableau given by quite young children in Form I). In these dramatic moments, as we call them, the children choose the incident and plan the grouping entirely by themselves, the teacher's part being to guess what the picture represents when she is *allowed* to come and look! With older girls this living interest takes the form of discussion and free interchange of thought and opinion, and often one finds that the point which has fired their imagination in the lesson has been discussed at home, or with friends, thus marking that it has become part of their mental life. Only the other day, on going through the English Matriculation Paper for September 1919, I read aloud the following question, "Write a letter to a friend in answer to his or her remark, 'Why should I read Shakespeare? I do not like him and he has done me no good.'" The indignation was great and deep, and an eager combative spirit was displayed.

The ideals inculcated by Miss Mason make for a school life of as free a nature as is compatible with common sense. Rules are minimised, marks are eliminated, the children's interest and busyness of mind make for natural order and obedience; and a spirit of comradeship and cooperation exists between teachers and pupils so that more or less self-government prevails. A class *can be*, and is, left to read by itself from the age of 12 years of age and up and the result is often shown by a test paper on the portion read. As an example of the result of such work I will read a Report of a girl of 15.

The Class read Ruskin's *Modern Painters* for 20 minutes, and wrote for the remaining 20 minutes of the lesson.

THE OPEN SKY

Who can describe the sky? Those changing moods that
vary from glaring noon-day heat to the soft grey dusk of
evening. Never the same for two minutes together, but
always changing—changing—changing. But it is not
always so restless. There may be days when the torn
shreds of clouds race forward before the wind, but then
there comes an evening when quiet peace reigns. The sun
sinks, leaving the west in a blaze of rosy colour which
gradually dies away to soft drowsy blue and grey. The
stars come out one by one, as though afraid to spoil that
glorious peaceful blue with their insistent twinkle, and the
soft dew falls to cover the sleeping earth.

And yet, all this beauty leaves many people unmoved.
They know the sky chiefly from pictures. If you asked
them to describe it, some scrap of blue, framed with gold
and hanging in some dusty corner, springs to their mind.
They do not think of looking upwards into the vastness
over their heads; for they do not see it in pictures. Few
artists can portray the feeling of never ending eternity
that the sky has. They paint a hard beautiful blue with
solid bunchy clouds. You look at it, and, instead of sailing
ever on and upwards, your gaze is brought up with a jerk
against a blue board.

Here we see the impression made on a sensitive young
mind by the reading of a beautiful passage: such store
should be within the reach of all; ours is it to see that it be
so,—the golden heritage due to those who seek.

What, know ye not two hungers be in man;
Hunger for bread allayed, then clamours mind
For knowledge, which is life.

May I close with Miss Mason's own words, which seem to
set forth the creed of all her teaching:—
THE SAVIOUR OF THE WORLD (Vol. VI, page 107)

THE KEYS OF KNOWLEDGE
(The Disciple)
Are now, no dried up wells hermetic seal'd,

As held they water of life? Go we with Keys,—
Official proclamation that with these
We could the court where knowledge is revealed

Ope to the thirsty scholar? Our own ease
Take we the while fair knowledge lies concealed
'Neath dust of verbiage, nor the fit key yield
To willing learner whom 'tis ours to please?

Believe we then that knowledge is our own
To give or to refuse, hold or impart,
Or, miser's store, nor use nor give away?

Lord make us understand terms of that loan
Of gracious knowledge, of delightsome Art,
For all men's use, Thou lodg'st with us today!

AN APPRECIATION FROM
A P.N.E.U. ELEMENTARY SCHOOL
by D. S. Golding[54][*]

A late lark twitters from the quiet skies;
And from the west,
Where the sun, his day's work ended,
Lingers as in content,
There falls on the old grey city
An influence luminous and serene,
A shining peace.

The smoke ascends
In a rosy and golden haze. The spires
Shine and are changed. In the valley
Shadows rise. The lark sings on. The sun,
Closing his benediction
Sinks—and the darkening air
Thrills with a sense of the triumphing night
Night, with her train of stars,
And her great gift of sleep.

---

[54] See also page 226.
[*] Headmistress of the Hanharn Road Girls' Elementary School, Kingswood, Bristol.

So be my passing!
My task accomplished and the long day done,
My wages taken, and in my heart
Some late lark singing,
Let me be gathered to the quiet west,
The sundown splendid and serene,
Death.

On the day that we received the news of Miss Mason's passing, one of our classes was learning that poem, and the children remarked how fitting were the words to the occasion, "splendid and serene." When one has read, as I have done, every word in the Memorial number of our magazine, the March PARENTS' REVIEW, there remains no doubt that the same great tribute, "splendid and serene," can be applied to the life of our Founder as well as to her passing.

Our children have never seen her, yet they look on her as Friend. There seems to be a personal relationship between them and her. I can understand it. It is, I think, their expression of the fact that was borne in on me during the Children's Gathering of 1920. Never shall I forget the feeling of fellowship experienced at the Service held on the Tuesday morning of that week in the old parish church at Whitby. There were children from various, and in some cases, remote parts of the country, grownup children like ourselves; children from Home Schoolrooms; children from P.U. SCHOOLS; five children from an Elementary School in County Durham; and in spirit *all* who longed to come and were not able. Under such categories some, perhaps, would have classified us. But the difference in our conditions and our circumstances was not the outstanding feature about us all. The wonderful thing *was* that we were all children of one school, and that school one large family with Miss Mason as its head.

The P.N.E.U. scheme has been of great service to me in my endeavour to create an atmosphere with which, I strongly feel, every efficient school should be surrounded;—an atmosphere of home, of a large family working in unity and co-operation for the greatest good of all its members. Month by month we are reminded that Education is an atmosphere as well as a discipline and a life. Our Founder never thought, as some think and do not hesitate to say, that "spirit" matters not. One of our aims must be to get the children to work because they love to work; to do right, not because of any reward or punishment which may follow the doing or not doing, but because they *want* to do the right thing; and the principles which underlie the P.N.E.U. methods help us to attain this goal.

Education is also a discipline; but upon what authority does true discipline depend? Not upon the might of external force, but rather upon that inward authority which can dispense with rule from outside. The P.N.E.U. motto does not contain the forced, "I *must*, because someone outside myself compels me." It is, I AM, I CAN, I OUGHT, I WILL. It is Miss Mason who has taught us not to belittle the powers of a child. Children so often can do what we could not do, because we have not in the process of building set up the pillar of careful attention. There is the foundation of the habit of self-discipline in the great concentration which the children are called upon to exercise. Not only do they narrate after a single reading; but what perhaps to those who have not ventured seems still more impossible, they *must* and *can*, without any revision, reproduce at an examination the knowledge which once and forever they have made their own.

It was the wideness of the P.N.E.U. scheme which at the beginning (our P.N.E.U. career started in 1918), gave me such satisfaction. I had always talked to my girls on all manner of subjects apart from the lessons of any set syllabus. Our school is situated in an urban industrial district: a large majority of the children are from homes where the father and the mother, too, work in a boot factory when employment can be obtained at all. With one or two rare exceptions, our girls do not belong to the company of favoured children whose parents are able to take an intelligent interest in them. English, as it should be spoken, does not exist for them in their home life, and their vocabulary is sadly limited. Knowing that their outlook on life was extremely narrow, I tried to make them realise that life held many interests of which they had never even dreamed; and that the more they could get into touch with things beyond their own horizon, the more enjoyable and purposeful their lives would become. Fulness of life makes for happiness, and it is part of my own credo that if we crowd into life as much of the beautiful as we can, there will be no room for things unworthy. But before the P.N.E.U. scheme was brought into our school—and I would like in passing to express gratitude to Mr. Household,[55] through whose enthusiasm and championship of the cause so many schools in Gloucestershire are able to share the privileges of Miss Mason's teaching—before the P.N.E.U. scheme was known to us, the personal opinions of the teacher were unavoidably very much in the foreground. The best of us can never hope to have given original thought to every subject of a school curriculum. This scheme offers the product of the original minds of noble thinkers. It gives children inspiring ideas which promote thought and enquiry; and the more a child thinks, the more he lives:—and this is the child's right. They study a period of English History, they read the contemporary French History, and the older girls take the History of the Literature and sometimes of the Architecture of the same period. The Literary reader and Shakespeare Play are chosen, too, to help. Here we have a store of varied interests offered to them.

I have with me a set of last term's examinations papers, worked by the most intelligent child at the top of our school. I could give you a very accurate estimate of the work the same child (13 years of age) would have done under the old régime. She would have answered any questions set just as thoroughly so far as she had gone. How far would that have been? History, Geography, Literature and Current Events would have found a place in her written work at the end of the term: and because she was an intelligent and hardworking pupil, I should have found reproduced most faithfully the information, the suggestions and ideas which had been given in one lesson, revised in another—(perhaps even in more than one other)—and again thoroughly revised before the examination day. Instead, she has had opened up to her great vistas. She has written answers bearing on Scott's *Ivanhoe*; Shakespeare's *King John*; the set period of English History tested by questions quite as advanced as those which we were given in the days of my apprenticeship; the contemporary French History; and General History as

---

[55] See pages 44 and 185.

taught by the treasures in the British Museum. She has studied Citizenship from more than one aspect, as the questions will show,—

    (1) What do you know of the government of Mansoul. How do Hunger and Thirst behave? Show that they may change in character.

    (2) Give an account of the way in which Brutus and Cassius prepared for the battle of the Philippian Fields. How did Lucilius save the life of Brutus?

    (3) What is our duty towards foreign countries?

    (4) "India is a continent and not a country." Explain this and say what you know about the peoples and religions of India.

Then comes Geography supplemented by readings from Mr. Household's book on Sea-Power; Nature Study; Architecture; Picture Study and Musical Appreciation. In connection with the last named subject, we had an hour's Musical Appreciation given us by a very able interpreter who, in addition to playing some of Brahms' music, and explaining how it was made, told the children in story form what the "Intermezzo" might convey. The next morning the set question was given to the girls; and the one whose papers are here told the story, but altered the details so that it became a different story, her own interpretation of the music. The question was:—"Write a few lines on any three of the compositions of Brahms you have enjoyed." I will give the answer as it stands, with the child's own spelling, punctuation, and paragraphing.

Brahms has written a great many beautiful compositions, but unlike some of the great musicians, the names that he has given to them, do not tell you anything about the music itself.

One of his pieces is called "Intermezzo," which does not tell anything at all about the really beautiful composition. First of all it is peaceful and quiet, and then it grows louder and becomes troubled, reminding you of the angry waves dashing against the pebbly shore, then once more it becomes peaceful, but with a note of triumph mingled in.

While we are listening to this piece of music, we can make up a story about it. Imagine a poor and dilapidated cottage, which you enter. What do you see? A toilworn mother rocking her babe to sleep. Now the babe sleeps, and the mother may rest, but instead of resting she allows her thoughts to return to the past, and she sighs. She thought of the time when she was young, and when many men had sought her love, but she rejected all of them and married a poor fisherman, because she loved him.

A rich man had wished her to be his bride, and he sneered at her, and said she would soon learn her mistake. "Was it a mistake?" the poor wife asked herself, her husband was lost at sea a year ago, and now she must struggle for life, alone, but she resolutely put this thought from her, and said, "God said we should marry for love, not for land or gold, I have obeyed His word, and I will be true to my dead husband's memory." As she spoke, the door opened, and a storm-beaten mariner entered. He was recognised in an instant, and the wife ran to him with open arms, "My husband," she cried, "but they told me you were drowned at sea."

"Nay, nay lass," said he comfortingly, "We saw the rats leave the ship, and so we packed our things in the two boats. Just when we had all got clear of it, the old tub went down. We started to row in the other boats but we got lost in the fog, although we managed to keep together. At morning we were picked up by a schooner, but as she was late in starting on her voyage, we had to go with her, and a mighty long voyage it was too," he added with a chuckle. "Never mind," said his wife, "All those trials are over now," then she added, "Come and see our baby, who was but a month old when you left us.

They went together to the cradle of the sleeping babe, and as they bent over it, peace returned to the woman's mind, for love had triumphed.

I think this story gives a fairly good idea of "Intermezzo," because it shows the peace, the troubled thoughts, and the triumph of peace and love, which come in everyone's life.

Brahms has also written some short pieces called "Waltzes," and some of these make you think of the people who lived long ago. The stately Greecian ladies, in their dresses of clinging white material, seem to come to life again, and to perform before you the dances which they danced before kings and heroes.

One of Brahms' long pieces is called *Rhapsody*. It is a glorious composition, one long sweep of music, and it is gone. This piece shows the joy of human nature, for it is a very happy composition, although in the middle the tune is lost, and this causes a thrill to run through you, but the tune soon comes back again, brighter and gayer perhaps than it was before, for

Brahms his notes deftly mingled,
And from all the rich chords singled,
The richest chords that he could find
And all of it was for mankind.

We can sing his music's praise,
For that has lived for many days,
And it gives our dark souls, light,
Turning into day the night.

It brings us nearer to God,
Showing us were the saints have trod,
Where they sit and play their lutes,
Sweeter than all earthly flutes.

Some may be inclined to think that the P.N.E.U. curriculum is too wide. It may be if we labour at it in our own way, expecting every child to remember everything that she has read. This is not Miss Mason's idea. "My plea is," she writes in SCHOOL EDUCATION, "that many doors shall be opened to boys and girls until they are at least 12 or 14, and always the doors of good houses ... that the young people shall learn what History is, what Literature is, what life is, from the living books of those who know. Surely here will be the beginning of an appreciation of wide reading which will broaden the child's outlook. It will achieve something even more important, for it will give that balance of judgment which is so vitally necessary.

I have heard philosophy defined as the quest of man for Truth. A study of the great philosophers of all ages (who each discovered part of the truth, he himself thinking he had discovered all), shows us that the right outlook on life needs the points of view of all of them. Truth must be followed along every line, with all the faculties which we possess; and the sanity of the conclusions we reach will depend proportionately on the number of avenues leading up to the conclusions.

The P.N.E.U. training encourages the child to look at things from many points of view; it will lead her to form her own opinions; and it gives her the courage to express what is in her thoughts.

Miss Mason has taught us great things: we must continually get back to the *principles* which she carried out, and which she has laid down for our guidance; for if we do, then the scheme of education which lay so near to her heart will indeed prove to be an atmosphere, a discipline, a life.

The words of Alfred Noyes come back to me. For, Michael Oaktree we can read the name of our Founder,

> One whose love
> Had never waned through all her 80 years.
> Her faith was hardly faith. She seemed a part
> Of all that she believed in. She had lived
> In constant conversation with the sun,
> The wind, the silence, and the heart of peace;
> In absolute communion with the Power
> That rules all action and all tides of thought,
> And all the secret courses of the stars;
> The power that still establishes on earth
> Desire and worship, through the radiant laws
> Of duty, love and beauty; for through these,
> As through three portals of the self-same gate,
> The soul of man attains infinity,
> And enters into Godhead.

Miss Mason's portrait is before us: her spirit still is with us. We feel diffident, maybe; we realise our imperfections; but her work shall continue, for we, in faith and highest hope, must make her work our own.

This is the sacred trust which she has left with us; and with all those who, through her work and life, shall feel constrained to help build "Jerusalem in England's green and pleasant land."

A TRIBUTE

L ady Aberdeen[56] in introducing the next speaker said: "I would have gone much further in order to be present today, and I feel much disappointed that I have been unable to be with you during these last days, so sacred to those who loved our great Founder and inspirer. To have missed the opportunity of hearing these tributes to her life and work is a great loss for me, but I look forward to reading them in the magazine, and I hope too that they, together with the articles which have already appeared in the wonderful March number, may be given a more permanent form so as to enable those of us who have not been present at this Conference to have the pleasure of possessing an account of these spontaneous testimonies of the transformation which one frail woman was able to effect in the training of children in thousands of homes, just by her vision, her understanding, and sympathy with child life. Her faith, her hope and her love, are indeed a wonderful lesson to all, and especially to those who have been privileged to come within the scope of her influence.

The world is so full of darkness and misery that the thought of what Miss Mason has done for thousands and hundreds of thousands of young lives will surely give us fresh courage in the realisation that they have been awakened in soul, mind and heart to the beauty and joy of cherishing all things that are lovely, and true, and of good report, and of consecrating their awakened and trained powers to a life of service. It is men and women of faith and love of the type of Miss Mason that the world needs for its redemption.

May we not hope and pray that these myriads who owe so much to her, will be roused to fresh life and effort by the renewed remembrance which these testimonies to the effects of her life-long devotion, and to the motives and power by

---

[56] See also page 32.

which she was sustained, will bring home to them; and thus beyond the veil she will be able to accomplish even more than during her beautiful life amongst us. It is for us to pass on her flaming torch, and surely these memorial meetings will do much in this direction.

It is very delightful to find an old friend in the old friend of the UNION who is going to give the address, and I have great pleasure in calling on Dr. Lyttelton."

SYMPATHY IN TEACHING[*]

The Honarary Reverend E. Lyttelton thought it would not be disputed that the subject was appropriate to the occasion and that it was of the highest importance to all who were interested in education or in children. Anyone who had been privileged to come across a teacher who had sympathy would know what it meant. Many of the great schoolmasters of England had had a power of moral sympathy, but often intellectual sympathy was wanting.

Miss Mason, unlike Arnold and some of the other great schoolmasters, had the gift of sympathy not only in training but in teaching. The great schoolmasters succeeded, on the whole, in character training more by the splendour of their own example than by the sympathy they had with the difficulties and troubles of young people. A parallel Dr. Lyttelton suggested of a sympathy like Miss Mason's—but in the moral department—was that of the last of the Eton Dames—Miss Jane Evans. In her portrait by Sargeant one could trace something of the humour, deep vision and force which impress one so much in Miss Mason's portrait. Humour was very necessary in the management of boys, and Miss Evans could not have done what she did, for 37 years and have made the house she governed one of the best in Eton during that time, without humour. She, like Miss Mason, saw the good in people before anyone else did and drew it out by appealing to it.

Schoolmasters would often deny that every child was eager to make tracks for truth, but Miss Mason perceived this eagerness and counted upon it to help her. She also

---

[*] From notes of the lecture.

treated English children as potential literary people. Why not? Why should they not have the faculty in which their forefathers excelled so grandly? By giving the children books of real worth to read in class she solved to a great extent the difficulty of class teaching. By this means and by means of music, one could be sure that every child in the class was working hard all the time.

The things to remember for our hope were these. These faculties, for music and for literature, were born in English children, though both had been scandalously neglected in schools for hundreds of years. In the time of Edward VI music was taught all over the country: but the schools were destroyed by the Duke of Somerset and nothing had been done till lately to supply their place. But each generation that was born came to us with faculties unimpaired by our neglect and as ready to respond as ever it was. One could not make an appeal through music and literature without getting a rich response, and this after all these centuries of neglect! How patient nature was with our blunders!

Those who were to achieve anything like the results that had been got by Miss Mason must share her own conviction that the great and the divine was in every child: as long as the teacher was convinced of that, there was a good chance that even an English schoolmaster might acquire by degrees that insight and hope without which nothing could be done.

CHARLOTTE MASON AND THE NATION'S CHILDREN
by H. W. Household, M.A.[57]*

I do not suppose that a single one of those who are present in this hall needs to be reminded of the duty that we owe to our Foundress to make her teaching widely known; for the sake of those who shall come after us, for the sake of the Nation's children. But there are, I am afraid, among the many members of the P.N.E.U. who are not present here, some who do not fully share the faith and the enthusiasm that possess us. We heard at a recent meeting of the Executive Committee, with regret though not wholly with

---

[57] See also page 44.
* Education Secretary for Gloucestershire.

surprise, of the considerable number of members who fall out periodically by resignation—a number which happily is always very substantially exceeded by the number of new recruits.

Now it is quite certain that no parent who had ever felt Miss Mason's influence on heart or mind, could dream of withdrawing from the UNION. Those who leave it have had but the slenderest connection with our cause. They have asked some friend, no doubt, how best they can provide a home education for their children, and they have been told to join the P.N.E.U. and to obtain an AMBLESIDE teacher, if they can, and if they cannot, then, as the next best thing, to get the programmes and, so far as may be, to follow the methods, and all will be well. Of the larger, wider cause which the UNION, learning from its Foundress, has at heart, the right education of the Nation's children, they know nothing. It may be that if they did know they would say that it was not their concern. But, of course, it is their concern, and for two reasons. The first is gratitude, the second self-interest. If they observe the progress of their children, and compare the education which they are receiving, with the education which they had themselves, gratitude to the illustrious lady who worked such a revolution in methods and results, should move them to do what in them lies to extend such benefits to all. And their own interest as citizens points the same way. We do not want perpetual class war; we do not want to share the fate of Russia.

It is hardly possible to take up a paper without reading some indictment, usually unintelligent and biased, of our public education, inspired most frequently by a wish (perhaps in these days not wholly unnatural, though I think unwise) to reduce its cost. At the same time we read, and still more often hear, bitter complaints of the ignorance and folly of popular leaders, and of the credulity of those who follow them. The critics wonder what will become of industry, society, learning, art, religion. They shudder and predict ruin for a later generation, and hope that they themselves may just escape the day. But it is futile to sit and wring our hands and play Cassandra, prophesying nothing but disaster. If things are going wrong, whose fault is it? Why, surely ours. No man or woman was ever yet a fool or ignorant by intention. Folly and ignorance are a consequence of lack of opportunity. It is for us to find the remedy. And there is only one. It is to educate. "Oh, but," replies the critic, "you have been doing that now for three or four generations at enormous cost, and look at the result. Those whom you teach to read do not read: those whom you train to think do not think." Ladies and gentlemen, we may have taught children the mechanical art of reading, but until lately we have not shown them how to read books, nor have we put books, real books, within their reach whether in school or out of it. And assuredly under such conditions we shall never train anyone to think. Until a bare 20 years ago we spent ridiculously little on our public education, and yet even that little has borne fruit a hundredfold. It gave us a people who could win the war, if it has not yet shaped them for the more difficult life of Peace.

The great fault of our public education has been that it was conceived and administered on mean penurious lines. Many have never really believed in it. To this day there still are many sceptics. I do not suppose they would go the length of saying that the nation would fare better if its workers were uneducated, but they certainly would say that the best education for them is something very simple and above all very cheap. And then, forsooth, they complain of their ignorance, credulity, and folly. How should folk so educated know any better?

A hundred years ago even those who meant well did not understand the people's need, or the pathetic futility of an education that begins and ends in the crude elements of reading, writing, and arithmetic. Put some poor graded 'reader' in the boy's hands. Can he get through half a dozen lines? If he can, it is well. Let him go. The State has done its duty, though he never reads again. That, for 60 or 70 years, was all that officially we aimed at doing.

And the teaching service—what was the philanthropist's ideal for that? Listen. I quote. "Under the monitorial system of Bell and Lancaster (they, remember, were philanthropists) schools containing as many as a thousand pupils might be taught at a cost of 5s. per head per annum by monitors who possessed the 'advantage' (as Bell considered it) of knowing nothing which was beyond their pupils' comprehension." (The

Teaching of English in England, 41, 42). Five shillings per
head for teachers, books, stationery, furniture, apparatus,
heating, lighting, cleaning, and all extras! There was not
much, be sure, for books. And that lack of books has
inspired—no, I must not so degrade the word—has fatally
obsessed the whole of the theory and practice of our public
education. The philosophers who shaped the theory which
underlay the methods accepted the impossible situation.
There were no books. So be it. Primary education was a
peculiar kind of education (one has never heard of any other)
into which books did not enter. That postulate once granted,
the rest follows. You had to shape a teacher who could teach
without books. He must be a good talker. He must be able to
impart information and elicit answers; pour in and pump
out. Truly an empirical philosophy, designed strictly to fit
what was, and not what should have been. So your
Herbartian doctrine (I quote from the preface to HOME
EDUCATION) "lays the stress of education—the preparation of
knowledge in enticing morsels, presented in due order—upon
the teacher."

And for the teacher, of course, training was far more
important than education. That he had had a liberal
education, and was a graduate in honours of an ancient
university, would not admit him to the elementary school. He
must be equipped with a hundred tricks of method that
would enable him, without books, to keep children quiet and
make them work. He must talk and question well, and use
the blackboard ably. He must be able to hold attention; to
make a large class move as one individual; to push all
through a ridiculous and soul-destroying examination on the
result of which his meagre pay depended. He must be a
disciplinarian, with an air of command, and a strong right
arm.

No wonder that graduates were warned off the primary
school. As teaching there was largely a matter of tricks it was
the Certificate of the Board of Education that was the
essential qualification. A degree would not serve. And this
ridiculous anomaly still survives. It has become so much a
matter of course that no one thinks to laugh. If they would,
laughter might perhaps end it.

But until Miss Mason taught us how to do it nobody ever dreamed of giving a liberal education—the first stage of a liberal education—to the workers' children in the elementary school, of giving them just the same education, in the same way, and out of the same books, that we give our own children. It is indeed high time that we did so. Matthew Arnold justly said that "culture unites classes." But we have never given it play. Culture has been reserved for the children of the well-to-do. The children of the workers have had no access to it, save the tiny percentage who mount the narrow ladder, and are lost forever to their class. Because the workers in the days of their youth knew nothing of humane studies, many among them regard those studies with suspicion. They think that they provide an intellectual buttress for a social system ordered in favour of the well-to-do. They suspect the great books of antiquity, as they suspect history in general, of a bias in favour of a social and economic system which—or the present consequences of which—they detest. A liberal education for all is the crying need of the times. Never was it so necessary as it is now. The children who leave our elementary schools and pass into industry at the early age of 14 will control the destiny of the country. The questions which it will fall to them to decide are questions of a complexity unknown to earlier generations, and upon the decision hang tremendous consequences. A wrong decision over Catholic Emancipation or Irish Disestablishment over Home Rule or Licensing Reform, did not involve as a consequence the collapse of credit, the ruin of industry, the death of millions, the disappearance of all the amenities and most of the machinery of civilised life. But all of those grim consequences may follow upon hasty and ill-judged decisions of the electorate today. And how shall people hope to form sound judgments upon the questions before them if they ignore history, and, with a gesture, sweep away the accumulated experience of mankind as worthless?

Herbart and his fellows shaped their philosophy of education to meet the conditions of the bookless school. They supplied a sanction for the procedure which the facts had forced upon the Training College. Although there are very many more books today than there used to be, they are still too often cheap 'readers' so constructed as to demand no real

effort of the child. The outlook and the methods of the
Training College are much more liberal than they were, but
the old idea that the child cannot work without the constant
intervention of the teacher still underlies the system. The
teacher must still talk endlessly. Inspectors, as he knows,
will require it of him, and will judge him by his capacity to do
so. Method is still all important. We start with the axiom, as
Miss Mason says, that "what a child learns matters less than
how he learns it," with the result that he is "in danger of
receiving much teaching with little knowledge." The child who
has once tasted freedom knows the difference. I was talking a
few weeks ago to the teacher-father of a little boy of 11, who
had recently passed from an elementary school, taught under
Miss Mason's methods, to a Secondary School. We were
discussing the teaching of history. "My boy," said the father,
"frets at the change. He says the master talks all the time,
and will not let him get on." There you have it. Yet that
master is a clever young man and an enthusiastic teacher
who loves his subject. The Inspectors are full of his praise.
He lectures very ably; but the lecture method is an utterly
wrong method for young pupils, and a boy who has been
accustomed to do his own work on the books is bored and
irritated. He wants to get on.

Miss Mason's philosophy of education began at the
opposite pole to that of her predecessors. She would not
shape her theory to meet intolerable conditions. She went
back to first principles. A bookless education was a
contradiction in terms, and she would have none of it. If
there were no books, no good books, to be had, in the
elementary school, she could not help either school or
teacher. That is why it was so long before she found her way
there. It seemed so impossible to get the books. Then came
that brave Drighlington experiment, for which we can never
be too grateful to Mrs. Steinthal and Miss Ambler. The
children had their opportunity, and they rose to it, as Miss
Mason knew they would. Since then a hundred schools have
shewn that in the Worker's child, even in the child of the
slums, are latent the powers and tastes of our own children.
There is no need of other and simpler books for them. They
will understand any book suitable to their age. There is no
need for endless talk, for endless questioning, and irritating

childish explanation of the obvious. They all stop the child from getting on with his work. "Given a book of literary quality suitable to their age, and children will know how to deal with it without elucidation." And what was suitable was to be by no means easy, for Miss Mason asked much of them. It was her way. The books are hard. But the more she asked, the more the children gave. And, though they never saw her, there were thousands who loved her, because she understood them and knew what they wanted. She had treated them as persons. She had respected them. They were in some way conscious of her high and gentle courtesy. Their outraged pride was soothed. They were her children, equal members of her worldwide school. The badge of inferiority had gone.

Their ability amazed their teachers, who had been brought up to think that as a class they were of inferior mentality; that they could do nothing without help, and would do nothing without something like compulsion. They were not prepared—we were none of us prepared—for Miss Mason's epoch-making discovery, the "great avidity for knowledge in children of all ages and of every class" for knowledge which is presented to them in more or less literary form. The children who were troublesome in our schools were simply not interested. And, after all, who are we that we should hold their interest, day in day out, through every lesson? Even if we were so completely masters of all subjects, and such adepts in the lecture method, that we could hold their interest, how would it better the children? They would have made no effort; they would have done nothing for themselves. That way they receive much teaching with little knowledge. If they read for themselves without interruption, interest is great. If they read but once, and then must narrate, concentration is intense. You can see the children thinking. And what is read once and then narrated becomes a part of the child's knowledge, and is usable thenceforth. So treated the children make astounding progress. We have resorted to the play way quite unnecessarily, and made things easy far too long. The children rejoice in the hard work if you will let them do it. When a child of 7 will take up *The Children of the New Forest* or Hans Andersen and read them at sight, as many of our children will (though it is a thing that you would not have dared to ask your top standard to do

30 years ago) what is the need of childish "readers" carefully arranged and written down to a level that does not exist unless by artificial means you make it. The children of 9 and 10 in many of our elementary schools now read and love Shakespeare and Scott (the plays and books of course are chosen so as to illustrate the period of history under study); they love Plutarch and the tales of Greece and Rome; the great names of classical antiquity both in myth and history are already familiar to them. Are we not justified in saying that these children, when they are grown men and women, will love books, real books of worth, and will know how to use them? And we in Gloucestershire, at any rate, are happy in the knowledge that they will have access to such books, thanks to the far-sighted beneficence of the Carnegie Trustees. Charlotte Mason and Andrew Carnegie will be blessed as pious founders by after generations in many a country village.

But I talk too much and too often of Gloucestershire. I will leave my county for once and speak of a school that I have never seen.

In one of the last letters that Miss Mason wrote to me (it is undated but the enclosure which she forwarded bears date the 29th of last November) she sent for me to read a letter that she had received from the Headmaster of a Boys' School in Middlesbrough. "I send you," she said, "a drop of cold water to taste and pass on. Those slum schools are miracles of grace are they not? They confirm us and cheer us in our work. The right note is struck I think."

This is the first opportunity that I have had to obey her, and pass on the refreshing draught. You shall judge whether the right note was struck.

"We are approaching the conclusion," says the writer, "of our third term's attempt to carry out P.N.E.U. methods, and whilst I know you already have some measure of the effect of these methods in Elementary Schools, I think further testimony will be of interest.

This is a slum school, 200 yards from the river and docks, surrounded by the lowest type of brothel, "doss" house, drinking bars, and farthest removed of any school in Middlesbrough from green fields and lanes.

Most of the children are unshod, ill-clad, underfed, and live in overcrowded rooms—very often unfurnished—without conveniences for the ordinary decencies of life. There is an entire lack of discipline—mental, moral, physical—in the homes and surroundings.

In the schools there is much repression and excessive corporal punishment (I often wonder if you *realise* the tawdry soulless sham that passes for education in many urban schools) and this school was no exception.

The day I took charge (2nd May, 1921), there was an uproar in the street. A boy had been severely punished; another had slipped out of school, and roused the neighbourhood. A semi-drunken slut rushed into the school "to twist the teacher's neck."

Daily squabbles with parents about punishments were taken by the staff as a matter of course.

Now teacher and scholar are bright and eager in their work. Irregularity and unpunctuality are reduced to a minimum and there is no corporal punishment. The work to the scholar is becoming a much more important thing than the teacher is. And there you have what is to me one of the most important features of the P.N.E.U. methods. They compel the teacher to study the child, in setting this task, and discovering the why of that failure: and with this study 'all other graces follow in their proper places.'

But I must go back to Gloucestershire. I cannot keep away, and I do not think that you really wish me to. Let me read what a little child of 6 years and 8 months old wrote a few weeks ago about *The Laurel Tree* after hearing Bulfinch read.

THE LAUREL TREE

December 1st, 1922

Apollo the great god of the rays of the sun was one day walking in the valley and as he was walking along its banks he saw Cupid the little god of love sitting on bank playing with his arrows and some of his arrows had points of gold and some of lead but they were all very small and to Apolo only looked like pretty Playthings and Apolo said of what use are those little arrows with mine I have just killed this big Serpent which lived in the caves at the bottom of the mountain Cupid did not like to hear his arrows made fun of so he left Apollo and flew away with them to the top of the mountain of Greece now just at this time the beautiful little girl of the river-god came walking though the valley it was the spot she loved best on earth even the flowers which grew there seem to now her and lift up there heads as she passed by she would clime mountain every morning to see the sun-god golden chiorareot rise and ride across the sky and would watch it sink to rest in the evning now just at this time little Cupid on the moutain above saw her coming and in a Play-ful mood shot a golden arow staight at her and in some way or other is made her afraid and she felt she must run away it was Cupids turn now so taking aim he shot golden arrow at Apolo and wounded him now just at thies time Apolo saw the little girl running as fast as she could though the valley Apolo was charmed with her beauty and called to her to stop as she would not Apolo ran quickly after her she ran on and on till she felt too weary to go any farther she lay down and called to her father the river-god to help her the flowing stream at once passed over her and when Apollo came up to the place where he last saw her there was only a beautiful laurel tree with glossy green leaves Apollo always loved that tree it was all that left to him of Daphne for that was her name he wore its leaves as a crown and as they were ever green so was his love for lost Daphne ever fresh and bright.

Teacher's Note:
    This child remembered the above story absolutely from memory without the slightest help of the teacher to assist in spelling a word.   —S.M.B.

And I have in mind a little country school of something under 50 children, with two teachers. For some years it had been on the border of inefficiency. There had been one incompetent teacher after another. The children could do nothing. In May 1921, the present master went there. He had been in one of our PARENTS' UNION SCHOOLS before, as an Assistant, and he introduced the programmes and the methods. In a single year he had worked a revolution, in the village as well as in the school. All had become allies and educationists.

Last November he sent me the exercise books of two boys. "When I came here," he said, "I found that both boys were real bad characters, and they were under police supervision. A.B. (age 11) is the eldest of five children whose mother went to the Lunatic Asylum just before I came, and he has a wretched father. M.N. is one of a family of seven. His mother is in the Workhouse, and his sister 15 years old keeps the house going. Both fathers are farm hands."

I will read you two passages from A.B's book. I do not say they are wonderful; but remember the boy's history; they are wonderful for him. The first is an extract from a piece of composition written after a single reading from *Hereward the Wake*, the second the closing paragraph of an original essay. Both were written last July within 15 months of that master going there.

One day as Hereward was slowly driving his steed on a lonely road he heard sounds of pattering feet coming behind him. He looked, and as he came nearer he recognised him, it was Martin Lightfoot. He soon caught up Hereward. 'What are you here for?' asked Hereward. 'Because I am going to follow you,' said Martin. 'Follow me? What can I do for thee?' said Hereward. 'I can do something for you. I can read and write, speak French, Irish, and Danish and I will tell you all my secrets,' said Martin. 'I ran away from the Monastery. So did you. I hated the Monks. So did you. And now I am with you I will live and die with thee,' said Martin.

The second passage closes a delightful essay of six pages on *Sunshine on Gloomy Days*.

Tomorrow, Thursday, we shall be delighted and happy as anyone, for our mothers are coming to see the work that we do and the joy and happiness we get out of it. This is what the P.N.E.U. does for children who love it.

So these children actually enjoy their work. Yet many educationists are still convinced that education must be an exacting and even repellent discipline, must be something so difficult and distasteful that the normal child will avoid it or escape from it whenever it can. That supposed necessity plays a large part in the argument for compulsory Latin; and, beyond question, it is largely responsible for our utter failure to train the intellect or cultivate the taste of so many of the boys who learn Latin at our Public Schools.

"Our English children," said the writer of *The English Secret*, a brilliant article in the Literary Supplement of the *Times* some months ago—"Our English children are not consumed with anxiety to learn anything; least of all has it ever crossed their minds that they must learn English."

Well, poor souls, in many of our Preparatory and Public Schools they are hardly permitted to see English: that they might learn it has never been allowed to cross their minds. And when the writer says that our English children are not consumed with anxiety to learn anything, he is surely a witness, an unconscious witness, to the failure of the orthodox curriculum and methods. Of course they are not consumed with anxiety to learn, just because they may not learn English, and get knowledge, for which they are naturally eager, through the use of books that are literature; just because they must learn what they can neither use nor understand.

Let him go to one of the schools that are following Miss Mason's programmes, and see whether our English children are not consumed with anxiety to learn. Even Public School boys can delight in learning. Not many months ago I was told, in a house where I was staying, of two boys who had come home there from school after illness during term time— normal boys with normal schoolboy tastes. They had found their sisters, under an AMBLESIDE teacher, using books the style and matter of which appealed to them, and voluntarily and without shadow of suggestion they joined their classes during the idle weeks. They had found a place where they could learn English, and through English many things that they wanted to know.

And it is interesting to note that in that village, as in a good many other villages in Gloucestershire, the labourer's child is using the same books, following the same programmes, as the squire's and the parson's. There is the first promise of a common school, a common culture, with its large fund of common interest. There is the "Liberal Education for All" that will give us an intelligent and thinking people.

I am convinced that we set too much store by the teaching of Latin and Greek. We make many boys learn Latin who would be much better employed in learning English. If the Elizabethans could have found in English all and more than all that can be found in Latin and Greek, can we believe that they, athirst like the Greeks themselves for knowledge and experience, would have tried to make boys spend priceless hours in learning the Latin that they would never use? Would they not have gone straight by the nearest road, the English road, for the thing they wanted—knowledge?

If a boy after his hard struggle with the language drops it before he has mastered it sufficiently to be able to read widely and with ease, what has he for his pains? He does not—eight out of ten do not—enjoy anything he reads. The constant effort to make sense kills interest. The beauties of Virgil are beyond him. He reads so little, and finds it so hard to read, that he seldom gets the story. He retains nothing. He would have gained much more from a good translation in a fraction of the time. And in another fraction of the time what might he not have learned through English? The true reward of time and labour spent upon the classics—the power to read with ease and a full understanding, for surely that is the only adequate reward—can hardly be achieved by any but those who take an Honours course at the University. For the rest time and labour have been largely wasted. "Intellectual discipline" there may have been, and "real mental effort" (*The Classics in Education*, page 119), but the boys have never caught the spirit of the Classics or drawn its real lesson from the tale of Greece and Rome. The beauty, the wisdom, the rich experience are unheeded. Voiced in English they would have made an irresistible appeal. Then all, and not merely a small section of a select class, would be able to enjoy them and to get some understanding of what the ancient world stood for, and the lessons which it has to teach. Culture, remember, unites classes. But the children of the Workers have never come in contact with culture, never tasted the humanities, except in those few elementary schools which Miss Mason has influenced. That is why Labour so often says that it has no time for culture. It must have time for culture, and it can only get it by beginning young. If we deny it the opportunity, and culture, in consequence, is pushed aside as unimportant, civilisation will be eclipsed once more, and we shall go down together into a dark age of barbarism and stark poverty, with its unimagined miseries.

Without culture Labour will never attain to a sympathetic imagination, or learn how human nature works. And without imagination it is impossible to handle wisely foreign or imperial affairs. He, for example, who would govern India must understand her; and he who would understand India must be able to think himself into another world of associations and ideas, far away from 20th century Glasgow or Manchester or Birmingham, and the men and institutions and ways of thought with which he is familiar there. The stunted education which in our folly we offer to the children of the Workers, the common textbooks, and the vain lecturing of half-educated teachers, will never wing them for such flights. Without imagination it is not possible so much as to begin the search for truth. Each man is sure that he has it here and now. Humility, a consciousness of ignorance, must precede enlightenment. Sympathetic imagination, the capacity to understand people and ideas hitherto unfamiliar to us, are a part of the legacy of Greece, in which all men may have their share through the medium of a common education in the mother tongue—that liberal education for all which Charlotte Mason would have us give. What a solvent of class differences, of suspicions, antipathies, and misunderstandings, such an education would prove itself! How inevitably they are perpetuated by the class education of today!

A TRIBUTE

The Lady Cottesloe in introducing the next speaker said,— "I want to say quite frankly and simply that I do not know what I should have done without the PARENTS' UNION and the PARENTS' UNION SCHOOL. Please forgive me if what I say is partly personal.

I married young, knowing almost nothing about either the training and education or the physical care of children. Shortly after my marriage, a friend told me of Miss Mason and of the UNION and of that wonderful book HOME EDUCATION. I can never estimate all that this has meant to me and to my eight children.

I can only forever thank God for the inspiration He has given through Miss Mason, through her books, through her TRAINING COLLEGE at AMBLESIDE, and through the PARENTS' UNION SCHOOL.

These, in our family, have been our mainstay and probably our greatest educational blessing through these 26 years. It will be 20 years this autumn since my eldest son joined the PARENTS' UNION SCHOOL with an AMBLESIDE governess. I have had seven children in it, at times with AMBLESIDE teachers, at times with other teachers. My youngest child is not yet old enough to join. One girl was in it from Form I to Form VI for about 11 years, and is now preparing for Oxford.

I thank God for the Training College. I have in more than one instance found in its teachers, women inspired by the Spirit of God to be such wonderful helpers as I could hardly have dared to hope for. But though it is undoubtedly an incalculable gain to have teachers who have been trained at AMBLESIDE, yet it is infinitely worthwhile to have our children in the PARENTS' UNION SCHOOL even with other teachers. One should, however, always bear in mind that perhaps no others, or very few others, can reveal to us the *full* beauty of the PARENTS' UNION SCHOOL and that it is unfair to criticise it, if the working of it is in amateur hands.

In this connection I would say that when the Headmaster of Westminster was speaking yesterday of the difficulty of getting such methods put widely into practice in our public schools, I was impressed with the need of a Men's Training College on the same lines as the Women's Training College at AMBLESIDE. How infinite—how incalculably far reaching— might be its influence for good in our schools and for humanity!

As to results, I find the PARENTS' UNION SCHOOL gives keenness, intelligence, and wide interests; that it gives an abiding interest in nature and that it gives useful and capable hands. I have found that when the children have gone on to school they have done well, and that their powers of expression are markedly good. This shews itself among them both in the writing of verse and of prose as well as in good letter writing, and in other ways. This I attribute largely to the good and well chosen literature, to the constant narrating, and to the dictation by the younger ones of examination answers. It is of course an inestimable gain in the home schoolroom to have well chosen books and a definite standard and programme of work. Self-understanding and self-management are also greatly helped—a very vital matter! For example, if such phases as the unbalanced kind of hero-worship arise, a well-trained PARENTS' UNION SCHOOL boy or girl should recognise them and be able wisely and sanely to deal with them, in himself or herself.

Above all, sane and vital spiritual life may, by God's grace, be fostered and nourished in the PARENTS' UNION SCHOOL.

One matter I should like to take this opportunity to emphasise with all possible force. I said that I married young knowing nothing of the care and training of children. I deeply desire to see more done to prevent this situation arising in the present generation. I fear something approaching it is still lamentably common. I should like to see more done in Forms V and VI to prepare girls for the future care of children. I had correspondence with Miss Mason about this, and an admirable beginning was made when HOME EDUCATION became one of the books for study in Form VI.* I should like to see this preparation for the future carried further,—i.e., preparation for the training and education of children— spiritual, mental and physical. Truby King's *Feeding and Care of the Baby* could be studied on the physical side. This is an excellent and in some ways a unique book and the writer has done a wonderful work for the little ones of the

---

* I learn that HOME EDUCATION is not at present on the P.U.S. programme. I would urge mothers and teachers to study it with their girls as an invaluable bit of preparation for life.

empire. I commend it as invaluable. A simpler one, on the same lines, will, I hope, be published this year.

I know only a beginning could be made in school days, but it might help to avert for others the bitterness with which one looks back to irreparable mistakes due to a tragic ignorance. Undoubtedly a good Mothercraft training should be considered as an essential part of a girl's education, but I fear that, although so vital, this is still far from being universally recognised.

Let me say again that my heart is full of thankfulness to God for all He has given to us and to our children and to humanity in her whose memory we venerate today, in the many who, through her, have been called to, and fitted for, their high calling, and in the many sided and glorious work which He inspired through her. She has handed on to us the torch, and that nothing may hinder the eager, straight running of the race to the goal, may the Spirit of Love and Truth and Courage Who possessed her, possess us too."

SCALE HOW
By E. A. Parish[*][58]

When an ex-student of the HOUSE OF EDUCATION hears the words SCALE HOW she is reminded of many things; she sees again a long and beautiful drive approaching a finely situated and beautiful house with doors and windows open to the sun, surrounded by a garden which, except in midwinter, is a blaze of colour and a veritable paradise for birds and students, flooded with sound, happy sound, made of birds' songs, the laughter of happy people and the voices of children passing to and from their work in the Practising School. Then, till now, the student has known that in the house was the sweet presence of Miss Mason, radiating love to her bairns, making all work joyous work, proving to each that she was capable of more than she had ever supposed possible. We try to think that the happy spirit of Miss Mason will always be in SCALE HOW and we must feel that it is the work of every ex-student to keep her memory fresh and to

---

[*] Principal of the HOUSE OF EDUCATION.
[58] See also page 60.

give to every future student such a knowledge of our Founder as will give something of the inspiration that used to flow from her.

SCALE HOW is the local name of the HOUSE OF EDUCATION which Miss Mason founded in 1892 as a Secondary Training College where women are trained for teaching in private families, in schools and classes or for any other guardianship of children to which they may be called. The way in which Miss Mason started the college was the way in which she did everything:—she did not wait for funds; she knew the thing had to be done so she did it.

At first she lived in rooms, having only four students, the training then took one year, the following year saw 13 students already housed in Springfield, a gabled house on the Rydal Road, with sitting rooms commanding a beautiful view of the surrounding hills, so beautiful "that it was an education in itself." Work was carried on in the Y.M.C.A. Institute, the Practising School occupying its main hall.

The curriculum was very much the same as it is at present though as Miss Mason gathered experience she concentrated more upon her own educational principles. By 1893 there were 24 students at work, Miss Mason having secured a strong staff of helpers, and this necessitated two more boarding houses and in 1895 Miss Mason was able to move to SCALE HOW.

One of the outstanding features of Miss Mason's teaching is its consistency. In no part of her written work, written during a period which covered more than 60 years, do we find any conflicting principle, the early writing contains the germ of the later, the later is entirely faithful to the early work, but what is more wonderful is the way in which she carried out her principles in her life. For the life of SCALE HOW *was* her life, the life the students lived with her was, so far as they could rise to it, her life.

Miss Mason regarded education not as a separate compartment, but as being as much a part of life as birth or growth, marriage or work; and she considered that it must leave the pupil attached to the world at many points of contact. And so it followed that many young women who went to the HOUSE OF EDUCATION to learn the art of teaching, found that as well, they were learning the art of living, and of living fully by means of the relationships they formed.

One of Miss Mason's principles is that method rather than system should be our way to our end, accordingly there was a great elasticity about the conduct of the college, and all the fortunes and misfortunes of daily life were woven in as so many opportunities.

Perhaps this principle was specially evident during Criticism lessons on Thursday mornings when Miss Mason would criticise a student for doing what was, apparently, precisely the thing another student has been criticised for not doing the previous Thursday, thus reducing us to despair. For what were we to do? and when we asked for the precise recipe we were told to "mix it with brains." Every lesson needs a special giving and the method is based upon broad principles which leave the teacher all the exercise of her own ingenuity.

Another of Miss Mason's principles is that children are born law abiding and we find as we follow her teaching that she never at any time had one law for a child and another for an adult, so, though she treated the students as children and the children in the practising school as students, from none of them would she exact implicit and unthinking obedience because from all alike she expected and obtained temperate conduct and self-control. This she obtained in the college by what the students themselves describe as the life of a "self-controlled community." It is the work of the Senior Monitress to see that life in the college goes on in such a way that the atmosphere is peaceful, though at times it may be called a little too merry, but, as one of them has said, "All are bound together by the fact that they are all working for one great cause." Every student has her own work to do and, in addition, her monitress duties, which when combined, help the college to run smoothly. One learns the place of authority at the school by teaching the children and at college by obeying the very few rules of the HOUSE and by giving entire obedience to the staff and to those students who, in carrying out their monitress duties, have authority over other students.

Last week I thought it well to consult with the present students on the various ways in which Miss Mason lived out her principles and taught her household to live out her principles at SCALE HOW. I cannot, as I should wish, offer tribute to them by name, but most of what I say here comes from one or other of them.

Miss Mason considered that Education was the Science of Relations, and of these relations those which mattered most were our human relations. This is how a student puts it:

> There is a distinct atmosphere about SCALE HOW which I think every student feels when she first arrives. It is an atmosphere of friendliness and understanding such as is not often felt in a school or college.

And another:

> When we come to SCALE HOW we are not instructed more carefully in any one subject than in any others. It may be that we do not become particularly proficient in any one of these subjects, there is no time for that, but there is time to awaken our interest in them, and it is awakened. We gain 'common information' which helps us to establish our relations with the world and with each other.
>
> Here we live the life of a community, practising obedience and consideration for others. When so many people live in so limited a space they are naturally interested in each other. We feel ourselves to be all one family and one spirit. Not only in this way do we form human relationships but also by the help of the books we read, the languages we learn and the art in which we become interested.
>
> We do not lack moral teaching. We learn the meaning of our duty towards our neighbour, we know that we owe it to the future to prepare a generation better than ourselves. All the time we are learning to know ourselves and this knowledge is important because it helps us to form relations with ourselves and without these we cannot hope to form proper relations with other people. We are taught to understand the power of habit. We are fitted for citizenship by being to a large degree, a self-governed community. We are encouraged by narration to

exercise our powers of speaking. We are taught that duty is not optional.

If we are to rise to the responsibilities of our human relationships we must be persons who are living a full rich life. We cannot have this joy for ourselves and we cannot pass on this joy to our pupils unless we are in touch at all points with the world in which we live, with the past and all that is implied in "the inheritance of the ages" and, in so far as we are concerned with shaping it, with the future. How in the short span of two years which pass so rapidly, are we to accomplish this?

"The new student," says one of them, "is at first amazed to find how little we specialize, perhaps she does not wish to teach mathematics and does not see why she should study them; perhaps she loves history and considers that the study of history alone is a life work. She does not yet understand that all subjects are so interwoven that one cannot fully be studied and understood apart from the rest and that is why so many subjects are taught at SCALE HOW."

A glance at the College prospectus will impress most people with the work that is to be done during the two years course.

- Ethics and the philosophy
- History
- Methods and principles of education
- Practical Education in the Practising School
- Languages: Greek, Latin, French, German and Italian

- Mathematics
- Nature Lore
- Physiology
- Hygiene
- English
- Physical Exercises
- Handicrafts
- Art
- Music and Singing

Then there are "SCALE HOW evenings," one of the special institutions of the college which have long been in practice and at which one of the students reads a paper dealing with an author, composer, painter, or sometimes with a place—the subject is chosen by the student and is usually the one which interests her most. One will take a visit to Rio, another will give the history of *Punch*, a third will give an account of

Alpine climbing and so on; very often the life of a poet or
novelist is taken and on all occasions extracts from the work,
or bearing on the subject, are read by various students.

Miss Mason considered leisure to be as important as
work, for it is during leisure that ideas are sifted and grow;
moreover "leisure out of doors, with all the wild things of
Nature, is soothing and restful to the tired mind; it gives a
time when ideas can grow." Accordingly leisure is an
important part of the students' life at SCALE HOW; half
holidays, Sundays, the last half hour before bedtime, the half
hour after the midday meal, all these are times when actual
work would be out of place. New and energetic students find
it difficult to understand that temperance in work is as great
a thing as temperance in play.

Dynamic relations, so important to the well balanced
healthy person, have their place in the life of SCALE HOW. Not
a day passes without opportunities for physical exercises
and, "What is more" says a student, "we are bound to make
use of them and we learn to dance, climb, play hockey and,
above all, walk."

In beautiful lakeland, walks are one of the greatest
delights, they furnish opportunities for the scientific work
that is done at SCALE HOW, which, being in the heart of the
Lake District, provides excellent opportunities for studying
Geology, Botany, Natural History, Physical Geography and
Historical and Literary associations. Time and opportunity
are given to explore and to become acquainted with the
district and help is also given in answering the problems
arising from the walks by the indoor study of Natural History,
Geography, Geology and Astronomy.

A student writes, "I think if anyone asked me what I liked
best about SCALE HOW I should say: the fact that all of us
love birds and butterflies, insects and flowers *and* that our
museum is a "perfect disgrace"—we have not a single stuffed
bird or snake, no lovely collections of butterflies and insects,
no pressed flowers or birds' nests or eggs, only a few rocks,
minerals and fossils. For the rest we spend the afternoons
with, and not hunting, catching and collecting birds, beasts
and flowers. I have almost, but not quite, given up wanting to
see the inside of a Buzzard and to compare his anatomical
structure with that of a Kestrel. Why do they fly so

differently? If you can only find the answer by hunting the Buzzard—then, go without the answer."

It must not be thought that Miss Mason as an invalid was unable to share these interests; she dined everyday with her students and compared her nature notes with theirs. You will know what her notes were like, through the beautiful article contributed to the March PARENTS' REVIEW by her faithful friend and coachman, Barrow.[59]

Students quickly come to see the truth of Miss Mason's principle, that relations with birds and animals are better formed with free creatures than with those in captivity.

"There are no pets at SCALE HOW and the garden is safe for all birds and for many squirrels; rabbits, bats, dogs, cats, horses, cows and sheep are amongst the animals studied on close terms, whilst a great deal is learned about their habits and lives in the lectures on Natural History and Biology."

Handicrafts form an important part of the training of the students, who have every opportunity given to them of using their minds and hands "to make all kinds of things and to realize the joy of creating original models in a large number of materials."

In considering the training which Miss Mason thought out for her students, one is reminded of her great insistence on willing effort. All work must be one's own work. Self education is the only education. But willing work can only come from the ideal, the vision, and this vision of the new era that must dawn when every English child comes into his birthright of wisdom and knowledge, is approached step by step, and that happens to the student which happened long ago to Dante when he found that the higher he climbed on the mountain the easier became his ascent.

When the new student arrives at SCALE HOW she is asked to do and learn many things which she is sure she knew long before and which she firmly believes she is wasting her time in repeating. It is useless to tell her that she must bathe in the waters of Jordan, all one can do is to engage her patience and tolerance till she sees that her Seniors who have begun their second year at the college, have discovered that they are the oarsmen of a great boat and the oarsman who neglects his work will impede the progress of the boat. With varying

---

[59] See page 79.

degrees of speed each student becomes interested in the progress of the boat, then she sees that its cargo is composed of the Gold of the Indies and after that, rather than lose the chance of holding an oar, she will do the smallest thing counting it an honour to press forward the work of so great a Teacher.

A student writes "Part at any rate of our great love for SCALE HOW is due to the fact that it has helped to make life so much fuller for us. It is incredible how fast two whole years can fly—years in which relations and living interests are established in every direction, interests undreamt of before we came. We seem to have come there so ignorant and to have learnt so much, and yet the little we have learnt can in no way compare either in amount or importance with the desire we have gained to learn more. These new interests are going to help us all through life. But they are ours only that we may share them, which is half the joy of interests. Now our chief source of wonder is "How did we get on before without them? Why did we allow the trees and the birds and flowers to mean so little to us? We grieve over lost opportunities and determine that in future we will lose no more."

THE P.N.E.U. FROM A
PREPARATORY SCHOOL STANDPOINT
By J. W. Clouston, M.A.*

I have been asked to tell you how the P.N.E.U. affects a Preparatory School—and though as a speaker, I cannot do justice to the subject, I can tell you my opinions formed after seeing Miss Mason's methods in my own school for the last 12 years.

We all recognise the far reaching effects of Miss Mason's methods, but I think one of the greatest gains is before boys come to a Preparatory School.

Now boys come to a Preparatory School so young that many parents think it is up to the School to accept full responsibility for a boy until he goes to his Public School.

---

* Headmaster of Stratton Park School, Nr. Bletchley.

This, I fear, is one of these superficial truths, which do not always bear examination.

In a well regulated nursery even infants are taught many habits for their future welfare—and no child is too young, for instance, not to be taught that he cannot always have what he wants, or that someone will pick him up and nurse him if he cries sufficiently strenuously. I did not refer, however, to these early lessons, which every mother should rejoice in imparting; but rather to these years before a child is old enough for school—or indeed for any instruction—as we term it.

Miss Mason's great point is that children really are human beings and should be treated as such. When a child cannot read—his only method of acquiring information is by questions. Is it treating him reasonably to refuse to answer these questions—or to delegate one's authority to a nurse, who in any case is not capable of answering many of the questions—but who generally is too busy and advises—rather strongly—that the thirster after knowledge should occupy himself with his bricks and his toy engine. A parent myself, I can sympathise with those who have to meet the avalanche of questions which sometimes threatens to overwhelm; but we must never lose sight of the fact that these questions should be answered, for the most intelligent child later is the one who was the most successful questioner of his parents before he went to school. Any effort to repress a child discourages him and makes him retire into his shell and develop a mental apathy, which, later on, is hard to dispel. Observation, a golden acquisition, and one on which Miss Mason rightly lays particular stress is acquired easiest in preschool days and parents cannot give their children too much help and encouragement to observe and to keep on observing.

There is, believe me, a great difference in children who come from a house where they are accustomed to see a great deal of their parents, and hear and note the hundred and one little things, which grownups had almost forgotten to impart. In the past boys were sent to a preparatory school—who did not know a single nursery rhyme—in my opinion an *awful omission*—nor had they acquired any aptitude for learning one—they did not know the names of the days of the week or the months of the year—indeed they often could neither read nor write, as this had been left to professional hands.

This—in very deed—meant preparing a boy for a Public School and it is, thanks to Miss Mason, that such a state of affairs does not exist today—or only in extreme cases. It is Miss Mason's life and work which, very largely, has made the parents see the importance of their early help and training and has forced them to realise that no one can take their place or accept the responsibility which they should be only too pleased to place on their own shoulders. It is here that Miss Mason's ideals first affect not only any Preparatory School which adopts a PARENTS' UNION programme, but all Preparatory Schools, and through them the Public Schools in an ever widening circle.

Secondly, Miss Mason has affected the Preparatory School by altering the outlook and standpoint of the teacher: to begin with she does not assume that boys dislike work and it is therefore necessary to disguise it as play, or to give them coloured bricks instead of units. At the risk of being thought heretical, I must confess I view with great mistrust the modern tendency to remove all difficulties—a poor training, surely, for a boy whose future life will consist of overcoming difficulties. I am sorry to say that when a boy dislikes work it is generally because the work is made so dull and uninteresting that it would bore an angel; again, and this is the whole mainspring of the question, Miss Mason insists that boys are human beings and must be treated as such.

Failure in the past, complaints of inattention and laziness, can be traced to the inability of teachers to see things as they are, and not as they would wish to see them. Many teachers will not let the children do the work, they want to do it for them by separating what they should learn from what they should not learn, and by making them absorb this residue, by notes, by explanations, by diagrams—in fact by any means that the brains of man can devise—but always on the understanding that the child should accept these particular scraps, which are thrown down for his consumption. Quite unconsciously, I honestly think, the Master so dominated the boy that the latter could not develop his own mind he merely tried to reproduce what he thought his teacher appreciated not what he wished to produce or what he could have produced, had his mind not been in subjection to another and a stronger. Speaking as an old Science teacher I value any piece of original thought, any piece of original work, however small, far more highly than if a boy repeated a whole textbook. But if the boys are to be fed on the boiled down bones of the authors and the opinions of the Critics, or the Master in charge can we wonder at the result? Can we not search in vain for the originality we have ourselves suppressed?

Anyone who has had to read or correct schoolboy essays will agree with me that one can foresee what 98% of the candidates will write. Why? Simply because they write what they fondly imagine appeals to the grownup mind. It is not what they really think, it is like, "Dear Mother, I hope you are quite well" a Shibboleth without which no letter could be complete. This is all due to the teacher; he must and will point out the moral of every story, and draw for his hearers the lesson of every deed and life.

In the Townsend Warner History Prize the other year, the boys were asked: "What King or Queen, in your opinion, did most harm to England and why?" and the examiners were dissatisfied with all but 5% of the answers. Everything considered it was not to be wondered at that the boys attacked only these characters that their own history books attacked and in the same way—poor King John not only had the misfortune to lose his kit, but to earn the contempt of generations of school boys. The few remaining candidates realising the value of the caution in your opinion decide to break a lance, fairly successfully, with such redoubtable old warriors as Henry V and Coeur-de-Lion.

Miss Mason believes in a boy reading, as far as is possible, from the text—and a full text—and not only forming his own opinions but acquiring a useful vocabulary at the same time. Many teachers say, "What is your opinion of Richard I?" but what they really mean is, "Kindly note *my* opinion of Richard I."

When I was at a Preparatory School I wrote Latin verse— or rather I didn't—but I attended a class where I was supposed to, and though I knew little or nothing about English verse and much less about Latin verse, I did my best to please the gentlemen in charge, more especially as any striking originality in my verse or concords shortened the time I could give that excellent institution cricket. I still remember how we used to sigh as we divided up the feet for a hexameter, and then proceeded to push and pull the words till they went in somehow, like a jigsaw puzzle. This was to produce in us a love and appreciation of the classical authors—what it did produce was a certain amount of low down cunning and a dislike for the Classical Authors that was only obliterated with the passage of time. English verse was not there for us to appreciate—much less criticise—it was there for us to learn, and like the "gallant 600" we did not reason why—we did it. And today there is a gentleman who proposes that Euclid should be printed in the original Greek so that the boys can learn Euclid and Greek at the same time, but to my way of thinking to learn neither Euclid nor Greek after very much time. Miss Mason always pleaded the cause of boys being given an opportunity of writing verse—and I heartily support it. Some will say, "But can they write verses?" I would reply: they certainly cannot if they never try and what is more they won't do it later in life if they have no early opportunity and training. I have known boys at my own school produce astonishing efforts for youngsters and what is far more important, these same boys have continued writing at a Public School and University and have produced very excellent verse. Under Miss Mason's ideals boys have very good verse supplied for their study and appreciation, and what is more natural than that they should sometimes wish to imitate it under sympathetic help and guidance. The gift of verse will not fall upon them later like manna from Heaven and it is this early opening that I also would plead for in every school. To criticise teachers generally causes them to take cover behind the fact that the hydra-headed examination is ever present, and in fairness I will admit that though a clever boy can be educated and pass examinations it is difficult to educate his slower brethren if they have to pass examinations as well. It is rather like the story of the man who would not enlist in the cavalry giving as his reason that, in the event of a retreat, he did not wish to be hampered with a horse.

Examinations, I fear, will be with us for some time yet but in spite of this drawback teachers can still read Miss Mason's ideas and strive to carry them out even through that disciplinary grounding which examinations have demanded of us. No good can be gained by treating boys as if they could not reason, in fact they will very soon cease to reason, it being far less exertion to listen to someone else doing it.

Take mathematics, even this can be robbed of much of its old dullness by a good teacher and more reasonable methods employed. The customary way to teach a boy fractions is not to show him any, but to keep him working out endless L.C.M.'s for which he can see no use and which bore him very much. Would it not be more reasonable and better to make him feel the use of a weapon, before it is placed in his hands? Personally, I believe in boys adding fractions at once with the same denominator at first, when the denominators are different they can only add the fractions with a great deal of thought. If now they are shown how to find the L.C.M., they not only remember it, but thoroughly appreciate it as the weapon that divided their difficulties.

To put the matter in a nutshell Miss Mason's methods make for originality of work and originality of thought; the older methods except in very gifted hands, did not: and as the race of tomorrow can only move forward through the children of today, we want originality of work and thought, for no amount of imitation or the blind reiteration of the thoughts of others will help to make the world any better than it is today.

I have dealt with Miss Mason's methods in general and with regard to teachers may I say a last word on the individual School? I need hardly point out the value to a school that adopts the PARENTS' UNION Programme and has the work examined each term by the authorities at AMBLESIDE. This is probably well known to all of you but I will just make one or two points which I put before my fellow Headmasters when I was asked to write an account of the PARENTS' UNION methods for the Preparatory Schools' Review. I dealt, in this case, with the teaching of English, after all the bedrock of Education and I pointed out once again the effect of giving the boys good books and not condensations. We are very careful that boys should associate with suitable companions or see suitable plays. Is it not equally important that they should see and read good English? Boys imitate much consciously and even more sub-consciously and I gave it as my opinion that P.N.E.U. trained boys are better read and have a far better vocabulary and style.

Another point is the use of the power of attention and of observation for not having preparation a boy is compelled to concentrate in class, or subsequent narration is impossible. Not only this, but boys learn their work not by an aimless repetition, but by allowing one point to bend up to another until they can visualise the whole.

One of my assistants, one of the best and most successful teachers, left me to start a school of his own. Later he wrote me:

> I am confirmed in my belief in the P.N.E.U. Not only do I find it a time saver, but my boys have a consecutive and connected view of the term's work, without revision. This is a recommendation in view of the number of subjects which find space in the timetable. The method too, stimulates interest, attention, and clarity of thought. As far as I am concerned the method has come to stay, and I am very pleased with the way my boys have increased not only the range of their vocabulary but also their powers of concentration.

As my correspondent wrote, it is indeed a method that has come to stay, for it is more than a method or a programme, it is in an idea which, in the hands of a practical teacher can be indefinitely expanded until it becomes a governing factor in a school's life. To conclude, I have been asked, "are you satisfied with the P.N.E.U. taught from the standpoint of the Entrance Examination to the Public Schools?" All my junior forms are taught on PARENTS' UNION methods and personally I am very satisfied with the results. As you know, Headmasters are not easy to convince, they have listened too often to the voice of the reformer who never taught a class in his life but who would like to spend his declining years in pointing out how others should do it. In these days when every school is in active competition and striving to affect a maximum efficiency no Headmaster would accept, or dare keep, what he had not thoroughly tried and proved. We test our boys, we test our teachers, indeed we test ourselves by what we can produce.

I have kept Miss Mason's methods in my school for over 12 years—and indeed you can rest assured it is because I am satisfied not only with what it has produced—but what I know it will continue to produce.

WHAT THE PARENTS' UNION SCHOOL DID FOR ME
By Michael A. E. Franklin[60]

On being asked to add something as a member of the PARENTS' UNION SCHOOL to the many expressions of appreciation which are to be delivered at the Conference, I accepted with some diffidence.

I do not consider myself qualified in any way to speak at any time to anyone about anything. Then, the subject about which I was asked to speak is not an easy one, and I want to treat it in an impersonal light, as if it were, "What the P.U.S. has done and is doing for all its Pupils."

I myself have been very fortunate in that even though I actually left the PARENTS' UNION SCHOOL nine years ago, yet I have been living ever since in a P.N.E.U. atmosphere, and have been afforded many opportunities of coming directly under the influence of its ideals.

Yet the value of the P.U.S. teaching is marked the more strongly when one considers that the mind-food that was given to me when a little boy, and the doors that the P.U.S. opened to me between the ages of 6 and 11 have been possessions for me ever since. Even things that have lain dormant since I left the P.U.S. have been ready at hand when needed.

Last year I was privileged to spend a few months at the University of Grenoble in the Dauphine, France. The pleasures and the value of this time were enhanced a hundred fold by the fact that in the P.U.S. I had learnt to keep a nature note book, and I was able to enjoy the wonderful flowers of the Alps in a manner in which, I believe, it would be impossible to do without the *friendship* with flowers and trees which the P.U.S. gives.

---

[60] Son of the Honorary Mrs. Henrietta Franklin. See also page 97.

There is rather an amusing story connected with these flowers. I was in the habit of bringing home to the little cottage where I was staying flowers to paint. One day I came in with a beautiful saffron lily. The gardener's wife asked me what I was going to do with it. I said I was going to paint it. To this she replied that she did not think the paint would stick on!

Again, in the picture galleries of Italy, when I came upon those pictures whose acquaintance I had made with the help of Mr. Mansell and the P.U.S., it made all the difference in the world. It was so nice when standing in front of the pictures to see in real life, as it were, something which one had already studied carefully, and about which a feeling of familiarity had arisen. While I was standing in front of Carpaccio's St. Ursula at the Academia in Venice, a French woman tourist burst into the room in which the walls were panelled with the St. Ursula series,—the one of St. Ursula in bed and the angel appearing to tell her to travel to England with nine thousand maidens, which is one of my favourite pictures, being placed opposite the door. She gave one look at the picture and exclaimed, "Ah, *quelle drôle d'Annunciation!*"[61] and burst out again.

It would appear time that the P.N.E.U. spread to France!

In the pension in which I was staying, there were six or seven quite young children whose only literature consisted of a catalogue of a French store and a vulgar paper of the nature of the English *Comic Cuts* or *Rainbow*. When I read to them the *Contes de Lundi* and some of the poems from Victor Hugo's *Legende des Siêcles*, making them narrate it, they simply loved it and responded in a most marvellous manner.

This is illustrative of the fact that the system is so good it can be used in a foreign language and in a foreign environment and that one so completely inexperienced as myself can obtain results by its use.

Curiously enough the little boy of four who sat upon my knee while I read (only because he could not be left alone to play) astonished me by narrating to me in childish French in a most wonderful way, matter to which I had not thought he would have listened, much less understood.

---

[61] What a funny annunciation!

Again in music, the musical appreciation which is taught in the P.U.S. makes one able to understand in some measure the work of a musician, as well as having one's senses pleased by it.

It has been asked if the P.U.S. tends as a preparatory school for boys to have a sufficiently high standard of work for the entrance into the public schools.

Headmasters, I am told, say that the P.U.S. boy upon his arrival in their schools, is not only equal to his fellows in intellect and learning, but often by far surpasses them. He is more ready by the training in concentration and quickness of perception given in the P.U.S., to adapt himself to his surroundings and to glean from the new work its fullest message. The number of scholarships that have been obtained by members of the P.U.S. testifies to that.

I have mentioned musical appreciation. There is also to be obtained in the P.U.S. that high standard of writing (to which mine is a very sad exception).

There is the Nature Study, the Picture Talk, there are the literary evenings, the reading of the historical novel with the history, the blending of the various subjects one with another.

There is the *spirit of fellowship* which the PARENTS' UNION SCHOOL gives. There is perhaps no stronger bond which binds one child with another than the bond of being schoolfellows.

To think that a child in Hong Kong, or in India (for I believe the P.U.S. has spread to almost every country over which the Union Jack is flying), and the child in Manchester or in London, are all doing the same work, loving the same books, the same pictures, and sharing common interests; this is indeed a bond of fellowship.

The P.U.S. is a kind of educational League of Nations.

I have been privileged to visit one or two elementary schools of which an ever growing number are working in the P.U.S., and there it is apparent what Miss Mason has done to spread the spirit of fellowship and to break down the barriers of class. To make the lives of the children of the world happier and to open to them all the doors through which hitherto only the rich have been able to pass, that indeed is a wonderful thing.

Let me say one or two words about Miss Mason and what she has done for us, her grandchildren, for her students were her "bairns," and we of the P.U.S. her grandchildren. We are before her portrait; let us look at her face, let us read in it the love that she had for each one of us, though so few were personally known to her. Let us feel that she was our teacher, she was our philosopher, she was our friend.

What I count one of my greatest possessions is the fact that I knew Miss Mason personally and was known to her.

She had in her frail body perhaps the greatest heart that has ever come into my life. She had what is the sign of a truly great brain, the power of giving the right amount of thought to the smallest detail and to the largest.

I feel she would not have us be sad or downcast. She, whose eyes were full of childlike merriment, who was possessed of a marvellous power of rejoicing, of seeing the Godsent joy of the world; she would not, I feel, have us sad or despair. She is, I am sure, with us today. Let her memory be as an inspiration to us her children.

Our badge is the lark, the symbol of the ascending power of man over himself, as it were, and over the evils that lie in his path. The lark, the "blithe spirit," Shelley calls it, and that is what I feel Miss Mason wanted us to be, blithe and joyous soarers in the world.

Let us feel the responsibility as well as be proud of bearing our motto and our badge.

Let us feel that in each one of us lies the power to do something for the great UNION of which we are members.

I should like here, to say how much good can, in my mind, be gained by the continuance of that fellowship of which I spoke, by joining the PARENTS' UNION SCHOOL ASSOCIATION. The joining of this should be almost automatic upon leaving the P.U.S.

Let us of the PARENTS' UNION SCHOOL show our gratitude to Miss Mason in the conduct of our lives, so that she would be proud of us as we are proud to have received of her teaching.

HENCEFORWARD
By R. A. Pennethorne*

One wonders whether parents and teachers following the work of the younger children in the P.U.S. noticed the curious coincidence by which the minds of those children were prepared for the great and personal loss which they, as well as we, have sustained. At the end of last year those children were hearing how Moses, the great leader, passed beyond; and Joshua and the children of Israel were left to enter into the Promised Land through the 'great door and effectual' opened unto them, and in spite of the many adversaries. This story is a text which we might well take as a sermon for ourselves. What would the natural and diplomatic modern world have thought should have been Joshua's behaviour under the circumstances? Surely to first make certain that his people *knew* the law they had been taught, were perfect in it, before attempting new and untried adventures in a world of difficulty. But on the contrary the people were at once led forth to fresh effort and new experience. Every great movement sooner or later must face the same test and the world comes asking the same question, "Know ye that the Lord has taken away your master from your head today?" And the true disciple answers, "Yea I know it—hold ye your peace" and prays for a *double* portion of that master's spirit.

Every great movement is faced with the same dangers—namely, that loyalty to a great past may degenerate into mere copying under changed and unsuitable circumstances, or, on the other hand, that apparent expediency may be considered instead of immutable principles.

Our own work must always be for the generations yet to come—we have always to answer the eternal question of the eternal child "What mean ye by these things?"—and upon our reply the future of the world depends. Now the educational world of England today is full of immediate problems—Jordans to cross—Jerichos to fall and valleys of Achor to be doors of hope. First, Jordan to cross. Now if any reproach is brought against us continually, deservedly or undeservedly, it is that the PARENTS' UNION SCHOOL is a wonderful training

---

* Organising Secretary of the P.N.E.U.

in English, but that its mathematics are beneath contempt and not worth discussing. The modern world of examination tests makes the whole future of individual children depend on whether or not they can pass through that dividing stream or find a *Pons Asinorum*[62] over it. Whether it be the elementary school child being tested for scholarships to the secondary school, or the preparatory schoolboy faced by 'Common Entry' or the girl or boy with matriculation or school-leaving certificate to be attained as the necessary prelude to a professional or university career we know that their chances are *nil* unless they can get through their mathematical papers. Now if it were true that by being prepared for life in the P.U.S. either boy or girl was thereby unfitted to prove to the world by the world's tests that it was ready to do the world's work—then we should have much to answer for. Now frankly the work in mathematics set in the P.U.S. was never intended to fit the elementary school child to get through the tests imposed upon it at the present early age. And therefore to our elementary schools we say that there is *no* obligation to follow that work where the children's interests require something different. (For example in Wales where the children pass early to the Intermediate Schools, none follow our arithmetic, and in Gloucestershire some do and some do not.) But what about the understanding and the rate of progression? Children trained under our scheme do generally grasp what they are doing and why—they do *not* always get so far by the time they are 14 as those children do working under ordinary schemes for whom 14 is "leaving age." But educationally *should* 14 be the leaving age? Where the scheme is followed in its entirety to 18 the final result can be tested in the ordinary way—girls from our big schools do successfully pass the ordinary public tests. Little-Go, 2nd Class Honours Matriculation, Senior Cambridge, etc., were some of those taken and reported to us last year. But the whole question must be considered upon higher ground. We are not merely an admirable teaching scheme—we are a great UNION formative of public opinion and with a great inspiration behind us. Do we share the world's estimate of the supreme importance and commercial value of 'arithmetic' as the final test of a boy or girl's use in this world? Now Miss

---

[62] A place that cannot be passed.

Mason very wisely called it for the little people not arithmetic but *number* and the modern thinker is coming to perceive that the old Cabbalists were nearer the truth than some who argue that we need only be taught what we shall *use*, so why trouble about the higher mathematics at all. One hopes the parents and the teachers have read with the children a book which Miss Mason quite recently added to the programmes called *Number Stories of Long Ago*. No child having revelled in that book but will have perceived that 'sums' have no arbitrary existence, and that number and shape, the power of working from known to unknown quantities are things inherent in the understanding of life itself and *one* mystery and wonder of delight.

Now how long can we as a society remain untouched by the great wave of feeling on the subject of English children's heavy burden in the ordinary conventional teaching and use of 'arithmetic'? (24 hour week and 5 hours arithmetic). Do we realise that continental children are free from the awful burden of our double system and can perform the actual operations through the metric system with ease and sureness and so can give more time to true mathematics and see where their work correlates to life and science and have more *time* to devote to the humanities. Only English children have to master both the metric system and that of $2/_{11}$ of 4s. 9¾d. and all the other awful intricacies of our legacy of local thought and practice in weights, measures and coinage. Teachers resent the limitations thus imposed. Chambers of Commerce lament them, but parents who are also rate-payers, voters, school managers and politicians have gone on calmly acquiescing. But each one of us *must* take thought. Do we realise the needs of the world and the true wonder and mystery of the subject, and do we believe our children can and should do so too or do we simply believe that there is some magic discipline in endless compound multiplications of money and long division? We *must* think and we shall perforce have to choose for the river is there and the children must cross it.

And then Jericho to be taken—the existing strong place manned by giants. Perhaps the most marvellous and encouraging chapter in our history has been the way in which the schools of the nation have entered the Union and done some of its most magnificent work. Yet to me as a schoolmistress and a school teacher, both under our own UNION and under the ordinary auspices, the most amazing thing is that parents suffer the 'ordinary' school, private or public, to go on being very 'ordinary' indeed and that, though over 100 secondary schools of all sizes work with us now, there are not *thousands*. *These* are the strongholds of the giants, the experts in their particular departments of academic attainments, the 'double first' man, or the brilliant woman. Now having been in and out of schools all up and down the country, famous or obscure, expensive or cheap, more and more, one is convinced that the very experts themselves are crying out for more freedom for the children, more unity of aim for themselves and more correlation of their individual efforts. Now all these things we can give them—but the natural fear arises in their hearts of surrendering their own liberty or not finding full scope for their own God-given talents. Now those who *do* work with us find all those things and we are proud to number among our ranks some who might certainly claim original genius—but let us appeal to the parents. When you want the best chance and the widest culture for your children and *continuity* of these things irrespective of the people who from time to time administer them, you can and do get this by starting the children at home in the P.U.S., and then sending them on to a school working *with* the P.U.S., and if more parents truly realised and required what it gives then *many* more schools would unite themselves to us. There is a great field and mission for starting P.U.S. classes and small schools in districts where there is now *nothing* for the children and by combination and UNION parents can begin if only on a small scale with a class held by an AMBLESIDE student which will eventually *grow* into a school, and we can proudly point to large well-known schools recognised by the Board of Education which spring from such an origin. *But* where there *is* an existing school on ordinary lines and yet there are *also* groups large or small of parents who are members of the UNION *then* I would say, to continue the parallel remember the story of the Gibeonites—*convert* the schools, and turn suspicion into love, understanding, appreciation, and *service*.

But there is a third and important problem which must be faced in the immediate future—namely, the teaching of history. Moses' method of preparing the people for their future was to retell to them their past. Now the PARENTS' UNION SCHOOL has here a very fine record of pioneer work to its credit—we alone have always done what Mr. Wells has been calling upon the world in general to do—taught universal history universally. The Books of Centuries which you will all have seen are the children's own records of that teaching. History of all subjects is the most difficult and the most dangerous as it may so readily degenerate into a mere teaching of opinion or a mere indulgence in 'gossip about the great of the earth.' The books we choose are designed to give children a fair survey of differing opinion and a solid ground work of fact—chronological and social—upon which to base citizenship which they also learn through the lives of heroes in *Plutarch's Lives*, the understanding of human nature through OURSELVES and the conditions of its every day practice through various books actually on 'citizenship.' *But* we have to reconsider our whole approach to the history of the past—have we so taught it through 'Drum and Trumpet' that the warrior and not the law-giver, the destroyer and not the constructor, has been the arch type of mankind in the eyes of our boys and girls? Except one little *League of Nation's* book suitable for the quite young child for whom the delightful *Our Island Story* already provides there is no book of history yet imbued with the *new* spirit of a chastened and repentant age which we can offer our children. Cannot we among the children of our UNION *train* the future historian who shall use this valley of Achor for a door of hope—who shall look back and see the hand of God in the happenings of the dark ages and on to the New Jerusalem even in 'England's green and pleasant land.' Cannot we raise up such a prophet and inspire such a writer? The final judgment of posterity upon any great leader must be the character of those who follow after—are we therefore going forward to meet the new wants of a new age with the serene confidence that "As I was with Moses so will I be with thee." Are we henceforward to be a great missionary body not merely enjoying our rich and splendid legacy from the past but liberally and generously sowing for the future and passing on to others the good things we treasure for our own children? Without that missionary spirit we must dwindle; with it we can prove that the future is always greater than the past and it will be the future of the children yet to come.

Henceforward then we must go on through the great door and effectual,—

> One the object of our journey,
> One the faith that never tires,
> One the earnest looking forward
> One the hope our God inspires.

Memorial Service
Thursday, March 29th, 1923

A Memorial Service was held at St. Martin's-in-the-Fields, Thursday, March 29th, 1923. 10:15 a.m. (by kind permission) for

Charlotte Maria Shaw Mason
Born January 1st, 1842
Died January 16th, 1923

ORDER OF SERVICE

Hymn	*The King of Love My Shepherd Is*

Address

The Sentences

Psalms 90

Lesson—Wisdom iii. 1-9

Veni Creator	Attwood

(To be sung by one voice, the congregation kneeling)

Lesson—Romans 8:18-28

The Prayers

Hymn	*O God, Our Help in Ages Past*
Nunc Dimittis	*The Blessing*

The service was arranged by the Rev. H. Costley-White and Mrs. Whitaker-Thompson,[63] and was taken by Mr. Costley-White (who read the prayers and gave the address), the Master of the Temple (who read the Lessons), and the Rev. F. Lewis. Mrs. Mellish sang the *Veni Creator* and Mr. Goldsborough played *Requiem Aeternam* (by Basil Harwood) as the congregation left the church.

In the course of his address Mr. Costley-White said that we were met to do honour to a very great, very clever, very good woman. She was herself the living example of her

---

[63] See page 40.

teaching that it is character that matters. She had a shrewd, saving north-country common sense which kept her idealism from ever becoming an unpractical fact.

He struck the note of thanksgiving by pointing out that we had met to thank God for the gift of a great and noble life with which we had been specially privileged to come in contact, and not to mourn the loss of a leader.

He laid stress on the fact that Miss Mason not only possessed wonderful powers but throughout her whole life, wherever she might be, made the fullest use of them in the service of others. In this connection he told the anecdote of how he was once driving with Miss Mason in her carriage near Rydal and he, thrilled with the beauty of the scenery, exclaimed, "Who would not be a poet in such surroundings?" To which Miss Mason replied with kindly irony, "Then you give no credit to Wordsworth for being a poet?"

The outstanding points of the address seemed to be:—

   i.   Praise for the inspiration of her life and work

   ii.   Our privilege in having come under her influence

   iii. Our consequent responsibilities.

Mere notes cannot even faintly give a sense of the reverence and gratitude which the address aroused in the hearts of all who heard it.

IMPRESSIONS

I

I have been asked to give my impressions of the P.N.E.U. Memorial Conference, and as a member of the audience on that occasion I am glad to add my little word of deep appreciation.

I went as a total stranger to all there, never having met Miss Mason or visited the College at AMBLESIDE, though I had some previous knowledge of her work.

It was a happy idea to have her portrait on the platform, smiling down upon us from among "a host of golden daffodils" and at the end of three days her features had become so familiar that she seemed to us who had not known her no longer a stranger but a friend. Her spirit seemed to fill the room and there was a consciousness that she "being dead, yet speaketh."

There is no need to comment on the various addresses which are to appear in print. Sufficient to say that one and all sounded a note of joy and thanksgiving for her great example and devoted life-work. There was "no sadness of farewell" about the Conference, which was what she would have wished, but rather a radiant hopefulness.

It was specially impressive to note the wonderful self-possession and confidence in the future of those who must have been dearest to her and to whom she had handed over her sacred trust.

It must have been hard to speak of one so much beloved before a large audience, but the quiet dignity with which it was done could not fail to touch all hearers and remind them that

> To live in hearts we leave behind
> Is not to die.

The Memorial Service at St. Martin's-in-the-Fields was a beautiful completion of three very happy and inspiring days and the exquisite singing of the *Veni Creator* will remain for long in our memories. I think all present came away with the intense conviction that a great spirit had passed beyond the veil and that Charlotte Mason was one of those of whom it may truly be said "Their works do follow them."

Ethel E. M. Peacey
Vice-Principal, Norland Institute
23rd April, 1923

II

When we entered Mortimer Hall for the first meeting of the Conference it seemed as though Miss Mason herself was there to greet us. On an easel on the platform was her portrait in colour; and from this her soul seemed to break forth to commune with ours.

Before her portrait was a beautiful jar which next day was filled with daffodils; and many, many more in other bowls appeared—wild daffodils gathered from the garden of SCALE

HOW by the loving hands of those whose hearts were sorrowful.

Triumphing over this sorrow must have been a feeling of thankfulness and joy that they had been privileged in other years to share with Miss Mason the life at AMBLESIDE.

It was more than interesting to listen to the speakers, each of whom touched on a different aspect from the others. Never shall I forget the telling testimony given with such deep feeling by Mr. Michael Franklin,[64] at one time a pupil himself in the P.U.S.; or the great tribute paid by the Rev. E. Lyttelton[65] who said that Miss Mason was a mistress in the art of both character training and intellectual training, a combination exceedingly rare. "It is women and men of faith and love like Miss Mason," said another, "who will redeem the world."

It was a joy to hear from Miss Kitching[66] something of Miss Mason as a child; and those of us who have never been to AMBLESIDE were grateful for Miss Parish's[67] loving description of the beauties and surroundings of SCALE HOW.

On the last day of the Conference the right note was struck—the note of progress and development. We know that our work is never standing still. We move forward or backward; we gain ground or lose it; and there is no doubt as to which we shall do if we follow the example of the one whose faith and enthusiasm carried her forward right on to the beginning of her fuller life beyond.

What a fitting close! A memorial service held in St. Martin's-in-the-Fields! It was a beautiful choice, for this simple, restful church standing in the midst of the life and whirl of London is typical of that inward peace which regulated the busy life of our Founder.

D. S. Golding[68]

---

[64] See page pages 97 and 215.
[65] See page 184.
[66] See pages 67 and 120.
[67] See pages 60 and 201.
[68] See also page 175.

An Epitaph

C.M.M.
January 1923

Homage and Remembrance to one who never forgot to remember each individual and all their joys and sorrows.

Hail and farewell to one who never let any, once known to her, slip out of her life and thought.

Honour to one who shewed that life and work were not for personal honour or gain, but for the service of humanity.

Life and more Life to one who showed that life was greater and better worth living with every day of our life.

Fame and Renown to one who found the profession of home teaching a byword and left it a vocation.

Recognition to one who recognised the full possibilities of each person born into the world.

Peace to one who taught that ends were not gained by 'jostling in the street.'

Joy to one who showed that cheerfulness and goodwill were both duty and pleasure.

Good harvesting to one who never looked at results but at efforts.

Fulfillment of desires to one who distinguished between low wants and high hopes.

Satisfaction to one who was too great of soul ever to say 'it is enough.'

Love to one who knew that love was an immortal gift and not an earthly chain.

Vision to one who looked through earth to heaven, where may there be *Reunion* for all who journey one step nearer to the goal of us all.

Index of Persons

INDEX OF PERSONS

INDEX OF PERSONS (continued)

INDEX OF PERSONS (continued)

INDEX OF PERSONS (continued)

www.ingramcontent.com/pod-product-compliance
Lightning Source LLC
LaVergne TN
LVHW091214080426
835509LV00009B/995